T0305789

Contract, Governance and Transaction Cost Economics

Contract, Governance and Transaction Cost Economics

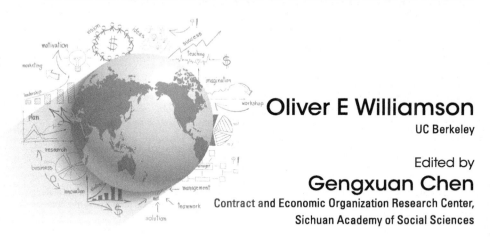

Oliver E Williamson
UC Berkeley

Edited by
Gengxuan Chen
Contract and Economic Organization Research Center,
Sichuan Academy of Social Sciences

We World Scientific

NEW JERSEY · LONDON · SINGAPORE · BEIJING · SHANGHAI · HONG KONG · TAIPEI · CHENNAI · TOKYO

Published by

World Scientific Publishing Co. Pte. Ltd.

5 Toh Tuck Link, Singapore 596224

USA office: 27 Warren Street, Suite 401-402, Hackensack, NJ 07601

UK office: 57 Shelton Street, Covent Garden, London WC2H 9HE

Library of Congress Cataloging-in-Publication Data

Names: Williamson, Oliver E., author. | Chen, Gengxuan, editor.

Title: Contract, government and transaction cost economics / by Oliver E Williamson, UC Berkeley ;
edited by Gengxuan Chen.

Description: New Jersey : World Scientific, [2017] | Includes bibliographical references.

Identifiers: LCCN 2017002273 | ISBN 9789813202078

Subjects: LCSH: Transaction costs. | Industrial organization (Economic theory) |
Institutional economics.

Classification: LCC HB846.3 .W54 2017 | DDC 338.5/1--dc23

LC record available at https://lccn.loc.gov/2017002273

British Library Cataloguing-in-Publication Data

A catalogue record for this book is available from the British Library.

Desk Editor: Shreya Gopi

Typeset by Stallion Press
Email: enquiries@stallionpress.com

Printed in Singapore

Preface

Oliver E. Williamson epitomized the New Institutional Economics, especially as the founder and promoter of Transaction Cost Economics. He brought the concept of transaction cost into the general analysis to be more "operational." Promoted by him who was said to rediscover the Coasian Theory, Coase's transaction cost theory has turned into an important school in modern economics, motivated academic innovation and great interdisciplinary studies that involve economics, organization theory and law, etc. The Royal Swedish Academy of Sciences awarded him the Nobel Prize in Economics in 2009 for "his analysis of economic governance, especially the boundaries of the firm." They describe his contribution as follows: "Provided a theory of why some economic transactions take place within firms and other similar transactions take place between firms, that is, in the marketplace. The theory informs us about how to handle one of the most basic choices in human organization. When should decision power be controlled inside an organization, and when should decisions be left to the market."

Williamson's research is practical and interdisciplinary. As he said, "when I looked back my research, I felt that being practical was very important." This point is obviously reflected in his articles, books and guidance to students. In addition, his research on economic organization and governance mechanism include the aspects of economics, organization theory, law and sociology. He is also a professor of Business, Economics, and Law. In my view, being practical and interdisciplinary is the key to build and develop transaction cost economics. Besides, another feature no doubt is emphasis of microperspective, calling for microfoundation in economic analysis. He summarized the research methods in transaction cost economics as "It examines economic organization in a way that is simultaneously microanalytic, comparative institutional, and economizing in its orientation." I am deeply aware of the features above in his research during my study in his works combined with our communication, and believe the readers of this book will have the same feeling. Moreover, I strongly agree that being practical, microanalytic, and interdisciplinary is beneficial to achieve the valuable economic research results.

To further develop and publicize Williamson's theories and Transaction Cost Economics, I have such a plan to edit this book, entitled "Contract, Governance, and Transaction Cost Economics." Besides the collected papers that are closely around the topic, this book is going to borrow Williamson's description to be the theme: "Transaction cost economies are realized by assigning transactions (which differ in their attributes) to governance structures (which are the organizational frameworks within which the integrity of a contractual relation is decided) in a discriminating way." Although Williamson's works have been published for years, most of his theories have great academic value to date. On the research and analysis of economic organization, its value I want to describe in three aspects:

Transaction — transaction, as the basic unit, analysis on lens of contract;
Governance — contemporary research of economic organization in governance mechanism;
Transaction Cost Economics — a new economic research branch that has broad application prospects.

What is referred to as the New Institutional Economics (Beside Economic History studies) developed in the West in two mainly complementary ways: Property Rights Theory and Transaction Cost Economics. Of the two, Property Rights Theory developed more rapidly. Transaction Cost Economics has nonetheless taken shape. Research on the New Institutional Economics in China began in the 1990s and has grown rapidly since. As between Property Rights Theory and Transaction Cost Economics, China has given much more attention to Property Rights Theory. Williamson suggests that adequate attention is needed on Transaction Cost Economics and believes that China will benefit by bringing Transaction Cost Economics to bear.

For the application of transaction cost economics, as Williamson appeals: "Transaction Cost Economics has many applications not only within the field of industrial organization but within most applied fields of economics — to include labor, public finance, comparative economic systems, and economic development and reform. Applications to business — to the fields of strategy, organizational behavior, marketing, finance, operations management, and accounting — are likewise numerous. Applications to the contiguous social sciences (especially sociology, political science, social psychology, and aspects of the law) have also been made. Such broad reach arises because any problem that originates as or can be reformulated as a contracting problem can be examined to advantage in transaction cost economizing terms." In my view, one of the most important contribution of Transaction Cost Economics is on the research of modern economic organization. From the perspective of traditional economic theories, the special economic organizational structure in China is inefficient, however in economizing transaction cost, it can be efficient or has comparative advantage, which could be theoretical basis and research origin to explain why China can build economic miracle in the incomplete marketization. These books advocate the application of transaction cost economics in Chinese economic reform, development and practice.

It is abundant in Williamson's academic achievements. To screen, collect, and read the great amount of his works is a tough job to the readers who are eager to understand and explore his theories. In addition, it is meaningful to help promote some valuable academic theories. Thus, after the consideration of the recent research in this field and the discussions with Prof. Williamson, we edit this book, which selects the important papers that are closely related to modern research of economic organization. The initial purpose of editing this book was to publish a Chinese translation version for Chinese scholars and students. Then, World Scientific Publishing Company, the publisher of this book, suggests that it is beneficial to Chinese scholars in reading the book of original language, which is why this English version is also published.

It needs to be clarified that every article collected in this book is independent from each other, as a result different articles cannot avoid similarities or the same description. But for the integrity and logic of each article and the purpose to edit this book, after repeat consideration, no corresponding changes are made in the articles.

Finally I would like to thank Prof. Williamson for his support in publishing this book, and the help and encouragement he gave to me. I will benefit for my entire life from his guidance and influence.

Gengxuan Chen
June 2016
Email:gengxuanchen@qq.com

Contents

Acknowledgements

We thank the following journals for the permission to reprint the chapters collated in this book.

1. Transaction Cost Economics: The Natural Progression
   American Economic Review 100 (June 2010): 673–690.

2. The Lens of Contract: Private Ordering
   American Economic Review 92 (May 2002): 438–443.

3. Calculativeness, Trust, and Economic Organization
   Journal of Law and Economics, Vol. 36, No. 1, Part 2, John M. Olin Centennial Conference in Law and Economics at the University of Chicago (April 1993): 453–486.

4. The Theory of the Firm as Governance Structure: From Choice to Contract
   Journal of Economic Perspectives, Vol. 16, No. 3 (Summer 2002): 171–195.

5. Pragmatic Methodology: A Sketch with Applications to Transaction Cost Economics
   Journal of Economic Methodology, 16 (2009): 145-157.

6. Transaction Cost Economics: How it Works; Where it is Headed
   De Economist 146 (1998): 23–58. Kluwer Academic Publishers.

7. The New Institutional Economics: Taking Stock, Looking Ahead
   Journal of Economic Literature Vol. XXXVIII (September 2000): 595–613.

Chapter 1

Transaction Cost Economics: The Natural Progression*

The research program on which I and others have been working has been variously described as the "economics of governance," the "economics of organization," and "transaction cost economics." As discussed in Section 1, governance is the overarching concept and transaction cost economics is the means by which to breathe operational content into governance and organization. The specific issue that drew me into this research project was the puzzle posed by Coase in 1937: What efficiency factors determine when a firm produces a good or service to its own needs rather than outsource? As

*This article is a revised version of the lecture Williamson delivered in Stockholm, Sweden, on December 8, 2009, when he received the Bank of Sweden Prize in Economic Sciences in Memory of Nobel.

Williamson: This paper has benefited from my presentation of an early draft to my colleagues and students at the University of California, Berkeley and from subsequent discussions with Tadelis. I have grave doubts that I would have undertaken the project described herein but for (i) my interdisciplinary training at Carnegie Mellon University (where economics and organization theory were joined), (ii) my experience as Special Economic Assistant to the Head of the Antitrust Division at the US Department of Justice (which revealed the need within the antitrust enforcement agencies to bring economics and organization theory together), and (iii) the opportunity to work these issues through with my students at the University of Pennsylvania when I resumed teaching. (Teaching is learning, especially if the students buy into the project.)

described in Section 2, my 1971 paper on "The Vertical Integration of Production" made headway with this issue and invited follow-on research that would eventually come to be referred to as transaction cost economics. The rudiments of transaction cost economics are set out in Section 3. Puzzles and challenges that arose and would require "pushing the logic of efficient governance to completion" are examined briefly in Section 4. Concluding remarks follow in Section 5.

1. An Overview

For economists, if not more generally, governance and organization are important if and as these are made susceptible to analysis. As described here, breathing operational content into the concept of governance would entail examining economic organization through the lens of contract (rather than the neoclassical lens of choice), recognizing that this was an interdisciplinary project where economics and organization theory (and, later, aspects of the law) were joined, and introducing hitherto neglected transaction costs into the analysis. A predictive theory of economic organization was the object. The puzzle of vertical integration was an obvious place to start.

1.1. *Governance*

Whereas textbook microeconomic theory was silent on the concept of good governance, Commons, who was a leading institutional economist during the first half of the twentieth century, formulated the problem of economic organization as follows: "The ultimate unit of activity ... must contain in itself the three principles of conflict, mutuality, and order. This unit is a transaction" (Commons, 1932, p. 4). Commons thereafter recommended that "theories of economics center on transactions and working rules, on problems of organization, and on the ... [ways] the organization of activity is ... stabilized" (Commons, 1950, p. 21).

   This conception of economics is to be contrasted with the neoclassical resource allocation paradigm in two important respects: first, whereas Commons viewed organization and the continuity of contractual relations as important, the resource allocation paradigm made negligible provision for either but focused instead on prices and output, supply and demand; second, whereas the price theoretic approach to economics would become the "dominant paradigm" during the twentieth century (Reder, 1999, p. 43), institutional economics was mainly relegated to the history of thought because it failed to advance a positive research agenda that was replete with predictions and empirical testing (Stigler as reported in Kitch, 1983, p. 170). Stalwarts notwithstanding, institutional economics "ran itself into the sand."

This does not imply, however, that institutional economics was lacking for good ideas. Indeed, the Commons Triple of conflict, mutuality, and order prefigures the concept of governance as herein employed — in that governance is the means by which to infuse order, thereby to mitigate conflict and realize mutual gain. Furthermore, the transaction is made the basic unit of analysis.

Buchanan (1975, p. 225) subsequently distinguished between lens of choice and lens of contract approaches to economic organization and argued that economics as a discipline went "wrong" in its preoccupation with the science of choice and the optimization apparatus associated therewith. If "mutuality of advantage from voluntary exchange is ... the most fundamental of all understandings in economics" (Buchanan, 2001, p. 29), then the lens of contract approach is an underused perspective.

The past 35 years have witnessed growing interest in the use of the lens of contract, to include both theories that emphasize *ex ante* incentive alignment (agency theory/mechanism-design, team theory, property rights theory) and those for which the *ex post* governance of contractual relations is where the main analytical action resides. Transaction cost economics is an *ex post* governance construction, with emphasis on those transactions to which Commons called attention — namely those for which continuity (or breakdown) of the exchange relation is of special importance. How did the attributes of such transactions differ from the ideal transaction, in both law and economics, of simple market exchange (where no such continuity relation was implied)? What were the governance ramifications?

Answers to these queries would entail reformulating the problem of economic organization in comparative contractual terms by (i) naming the key attributes with respect to which transactions differ, (ii) describing the clusters of attributes that define alternative modes of governance (of which markets and hierarchies are two), (iii) joining these parts by appealing to the efficient alignment hypothesis, wherein (iv) predictions would be derived to which empirical tests would be applied, and (v) public policy ramifications would be worked up. Antecedent to the foregoing, the contract relevant attributes of human actors would be named and explicated.

1.2. *Organization*

Whereas the neoclassical theory of the firm treated the firm as a black box for transforming inputs into outputs according to the laws of technology, this was not, as Demsetz (1983, p. 377) observed, an all-purpose construction. It is a "mistake to confuse the firm of [neoclassical] economic theory with its real-world namesake. The chief mission of neoclassical economics is to understand how the price system coordinates the use of resources, not the inner workings of real firms."

Although Demsetz did not make the case that economics and organization theory should be joined in a combined effort to understand firm and market organization of a real world kind, that is nevertheless the research need and opportunity as I perceived it — in no small measure because of my training (1960–1963) in the Ph.D. program at the Graduate School of Industrial Administration, Carnegie Mellon University. This remarkable program in interdisciplinary social science made the case that organization theory should both inform and be informed by economics.[1] Simon, March, and Cyert played especially important roles[2] in putting this across. Considerations of bounded rationality, the specification of goals,[3] intertemporal regularities (wherein organization takes on "a life of its own"), the critical importance of adaptation, the reliance within the operating parts on routines, and, more generally, the "architecture of complexity" were all basic concepts that would prove to be pertinent to an understanding of incomplete contracting and complex organization. Had the governance of contractual

---

[1] Jacques Dreze speaks for me, and, I am sure, for many others in his statement that "Never since [my visit to Carnegie Mellon] have I experienced such intellectual excitement" (1995, p. 123). Nobel Laureates in economics from the small group of faculty and students at CMU include Herbert Simon, Franco Modigliani, Merton Miller, Robert Lucas, Edward Prescott, and Finn Kydland.

[2] Classic books by Carnegie Mellon faculty that feature economics and organization theory include *Models of Man* (Simon, 1957b), *Organizations* (March and Simon, 1958), and the *Behavioral Theory of the Firm* (Cyert and March, 1963).

[3] One way to introduce organizational considerations is to change the objective function of the firm by supplanting the neoclassical assumption of profit maximization with various forms of "managerial discretion" — such as sales maximization (Baumol, 1959), growth maximization (Marris, 1964), or expense preference (Williamson, 1964). These efforts to introduce "realism in motivation" yielded few predictions and resulted in little empirical testing.

relations come under study at Carnegie Mellon, there is no question that this would have been examined in an interdisciplinary way.

1.3. *Transaction Costs*

Coase, in his classic 1937 paper on "The Nature of the Firm," was the first to bring the concept of transaction costs to bear on the study of firm and market organization. The youthful Coase (then 27 years old) uncovered a serious lapse in the accepted textbook theory of firm and market organization. Upon viewing firm and market as "alternative methods of coordinating production" (Coase, 1937, p. 388), Coase observed that the decision to use one mode rather than the other should not be taken as given (as was the prevailing practice) but should be derived. Accordingly, Coase (1937, p. 389) advised economists that they needed:

> … to bridge what appears to be a gap in [standard] economic theory between the assumption (made for some purposes) that resources are allocated by means of the price mechanism and the assumption (made for other purposes) that allocation is dependent on the entrepreneur-coordinator. We have to explain the basis on which, in practice, this choice between alternatives is effected.

The missing concept was "transaction cost."

The lapse to which Coase referred had little immediate effect (Coase, 1988, p. 23) and failed to take hold over the next 20 years, during which period the implicit assumption of zero transaction costs went unchallenged. Two important articles in the 1960s would upset this state of affairs. Upon pushing the logic of zero transaction costs to completion, the unforeseen implications of this standard assumption were displayed for all to see.

The first demonstration was Coase's 1960 article on "The Problem of Social Cost." Upon reformulating the externality problem in contractual terms and pushing the logic of zero transaction cost reasoning to completion, he realized an astonishing result: "Pigou's conclusion (and that of most economists of that era) that some kind of government action (usually the imposition of taxes) was required to restrain those whose actions had harmful effects on others (often termed negative externalities)" was incorrect (Coase,

1992, p. 717).[4] That is because if transaction costs are zero then the parties to tort transactions will costlessly bargain to an efficient result whichever way property rights are assigned at the outset. In that event, the emperor really did have no clothes: externalities and frictions of other kinds would vanish. That being preposterous, the real message was this: "study the world of positive transaction costs" (Coase, 1992, p. 717).[5] Arrow's 1969 examination of "The Organization of Economic Activity: Issues Pertinent to the Choice of Market versus Nonmarket Allocation" likewise revealed a need to make a place for positive transaction costs, both with respect to market failures and in conjunction with intermediate product market contracting: "the existence of vertical integration may suggest that the costs of operating competitive markets are not zero, as is usually assumed in our theoretical analysis" (Arrow, 1969, p. 48).

But whereas pushing the logic of zero transaction costs to completion would reveal the need to make provision for positive transaction costs, there were three problems. First, upon opening the "black box" of firm and market organization and looking inside, the black box turned out to be Pandora's Box: positive transaction costs were perceived to be everywhere. That would prove to be a curse, in that some form of transaction cost could be invoked to explain any condition whatsoever after the fact, as a result of which appeal to transaction costs acquired a "well deserved bad name" (Fischer, 1977, p. 322). Second, it does not suffice to show that some types of transaction costs are demonstrably great. Unless these costs differ among modes (say, as between markets and hierarchies), such a demonstration lacks comparative contractual significance. Third, transaction costs that pass the test of comparative contractual significance need to be embedded in a conceptual

---

[4] Even the Chicago School, which had grave reservations with overreaching uses of externality arguments, was resistant to Coase's claims that externalities vanished under zero transaction cost conditions. For a discussion of Coase Versus Chicago, see Kitch (1983, pp. 220–221).

[5] Not everyone agrees. Some economists take the "Coase Theorem" (the first 15 pages of Coase 1960) to imply that costless renegotiation accurately describes contracting in practice. However, the following 29 pages in Coase (1960) reveal that the zero transaction cost assumption is not only wrong but undermines our understanding of complex economic phenomena. Express provision for positive transaction costs would thereafter need to be made if externalities and other real world contractual phenomena are to be accurately understood. Coase reaffirmed that this was his purpose in his Nobel Prize Lecture (Coase, 1992, p. 712).

framework from which predictions can be derived and empirically tested. The unmet need was to focus attention on key features and provide operational content for the intriguing concept of positive transaction costs.

2. The Vertical Integration of Production

What I have referred to as the "Carnegie Triple" (Williamson, 1996, p. 25) is this: be disciplined; be interdisciplinary; have an active mind. Being disciplined means to take your core discipline seriously and work at it on its own terms. Being interdisciplinary means to appeal to the contiguous social sciences — if and as the phenomena understudy cross disciplinary lines. Having an active mind entails asking the question, "What is going on here?" rather than pronouncing "This is the law here."[6] The Carnegie Triple would serve me well when I named industrial organization as my field, even though I had never taken an industrial organization course at Carnegie Mellon (or elsewhere), and I went on the job market.

Coase (1972, p. 62) described the leading industrial organization textbooks in the 1960s as "applied price theory" — with which I agree, but with a caveat: the structure-conduct-performance paradigm also played an important role in the "Harvard School" approach to the field. The organization of markets (especially with respect to the number and size distribution of firms and the condition of entry) thus figured prominently, but the organization of firms was ignored. Because firms were production functions for transforming inputs into outputs according to the laws of technology, the IO public policy lesson was this: except as contracting practices and organizational structures had a physical or technical basis, nonstandard and unfamiliar forms of contract and organization were regarded as deeply problematic and presumptively anticompetitive.[7]

---

[6] For a discussion of these distinctions, see Roy D'Andrade (1986).

[7] Coase (1972, 67) described the prevailing monopoly predilection as follows: One important result of this preoccupation with the monopoly problem is that if an economist finds something — a business practice of one sort or other — that he does not understand, he looks for a monopoly explanation. And as in this field we are very ignorant, the number of ununderstandable practices tends to be rather large, and the reliance on a monopoly explanation, frequent.

By contrast with this one-sided interpretation of deviations from the norm under the prevailing IO orientation, the Carnegie Mellon perspective on contractual and organizational variety was that such could also serve efficiency purposes. This difference in perspectives would forcefully register when I served in 1966–67 as the Special Economic Assistant to the Head of the Antitrust Division of the US Department of Justice, especially when I was asked to comment on an early draft of the Schwinn brief. The issue was one of vertical market restrictions, and the brief advanced the argument that the franchise restrictions imposed by the bicycle manufacturer Schwinn on its (nonexclusive) franchisees were anticompetitive. My view was more cautious. Not only was it unclear to me that the restrictions had anticompetitive effects, but a case could be made that the restrictions in question served the purpose of preserving the integrity of the franchise system — additionally or instead (Williamson, 1985, pp. 183–189). Alas, the principal architects of the Schwinn brief viewed the case as an opportunity to apply the "then prevailing thinking of the economics profession on restricted distribution" (Posner, 1977, p. 1). This anticompetitive interpretation succeeded in arguments before the US Supreme Court.[8]

By reason of what I perceived to be truncated and defective reasoning with Schwinn and other cases,[9] I decided to revisit vertical integration and vertical market restrictions when I resumed teaching at the University of Pennsylvania. The graduate students and I worked our way through the literature and, some very good papers notwithstanding (Fellner, 1947; McKenzie, 1951; Stigler 1951), satisfied ourselves that organizational economies played no significant role. I therefore decided to revisit vertical integration from a combined economics and organization theory perspective.

My paper on "The Vertical Integration of Production: Market Failure Considerations" differed from orthodoxy in the following respects: (i) I examined economic organization through the lens of contract (rather than orthodox lens of choice), (ii) described cognition in terms of bounded

---

[8] Interestingly, the Supreme Court effectively reversed Schwinn a decade later as the limits of "prevailing thinking" became increasingly clear.

[9] I do not, however, mean to suggest that my disagreements were common. The leadership and staff in the Antitrust Division in the late 1960s were superlative.

rationality, on which account all complex contracts are incomplete, (iii) made provision for strategic behavior (defection from the spirit of cooperation) when an outsourced good or service experienced disturbances for which the stakes are great, (iv) treated adaptation as the main efficiency purpose of economic organization, and (v) distinguished between investments in generic assets and specific assets, where a bilateral dependency relation between supplier and buyer stages was ascribed to the latter. Taken together, the argument comes down to this: efficient intermediate product market exchange is usually well served by simple market contracting if the assets are generic; but the advantage shifts to hierarchy as bilateral dependency (and the resulting risk of costly maladaptations) builds up by reason of asset specificity and outlier disturbances.

Although I initially regarded this chapter as a standalone effort to solve the puzzle of the boundaries of the firm and expand our understanding of vertical integration, it turned out that vertical integration would become a paradigm for the study of complex contract and economic organization. The combination of incomplete contracts, bilateral dependency (contingent on asset specificity), and defection from the norm of coordinated adaptation when a contract experiences significant disturbances (for which the stakes are great) had application to a wide range of phenomena that were interpreted as variations on a theme.

The initial trick was to think contractually, which for many phenomena was easy but for others required that the phenomenon be reformulated in contracting terms. This, however, was merely the first step. The key concepts needed to be operationalized; a predictive theory needed to be worked up; and, as gaps and omissions arose, the logic of positive transaction costs would need to be pushed to completion. The first two are addressed in Section 3 and the last in Section 4.

3. The Rudiments

Upon realizing that this approach to the study of economic organization had broad application, I needed to work up the basic mechanisms and the underlying logic more systematically. The rudiments are described in three clusters: key conceptual moves; key operational moves; and applications. Common to all three clusters is the need to examine economic organization at a more micro-analytic level of analysis, which is consistent with Simon's observation that:

> In the physical sciences, when errors of measurement and other noise are found to be of the same order of magnitude as the phenomena under study, the response is not to try to squeeze more information out of the data by statistical means; it is instead to find techniques for observing the phenomena at a higher level of resolution. The corresponding strategy for economics is obvious: to secure new kinds of data at the micro level (Simon, 1984, 40).

What follows is a very compact summary.

3.1. *Conceptual Moves*

The basic moves here are to elaborate upon (i) the attributes of human actors (ii) adaptation and to introduce and (iii) contract laws (plural).

Human Actors — If "Nothing is more fundamental in setting our research agenda and informing our research methods than our view of the nature of the human beings whose behavior we are studying" (Simon 1985, p. 303), then social scientists are challenged to name the cognitive, self-interest, and other attributes of human actors on which their analyses rest.

The cognitive assumption that Simon (1991, 1957) has characterized as his "lodestar" is bounded rationality, which he describes as behavior that is "intendedly rational, but only limitedly so." Human actors, so described, are neither hyperrational nor irrational but are attempting effectively to cope with complex contracts that are incomplete.

Incompleteness notwithstanding, transaction cost economics also makes provision for "feasible foresight," as reflected in Shultz's remarks about how his "training in economics has had a major influence on the way I think about public policy tasks, even when they have no particular relation to economics. Our discipline makes one think ahead, ask about indirect consequences, take note of variables not directly under consideration" (Shultz, 1995, p. 1). This is a recurrent theme in the discussion in Section 4 of pushing the logic to completion. I merely observe here that many economists and others within the social science community (Michel's 1962; March and Simon, 1958) practice feasible foresight, although this is an underused perspective.

My interpretation of Simon's description of self-interest seeking as "frailty of motive" (Simon, 1985, p. 303) is that most people will do what they say (and some will do more) most of the time without self-consciously asking whether the effort is justified by expected discounted net gains. If they slip, it is a normal friction and often a matter of bemusement. The proposition that routines describe the behavior of most individuals most of the time contemplates (nonstrategic) benign behavior.

But while accurate descriptions of what is going on "most of the time" are plainly essential, much of what is interesting about human behavior in general and organizations in particular has reference not to routines but to exceptions. Indeed, once good routines have been developed, the chief role of management is to deal with exceptions. In the context of outsourcing, such exceptions arise from contractual incompleteness in combination with consequential disturbances that push the parties to an interim agreement off of the contract curve. Strategic considerations — which arise by reason of information asymmetries, bilateral dependencies, weaknesses of property rights, and the costliness of court enforcement of contracts — will now come into play if, rather than mere frailty of motive, opportunism is the operative condition.

Adaptations — Both the organization theorist Barnard and the economist Hayek took adaptation to be the main purpose of economic organization, but with differences. Finding little in the social sciences that informed the study of internal organization (hierarchy) as he had experienced it, Barnard undertook to craft the relevant concepts himself in his path-breaking book, *The Functions of the Executive* (Barnard, 1938), where he focused on coordinated adaptation as accomplished in a "conscious, deliberate, purposeful" way through the use of administration. Hayek, by contrast, celebrated the "marvel of the market" (Hayek, 1945, p. 527) where autonomous adaptations are implemented spontaneously in response to changes in relative prices.

The challenge for the economics of governance was to recognize that adaptations of both kinds are important and to make selective provision for each. Rather, therefore, than be trapped in the old ideological divide between markets or hierarchies, transaction cost economics treats the two as alternative modes of governance, markets, and hierarchies, both of which have distinctive roles to play in a well working economy. The heretofore maligned mode of hierarchy is now awarded coequal status with the marvel of the market, the object being to deploy each appropriately.

Contract Laws (Plural) — As against the standard practice of there being one all-purpose law of contract, Llewellyn, who was a leader in the Legal Realism Movement in the United States, moved beyond the concept of contract as legal rules (with court enforcement) by introducing the idea of "contract as framework," predominantly as implemented by private ordering. Specifically, the "major importance of legal contract is to provide ... a framework which almost never accurately indicates real working relations, but which affords a rough indication around which such relations vary, an occasional guide in cases of doubt, and a norm of ultimate appeal when the relations cease in fact to work" (Llewellyn, 1931, pp. 736–737). This last condition is important, in that recourse to the courts for purposes of ultimate appeal serves to delimit threat positions. The more elastic concept of contract as framework nevertheless supports a (cooperative) exchange relation over a wider range of contractual disturbances than would a strict legal rules construction. As discussed below in conjunction with pushing the logic to completion, the contract law regime of "forbearance" has similar purposive origins.

Suffice it to observe here that adaptations (of autonomous and coordinated kinds) are taken to be the central purpose of organization; and viable modes of governance differ in contract law respects.

3.2. *Key Operational Moves*

The three key operational moves are to (i) name the attributes of the unit of analysis, (ii) do the same for modes of governance, and (iii) advance the efficient alignment hypothesis.

Unit of Analysis — Various units of analysis have been proposed for studying organizations, yet efforts to name the defining attributes of proposed units are rare. The unit of analysis in the transaction cost economics set-up is the transaction — as recommended by Commons (1932) and as is implicit in Coase (1937, 1960). For transaction cost economizing purposes, the critical dimensions of transactions are complexity, the condition of asset specificity, and the disturbances to which a transaction is subject. As among these three, the attributes of transactions that have been most important to an understanding of the governance of contractual relations are the conditions of asset specificity and outlier disturbances for which unprogrammed adaptations are needed.[10]

Although Marschak had made perceptive reference to specialized human and locational conditions and observed that "the problem of unique or imperfectly standardized goods ... had been neglected in the textbooks" (Marschak, 1968, p. 14), the wide reach of asset specificity — to include physical, human, site specific, dedicated, brand name capital, and episodic (or temporal) forms — would become evident only as the concerted study of transaction cost economics got under way. Relevant in this connection is that different types of hazards accrue to different forms of asset specificity, which variations have significant organizational ramifications. Whatever the particulars, the basic regularity that is associated with transactions that are supported by investments in specific assets is that these assets cannot be redeployed to alternative uses and users without loss of productive value (Williamson, 1971, 1975, 1976, 1985; Klein et al., 1978).

Intertemporal considerations are relevant in this connection. Thus although some conditions of asset specificity are evident from the outset, others evolve during contract implementation. (Human asset specificity that arises because of learning by doing is an example of the latter.) Whatever the source of the condition of asset specificity, the condition of nonredeployability, to which I refer above, has the effect of transforming what may have been a large numbers bidding competition at the outset into a small numbers exchange relationship during the period of the contract and at the contract renewal interval. Such transformations compromise the efficacy of simple

---

[10] Note, however, that complexity plays a crucial role in the following respect: all complex contracts are incomplete by reason of bounded rationality. Not all incompleteness, however, is consequential. I associate consequential incompleteness mainly with outlier disturbances for which the stakes are great (because the parties are bilaterally dependent), on which account asset specificity and uncertainty are the defining features. Inconsequential incompleteness is that range of disturbances over which Llewellyn's "contract as framework" can be presumed to work well, often with the support of credible contracting mechanisms. It is also, however, useful to recognize that incompleteness becomes more severe as the number of features of a transaction (precision, linkages, compatibility) across which adaptations are needed increase and as the number of consequential disturbances that impinge on these features increase, which disturbances increase with the length of the contract.

market exchange, which is supplanted by longer term contracts (as supported by credible commitments) or, in the limit, by unified ownership of successive stages with recourse to hierarchy.[11]

Modes of Governance — Markets and hierarchies are the two polar modes to which Coase referred in his 1937 paper and are the governance alternatives on which I focus in my paper on the vertical integration of production. This is wholly in the spirit of the first precept of pragmatic methodology: keep it simple (Solow, 2001; Snowdon and Vane, 1997). It is noteworthy, however, that transaction cost economics has subsequently introduced the hybrid mode (Williamson, 1991; Menard, 1996) and has furthermore moved beyond intermediate product market contracting to interpret a wide range of commercial (and some noncommercial) phenomena as variations on a theme.

The critical dimensions for describing alternative modes of governance, of which markets and hierarchies are two, are incentive intensity (which is strong in autonomous stages that appropriate their streams of net receipts and is weak under cost-plus reward schemes), administrative command and control (which is strong if successive stages are under unified ownership and are subject to coordination and dispute resolution by a common "boss"), and contract law regime, which is strong under a legal rules (court ordered) contract law regime but is weak if disputes between successive stages are settled by private ordering (where the firm is its own final court of ultimate appeal).

Assuming that each of these three dimensions of governance can take on either of these two values, weak (0) or strong (+), and that we focus on polar modes (market and hierarchy), there are $2^3 = 8$ possible combinations. Which are the internally consistent combinations that describe market and hierarchy? As discussed elsewhere (Williamson, 1991), the syndrome that describes the market is strong incentive intensity, weak command and control at the interface, and strong (legal rules) contracting. The syndrome that

---

[11] Note that because asset specificity is a design variable, the good or service to be delivered could be redesigned so as to reduce asset specific features, albeit at a sacrifice in performance of the good or service in question (Riordan and Williamson, 1985). Note also that whereas the emphasis on individual (bilateral) transactions serves the purpose of analytical simplicity, groups of related transactions sometimes pose sequencing problems. This introduces systems considerations for which real time coordination complexities need to be factored in. (See note 18, *infra*.)

describes hierarchy, by contrast, is weak incentive intensity, strong administrative command, and control at the interface, and weak contract law regime (forbearance law). So described, market and hierarchy are polar opposites.

Efficient Alignment — Transaction cost economics appeals to the efficient alignment hypothesis to predict which transactions go where — to wit, transactions, which differ in their attributes, are aligned with governance structures, which differ in their cost and competences, so as to effect a (mainly) transaction cost economizing outcome. The basic prediction for generic transactions for which asset specificity is nil and the adaptive needs can be ascertained and implemented autonomously is that these will be procured in the market. Such transactions correspond to the ideal transactions in both law and economics. Transactions, by contrast, that are supported by significant investments in transaction specific assets and are subject to incompleteness (by reason of bounds on rationality) will experience malcoordination when beset by significant disturbances for which defection from cooperation can be projected as the stakes increase. Such transactions will benefit from unified ownership and coordinated adaptations as implemented by hierarchy.

3.3. *Applications*

Economic theories take on added significance if and as (i) the predictions are borne out by the data, (ii) variations on a theme are worked out, and (iii) public policy ramifications accrue and are displayed.

Empirical — Transaction cost economics both makes predictions and submits them to empirical testing. Not only did empirical tests of transactions cost economics number over 800 in 2006, but they have been broadly corroborative (Macher and Richman, 2008). Indeed, "despite what almost 30 years ago may have appeared to be insurmountable obstacles to acquiring the relevant data (which are often primary data of a microanalytic kind), today transaction cost economics stands on a remarkably broad empirical foundation" (Geyskens, Steenkamp, and Kumar, 2006, p. 531). There is no gainsaying that transaction cost economics has been much more influential because of the empirical work that it has engendered (Whinston, 2001).

Variations on a Theme — Transaction cost economics has many applications not only within the field of industrial organization but within most applied fields of economics as well — to include labor, public finance, comparative economic systems, and economic development and reform. Applications to business — to the fields of strategy, organizational behavior, marketing, finance, operations management, and accounting — are likewise numerous. Numerous applications to the contiguous social sciences (especially sociology, political science, social psychology, and aspects of the law) have also been made. Such broad reach arises because any problem that arises as or can be reformulated as a contracting problem can be examined to advantage in transaction cost economizing terms.

Public Policy[12] — Although transaction cost economics has had numerous applications to public policy toward business (antitrust, regulation, corporate governance) and in some degree in the study of agriculture, public health, public bureaus, and economic development and reform, it is, in my judgment, an underused public policy perspective — especially in the design of public bureaus, of which the Department of Homeland Security in the United States is a recent example (Cohen, Cuellar, and Weingast, 2006). An efficiency assessment of feasible alternatives is too often scanted by a political process where public bureaus are designed with reference to immediate political purposes.

4. Pushing the Logic to Completion

Pushing the logic to completion is accomplished by combining the second and third precepts of pragmatic methodology — namely, "get it right" and "make it plausible" (Solow, 2001, p. 111). Getting it right "includes translating economic concepts into accurate mathematics (or diagrams, or words) and making sure that further logical operations are correctly performed and verified" (Solow, 2001, p. 112); and plausible simple models of complex phenomena are expected to "make sense for 'reasonable' or 'plausible' values of the important parameters" (Solow, 2001, p. 112). Also, because "not everything that is logically consistent is credulous" (Kreps, 1999, p. 125), fanciful constructions that lose contact with the phenomena are suspect — especially if alternative and more veridical models yield refutable implications that are

---

[12] Applications of transaction cost economics to public policy are reported in Williamson (1985, 2003, 2008, 2009).

congruent with the data. Combining precepts 2 and 3, the argument comes down to this: push the logic to completion, as tempered by considerations of feasibility.

Pushing the logic of zero transaction cost to completion with respect to externalities (Coase) and vertical integration (Arrow) revealed that routine recourse to this simplifying assumption led to counterfactual predictions, as a result of which economists and other social scientists were encouraged to push the logic of positive transaction costs to completion — both in general and as revealed by gaps or omissions that would become evident as the transaction cost economics setup evolved. Four such conditions are examined here: the impossibility of selective intervention, which bears on limits to firm size; the concept of remediableness, which has massive public policy ramifications by insisting on feasible, implementable solutions; credible contracting, which is a robust concept for expanding the range within which mutual gains from trade can be projected; and the test of scaling up to ascertain whether successive application of the simple (toy) model on which the analysis rests yields a scaled up version that approximates the phenomenon in question. Also, I briefly discuss the natural progression.

4.1. *Selective Intervention*

The limits to firm size puzzle, as posed by Knight (1933) and Coase (1937), is this: Why can't a large firm do everything that a collection of smaller firms can do and more? Lewis answers a variant of this puzzle as follows: because an established firm can always "use the input exactly as the newer entrant would have used it [and can furthermore] improve on this by coordinating production from his new and existing puts" the large firm will always realize greater value (Lewis, 1983, p. 1092). Transaction cost economics examines this argument by postulating two mechanisms — replication and selective intervention — which, if they could be implemented, would support the all-purpose superiority of larger firms.

Thus, suppose that two successive stages of production are combined with the understanding that (i) the acquired stage will operate in the same autonomous manner post acquisition as in the preacquisition status (by replication) except as (ii) the acquiring stage intervenes selectively, always but only when expected net gains can be ascribed to coordinated adaptations.

In that event, the combined firm can never do worse (by replication) and will sometimes do better (by selective intervention). Accordingly, more integration is always better than less — which is to say that, upon repeated application of this logic, everything will be organized in one large firm. Wherein does the implementation of this logic break down?

Assuming that the buyer stage acquires the supplier stage, the four conditions for implementing replication and selective intervention are these: (i) the buyer stage as acquirer (owner) promises the acquired supplier that the acquired stage will continue to appropriate its net receipts (as reduced by overhead, maintenance, user and capital depreciation charges) in all state realizations — thereby to preserve high powered incentives; (ii) the supplier promises to utilize the supply stage assets, the ownership of which has been transferred to the buyer, with "due care"; (iii) the buyer promises always and only to exercise authority (fiat) when expected net benefits can be ascribed to selective intervention; and (iv) the buyer promises candidly to reveal and divide the benefits that accrue to selective intervention as stipulated in the acquisition agreement. The problem is that none of these promises is self-enforcing. To the contrary, in the absence of three-way common knowledge (to include a costless arbiter),[13] each condition will be compromised. Contributing factors include (i) the owner (buyer) controls the accounting system and, within limits, can declare depreciation, transfer prices, and benefits so as to shift net receipts to its advantage, (ii) failures of due care become known only with delay and are difficult to prove, (iii) the buyer can also falsely declare state realizations to favor its own stream of net receipts, and (iv) in consideration of the foregoing, the division of benefits under selective intervention can be compromised. Also, (v) the political game is now played in a larger firm that is more susceptible to bureaucratic ploys and political positioning than in smaller firms.

The details of this brief sketch are reported elsewhere (Williamson, 1985, Chapter 6). Suffice it to observe that the breakdowns referred to above are often intuited by many intelligent businessmen and their lawyers, who

---

[13] The need for three-way common knowledge, to include the arbiter, is yet another example of pushing the logic to completion (Williamson, 1975, pp. 21–34). The assumption that two-way common knowledge suffices is nonetheless widely held

recognize the tradeoffs and factor them into the decision to integrate (or not). The lesson for social scientists is that markets and hierarchies differ in discrete structural ways, and we need to come to terms with the strengths and weaknesses of each.

4.2. *Remediableness*

The remediableness criterion serves as a reality check on the practice among public policy analysts of assuming that transaction costs in the public sector are zero. Not only is that nonsense, but standard public policy proceeded in an asymmetric way: private sector contracting experienced market failures, by reason of positive transaction costs, but there was no corresponding concept for public sector failures.[14] Little surprise, then, that convoluted public policy prescriptions were often (unwittingly) anchored in asymmetric application of zero transaction cost reasoning, of which regulation is an example (Coase, 1964).

The remediableness criterion is an effort to deal symmetrically with real world institutions, both public and private, warts and all. The criterion is this: an extant mode of organization for which no superior feasible form of organization can be described and implemented with expected net gains is presumed to be efficient (Williamson, 1996).

Because all feasible modes of organization are flawed, the feasibility stipulation precludes all appeals to the fiction of zero transaction costs (in any sector whatsoever — public, private, nonprofit, etc.) from the very outset. The implementation stipulation requires that the costs of implementing a proposed feasible alternative (one that is judged to be superior to an extant mode in a *de novo* side by side comparison) be included in the net gain calculus. The presumption that an extant mode is efficient if the expected net gain is negative can nevertheless be rebutted by showing that the obstacles to implementing an otherwise superior feasible alternative are "unfair."

---

[14] Albeit a caricature, "normative public policy analysis began by supposing that … policy was made by an omnipotent, omniscient, and benevolent dictator" (Dixit, 1996, p. 8) which, in transaction cost terms, assumes the absence of implementation obstacles, bounds on rationality and opportunism, respectively.

Fairness of both political and economic kinds come under review. Thus whereas political obstacles that are judged to be fair in circumstances where politics properly trumps economics (Stigler, 1992) survive, those that have unacceptable political origins (e.g., are unfairly discriminatory) do not. Likewise, whereas some economic obstacles, such as sunk costs that have been incurred by the incumbent, may warrant delaying the introduction of a superior feasible alternative, those that are judged to be unfair (e.g., predatory behavior) will be challenged.[15]

The upshot is that the remediableness criterion is an effort to disallow asymmetric efficiency reasoning of a zero transaction cost kind and force the relevant efficiency issues for the making of public policy — namely, feasibility, implementation, and rebuttal — to the top.

4.3. *Credible Commitments*

The concept of credible threat figures prominently in the study of rivalry (between nation states, in politics, and in business), where the main purpose of a credible threat is to deter the use of some instruments (e.g., nuclear weapons), thereby to deflect competition to other venues (Schelling, 1960) or to deter the appearance of competition altogether. The use of cost effective credible commitments to support exchange is related but different.

The basic proposition is this: absent the use of credible commitments to support exchange, the contractual hazards associated with many transactions would be perceived to be excessive. Generic investments would replace transaction specific investments if the latter pose too great a risk. Some transactions would be taken into firms. Some would never materialize.

Credible commitments sometimes come into place spontaneously, as where a history of good experience with a trader leads to a positive reputation effect. Often, however, credible commitments take shape as economic

---

[15]To be sure, unfair obstacles to implementation may persist even after a showing that these stand in the way of progress. Obstacles to efficiency nevertheless invite dissent. Some can be overturned by the cumulative force of movements, of which the civil rights movement is an example, and others by perfecting definitions of unfair competition.

actors consciously agree upon mechanisms that provide added assurance.[16] These can take the form of information disclosure and auditing mechanisms, the development of specialized dispute settling mechanisms, whereby the parties rely more on private ordering than court ordering (Llewellyn, 1931; Macaulay, 1963; Summers, 1969; Macneil, 1974; Galanter, 1981), and sometimes involve creating hostages to support exchange (Williamson, 1983).[17]

Credibility supports also vary with the institutional environment as among political jurisdictions (Levy and Spiller, 1994), to which the literature on positive political theory is relevant. Also relevant to the economics of governance is the concept of contract laws (plural), an example of which is the concept of "forbearance law" to describe the contract law regime within hierarchy[18] (Williamson, 1991, p. 274):

The implicit contract law of internal organization is that of forbearance. Thus, whereas courts routinely grant standing to firms should there be disputes over prices, the damages to be ascribed to delays, failures of quality, and the like, courts will refuse to hear disputes between one internal division and another over identical technical issues. Access to the courts being denied, the parties must resolve their differences internally. Accordingly, hierarchy is its own court of ultimate appeal.

The concept of forbearance law regime was introduced to fill a logical gap in the theory of governance. As with other forms of contract law, the

---

[16] The 32-year coal supply agreement between the Nevada Power Company and the Northwest Trading Company is illustrative (Williamson, 1991).

[17] Efforts to enhance credibility sometimes take strange forms, presumably because the parties are unable to do better. Thus consider the recently unearthed tablets in Mesopotamia (dated around 1750 B.C.) which reveal that self-inflicted curses were used to deter the breach of treaties. One of these reads as follows:

When you ask us for troops, we will not withhold our best forces, we will not answer you with evasions, we shall brandish our maces and strike down your enemy ...

As wasted seeds do not sprout, may my seed never rise, may someone else marry my wife under my eyes, and may someone else rule my country (*China Daily*, March 22, 1988, p. 1).

[18] Note that forbearance law precludes court jurisdiction over most internal decision making to which internal consequences accrue, but court jurisdiction does apply to externalities.

efficacy of forbearance law varies with the integrity of the institutional environment (nation state) of which it is a part.

4.4. *Scaling Up*

The object of a simple model is to capture the essence, thereby to explain hitherto puzzling practices and make predictions that are subjected to empirical testing. Often, however, simple models can also be "tested" with respect to scaling up. Does repeated application of the basic mechanism out of which the simple model works yield a result that recognizably describes the phenomenon in question?

The test of scaling up is usually ignored, possibly out of awareness that scaling up cannot be done. Sometimes it is scanted, possibly in the mistaken belief that scaling up can be accomplished easily. My position is that claims of real world relevance, including public policy relevance, of any proposed theory of the firm that cannot be shown to scale up from toy model status to approximate the phenomenon of interest (e.g., the modern corporation) should be regarded with caution.[19]

With respect to the transaction cost theory of the firm as governance structure the question is this: Does successive application of the make or buy decision, as it is applied to individual transactions in the transaction cost economics set-up, scale up to describe something that approximates a multistage firm? Note that transaction cost economics assumes that the transactions of principal interest are those that take place at the interface between (rather than within) technologically separable stages. Upon taking the technological "core" as given, one focuses attention as a series of separable make or buy decisions — backward, forward, and lateral — to ascertain which should be outsourced and which should be incorporated within the ownership boundary of the firm. So described the firm is the inclusive set of

---

[19] Jensen and Meckling (1976) posed the question of whether their simple model of entrepreneurial ownership scaled up to deal with the diversely owned modern corporation. They conjectured that it did apply but deferred a demonstration of scaling up to a later paper. Alas, that paper never appeared. Jensen and Meckling nevertheless candidly perceived the need for scaling up.

transactions for which the decision is to make rather than buy — which does implement scaling up, or at least is an approximation thereto (Williamson, 1985).[20]

4.5. *The Natural Progression*

Transaction cost economics is sometimes criticized because it has not been fully formalized, to which I have three responses: transaction cost economics, like many other theories, has undergone a natural progression; full formalization is a work in progress; and premature formalization runs the risk of a disconnection with the phenomena.

Theories commonly progress from informal to preformat to semiformal to fully formal stages of development — broadly in the spirit of Kuhn (1970). The informal stage of transaction cost economics was the literature from the 1930s (especially Commons and Coase) where errors or omissions in the neoclassical set-up were described. Preformat work got under way in the 1970s, where new concepts for reinterpreting vertical integration, vertical market restrictions, labor market organization, franchise bidding for natural monopoly, and the like were forged and the conditions for efficient alignment were worked out. Semiformal work, in the 1980s and since, deal with

---

[20] There is, however, a caveat: scaling up, so described, does not make allowance for systems complications of the kind that arose in conjunction with Boeing Aircraft's production of the 787 Dreamliner, where outsourcing confusion was rampant (Sanders, 2009, "Boeing CEO's Bumpy Ride," *Wall street Journal,* November. 5. *http://online.wsj.com.*). With the benefit of hindsight, malcoordination among outsourced transactions led to costly delays which possibly could have been averted if related components for which real time coordination would prove to be crucial had been produced internally. The requisite apparatus to address the systems complications that can arise among groups of related transactions has yet to be worked up within transaction cost economics.

Applications of transaction cost economics would, however, have avoided the most serious outsourcing error made by Boeing: the decision to outsource the highly specialized fuselage to Vought Aircraft Industries. This transaction required significant investments in specific assets and would pose a series of adaptation problems during contract implementation (Tadelis, 2010a). Boeing subsequently rectified this condition by acquiring Vought (Sanders, 2009, "Boeing Takes Control of Plant," *Wall street Journal,* December 23, pp. B2).

credible contracting, hybrid modes, the dimensionalization of transactions and governance structures, a multiplicity of applications within business and economics and the contiguous social sciences (to include public policy), and extensive empirical testing. Full formalism also got under way in the 1980s and is still in progress. The path-breaking paper by Grossman and Hart (1986) and the follow-on paper by Hart and John Moore (1990) and others in this tradition — which deal with some types of transaction costs (but is more often referred to as the property rights literature) — have been very influential. Subsequent significant work by Tadelis and his coauthors (Bajari and Tadelis, 2001; Tadelis, 2002; Levin and Tadelis, forthcoming; Tadelis, 2010a) is likewise in progress.

5. Concluding Remarks

What I describe as the transaction cost economics project had its origins in the puzzle posed by Coase in 1937: What explains the boundaries of the firm? I addressed this by taking the vertical integration decision to be the focal transaction and, upon reformulating it as a contracting problem, asked the following question: When and why should a firm acquire a technologically separable component by outsourcing rather than producing to its own needs — where outsourcing entails contracting out and own-production to contracting within. This question was addressed as an efficiency issue by selectively combining economics with organization theory. Albeit intended as a standalone research project, the vertical integration set-up would open windows to a wide array of economic activities that arose as or could be reformulated in comparative contractual terms.

With the benefit of hindsight, transaction cost economics has undergone a natural progression. The informal stage got started in the 1930s with Coase's challenge to the profession that firm and market organization should be derived rather than (as was then the practice) taken as given, to include the suggestion that the missing concept was transaction cost. This latter was buttressed by demonstrations (by Arrow and Coase) in the 1960s that much of standard economics was reduced to irrelevance upon pushing the logic of zero transaction costs to completion.

The preformal stage began in the 1970s with the application of the lens of contract/governance to vertical integration. Interim contracts that were incomplete (by reason of bounds on rationality) would experience maladaptation hazards if the parties were bilaterally dependent (by reason of transaction specific investments) in the face of disturbances for which the stakes are great (strategic defection). This economics of governance approach would subsequently have wide application as other contractual phenomena were interpreted as variations on a theme.

The semiformal stage gave added prominence to the defining attributes of alternative modes of governance (market, hybrid, and hierarchy) as these relate to differing adaptive needs, of autonomous and coordinated kinds, among different transactions. A series of puzzles arose as this operationalization effort progressed — of which the efficacy of selective intervention was one and scaling up was another, for which the answers would be revealed by pushing the logic of economic organizations to completion. Beginning in the early 1980s' and growing exponentially thereafter, an ambitious effort at empirical testing got under way. Applications to public policy are likewise numerous and growing. Fully formal research of a transaction cost economics kind has taken shape, and more is in progress.

I conclude that selectively combining law, economics, and organization to study the governance of contractual relations from a transaction cost economizing perspective has been instructive; and I project that research of this kind will continue to develop in conceptual, theoretical, empirical, and public policy respects. Research in transaction cost economics faces an interesting, challenging future.

References

Arrow, Kenneth J. 1969. "The Organization of Economic Activity: Issues Pertinent to the Choice of Market Versus Nonmarket Allocation." In *The Analysis and Evaluation of Public Expenditure: The PPB system*, pp. 59–73. Washington, DC: US Government Printing Office.

Bajari, Patrick and Steven Tadelis. 2001. "Incentives Versus Transaction Costs: A Theory of Procurement Contracts." *RAND Journal of Economics*, 32(3), pp. 387–407.

Barnard, Chester Irving. 1938. *The Functions of the Executive*, Cambridge, MA: Harvard University Press.

Baumol, William J. 1959. *Business Behavior, Value and Growth*, New York: Macmillan.

Ben-Porath, Yoram. 1980. "The F-Connection: Families, Friends, and Firms and the Organization of Exchange." *Population and Development Review*, 6(1), pp.1–30.

Buchanan, James M. 1975. "A Contractarian Paradigm for Applying Economic Theory." *American Economic Review*, 65(2),pp. 225–230.

Buchanan, James M. 2001. "Game Theory, Mathematics, and Economies." *Journal of Economic Methodology*, 8(1), pp. 27–32.

Coase, Ronald H. 1937. "The Nature of the Firm." *Economica*, N.S., 4(16): 386–405, Reprinted In *The Nature of the Firm: Origins, Evolution, Development*, 1991, eds. Oliver E. Williamson and Sidney Winter, pp. 18–33. New York: Oxford University Press.

Coase, Ronald H. 1960. "The Problem of Social Cost." *Journal of Law and Economics*, 3(1): 1–44. (3), pp.194–197.

Coase, Ronald H. 1964. "The Regulated Industries: Discussion." *American Economic Review*, 54 (May), pp. 194–197.

Coase, Ronald H. 1972. "Industrial Organization: A Proposal for Research." In *Economic Research: Retrospect and Prospect*, Vol. 3, ed. V.R. Fuchs, pp. 59–73. New York: National Bureau of Economic Research.

Coase, Ronald H. 1988. "The Nature of the Firm: Influence." *Journal of Law, Economics, and Organization*, 4(1), pp. 33–47.

Coase, Ronald H. 1992. "The Institutional Structure of Production." *American Economic Review*, 82(4), pp. 713–719.

Cohen, Dara K., Mariano-Florentino Cuellar, and Barry R. Weingast. 2006. "Crisis Bureaucracy: Homeland Security and the Political Design of Legal Mandates." *Stanford Law Review*, 59(3), pp. 673–760.

Commons, John R. 1932. "The Problem of Correlating Law, Economics, and Ethics." *Wisconsin Law Review*, 8, pp. 3–26.

Commons, John R. 1950. *The Economics of Collective Action*. New York: Macmillan.

Cyert, Richard M. and James G. March. 1963. *A Behavioral Theory of the Firm*. Englewood Cliffs, NJ: Prentice-Hall.

D'Andrade, Roy. 1986. "Three Scientific World Views and the Covering Law Model." In *Metatheory in social science: Pluralisms and subjectivities*, eds. Donald W. Fiske and Richard A. Schweder, pp. 19–41. Chicago: University of Chicago Press.

Demsetz, Harold. 1983. "The Structure of Ownership and the Theory of the Firm." *Journal of Law and Economics*, 26(2), pp.375–390.

Dixit, Avinash K. 1996. *The Making of Economic Policy: A Transaction-Cost Politics Perspective*, Cambridge, MA: MIT Press.

Dreze, Jacques H. 1995. "Forty Years of Public Economics: A Personal Perspective." *Journal of Economic Perspectives*, 9(2), pp. 111–130.

Fellner, William. 1947. "Prices and Wages under Bilateral Oligopoly." *Quarterly Journal of Economics*, 61(4), pp. 503–532.

Fischer, Stanley. 1977. "Long-Term Contracting, Sticky Prices, and Monetary Policy: A Comment." *Journal of Monetary Economics*, 3(3),pp. 317–323.

Galanter, Marc. 1981. "Justice in Many Rooms: Courts, Private Ordering, and Indigenous Law." *Journal of Legal Pluralism and Unofficial Law*, 19(1), pp. 1–47.

Geyskens, Inge, Jan-Benedict E.M. Steenkamp, and Nirmalya Kumar. 2006. "Make, Buy, or Ally: A Transaction Cost Theory Meta-Analysis." *Academy of Management Journal*, 49(3), pp. 519–543.

Grossman, Sanford J., and Oliver D. Hart. 1986. "The Costs and Benefits of Ownership: A Theory of Vertical and Lateral Integration." *Journal of Political Economy*, 94(4),pp. 691–719.

Hart, Oliver D., and John Moore. 1990. "Property Rights and the Nature of the Firm." *Journal of Political Economy*, 98(6),pp. 1119–1158.

Hayek, Friedrich. 1945. "The Use of Knowledge in Society." *American Economic Review*, 35(4), pp. 519–530.

Jensen, Michael C., and William H. Meckling. 1976. "Theory of the Firm: Managerial Behavior, Agency Costs and Ownership Structure." *Journal of Financial Economics*, 3(4), pp. 305–360.

Kitch, Edmund W. 1983. "The Fire of Truth: A Remembrance of Law and Economics at Chicago, 1932–1970." *Journal of Law and Economics*, 26(1), pp. 163–233

Klein, Benjamin, Robert G. Crawford, and Armen A. Alchian. 1978. "Vertical Integration, Appropriable Rents, and the Competitive Contracting Process." *Journal of Law and Economics*, 21(2), pp. 297–326.

Knight, Frank H. 1921. *Risk, Uncertainty, and Profit*. New York: Houghton Mifflin.

Knight, Frank H. 1933. *Risk, Uncertainty, and Profit*. London: London School of Economics and Political Science (Orig. pub. 1921).

Kreps, David M. 1999. "Markets and Hierarchies and (Mathematical) Economic Theory." In *Firms, Markets, and Hierarchies: The Transaction Cost Economics Perspective*, eds. Glenn R. Carroll and David J. Teece, pp. 121–155. Oxford: Oxford University Press.

Kuhn, Thomas S. 1970. *The structure of scientific Revolutions*, 2nd edn., Chicago: University of Chicago Press.

Levin, Jonathan, and Steven Tadelis. Forthcoming. "Contracting for Government Services: Theory and Evidence from U.S. Cities." *Journal of Industrial Economics*.

Levy, Brian, and Pablo T. Spiller. 1994. "The Institutional Foundations of Regulatory Commitment: A Comparative Analysis of Telecommunications Regulation." *Journal of Law, Economics, and Organization*, 10(2), pp. 201–246.

Lewis, Tracy R. 1983. "Preemption, Divestiture, and Forward Contracting in a Market Dominated by a Single Firm." *American Economic Review*, 73(5), pp. 1092–1101.

Llewellyn, Karl N. 1931. "What Price Contract? An Essay in Perspective." *Yale Law Journal*, 40(5), pp. 704–751.

Macaulay, Stewart. 1963. "Non-Contractual Relations in Business: A Preliminary Study." *American sociological Review*, 28(1), pp. 55–67.

Macher, Jeffrey T., and Barak D. Richman. 2008. *"Transaction Cost Economics: An Assessment of Empirical Research in the Social Sciences."*

Macneil, Ian R. 1974. "The Many Futures of Contracts." *Southern California Law Review*, 47(3), pp. 691–816.

March, James G., and Herbert A. Simon. 1958. *Organizations*. New York: John Wiley & Sons.

Marris, Robin L. 1964. *The Economic Theory of Managerial Capitalism*. New York: Free Press.

Marschak, Jacob. 1968. "Economics of Inquiring, Communicating, Deciding." *American Economic Review*, 58(2), pp. 1–18.

McKenzie, Lionel W. 1951. "Ideal Output and the Interdependence of Firms." *Economic Journal*, 61(244), pp. 785–803.

Menard, Claude. 1996. "Why Organizations Matter: A Journey Away from the Fairy Tale." *Atlantic Economic Journal*, 24(4), pp. 281–300.

Michels, Robert. 1962. *Political Parties*. New York: Free Press.

Posner, Richard A. 1977. *Economic Analysis of Law*. 2nd edn., Boston: Little, Brown.

Reder, Melvin W. 1999. Economics: *The Culture of a Controversial Science*. Chicago: University of Chicago Press.

Riordan, Michael H., and Oliver E. Williamson. 1985. "Asset Specificity and Economic Organization." *International Journal of Industrial Organization*, 3(4), pp. 365–378.

Schelling, Thomas C. 1960. *The strategy of Conflict*. Cambridge, MA: Harvard University Press.

Shultz, George P. 1995. "Economics in Action: Ideas, Institutions, Policies." *American Economic Review*, 85(2), pp. 1–8.

Simon, Herbert A. 1957(a). *Administrative Behavior*. 2nd edn., New York: Macmillan.

Simon, Herbert A. 1957(b). *Models of Man: Social and Rational*. New York: John Wiley & Sons.

Simon, Herbert A. 1984. "On the Behavioral and Rational Foundations of Economic Dynamics." *Journal of Economic Behavior and Organization*, 5(1), pp. 35–55.

Simon, Herbert A. 1985. "Human Nature in Politics: The Dialogue of Psychology with Political Science." *American Political Science Review,* 79(2), pp. 293–304.

Simon, Herbert A. 1991. *Models of My Life.* New York: Basic Books.

Snowdon, Brian, and Howard R. Vane. 1997. "Modern Macroeconomics and Its Evolution from a Monetarist Perspective: An Interview with Professor Milton Friedman." *Journal of Economic Studies,* 24(4–5), pp. 192–222.

Solow, Robert M. 2001. "A Native Informant Speaks." *Journal of Economic Methodology,* 8(1), pp. 111–112.

Stigler, George J. 1951. "The Division of Labor Is Limited by the Extent of the Market." *Journal of Political Economy,* 59(3), pp. 185–193.

Stigler, George J. 1992. "Law or Economics?" *Journal of Law and Economics,* 35(2), pp. 455–468.

Summers, Clyde W. 1969. "Collective Agreements and the Law of Contracts." *Yale Law Journal,* 78(4), pp. 525–575.

Tadelis, Steven. 2002. "Complexity, Flexibility, and the Make-or-Buy Decision." *American Economic Review,* 92(2), pp. 433–437.

Tadelis, Steven. 2010a. "Transaction Cost Economics." Unpublished.

Tadelis, Steven. 2010b. "Williamson's Contribution and Its Relevance to 21st Century Capitalism." *California Management Review,* 52(2), pp. 159–166.

Whinston, Michael D. 2001. "Assessing the Property Rights and Transaction-Cost Theories of Firm Scope." *American Economic Review,* 91(2), pp. 184–188.

Williamson, Oliver E. 1964. *The Economics of Discretionary Behavior: Managerial Objectives in a Theory of the Firm.* Englewood Cliffs, NJ: Prentice-Hall.

Williamson, Oliver E. 1971. "The Vertical Integration of Production: Market Failure Considerations." *American Economic Review,* 61(2): 112–123.

Williamson, Oliver E. 1975. *Markets and Hierarchies: Analysis and Antitrust Implications.* New York: Free Press.

Williamson, Oliver E. 1976. "Franchise Bidding for Natural Monopolies-in General and with Respect to CATV." *Bell Journal of Economics,* 7(1), pp. 73–104.

Williamson, Oliver E. 1979. "Transaction Cost Economics: The Governance of Contractual Relations." *Journal of Law and Economics,* 22 (2), pp. 233–261.

Williamson, Oliver E. 1983. "Credible Commitments: Using Hostages to Support Exchange." *American Economic Review,* 73(4), pp. 519–540.

Williamson, Oliver E. 1985. *The Economic Institutions of Capitalism.* New York: Free Press.

Williamson, Oliver E. 1991. "Comparative Economic Organization: The Analysis of Discrete Structural Alternatives." *Administrative Science Quarterly,* 36 (2), pp. 269–296.

Williamson, Oliver E. 1996. *The Mechanisms of Governance.* Oxford: Oxford University Press.

Williamson, Oliver E. 2000. "The New Institutional Economics: Taking Stock, Looking Ahead." *Journal of Economic Literature*, 38(3), pp. 595–613.

Williamson, Oliver E. 2002. "The Theory of the Firm as Governance Structure: From Choice to Contract." *Journal of Economic Perspectives*, 16(3), pp. 171–195.

Williamson, Oliver E. 2003. "Examining Economic Organization through the Lens of Contract." *Industrial and Corporate Change*, 12(4), pp. 917–942.

Williamson, Oliver E. 2008. "Corporate Boards of Directors: In Principle and in Practice." *Journal of Law, Economics, and Organization*, 24(2), pp. 247–272.

Williamson, Oliver E. 2009. "Opening the Black Box of Firm and Market Organization: Antitrust." In *The Modern Firm, Corporate Governance and Investment*, eds. Per-Olof Bjuggren and Dennis C. Mueller, pp. 11–42. Northampton, MA: Edward Elgar.

Chapter 2

The Lens of Contract: Private Ordering*

Buchanan (2001, p. 29) avers that "mutuality of advantage from voluntary exchange is ... the most fundamental of all understandings in economics." He further contends that this fundamental understanding is better realized by examining economics through the lens of contract rather than the lens of choice (Buchanan, 1975). Because the latter has been the reigning paradigm in economics during the twentieth century (Robbins, 1932; Reder, 1999), the lens of contract is (understandably) less fully developed. Interest in contractual approaches has nevertheless been building up, whence the gap between these two has been closing. This chapter sketches some of these developments, with emphasis on private ordering.

1. The Lenses of Choice and Contract

The science of choice is what Robbins (1932) had reference to in his famous book, The Nature and Significance of Economic Science. As therein prescribed, "Economics is the science which studies human behavior as a relationship between ends and scarce means which have alternative uses"

---

*Walter A. Haas School of Business, University of California, Berkeley, CA 94720-1900. The paper has benefited from the advice of Steven Tadelis and from the participants in the Institutional Analysis Workshop at Berkeley.

(Robbins, 1932, p. 16), or as recently restated by Reder (1999, p. 43), economics is the science that deals with the "allocation of scarce resources among alternative uses for the maximization of want satisfactions. "The theory of consumer behavior and the theory of the firm-as-production-function are the main constructions, where utility maximization and profit maximization are the objectives ascribed to each, respectively. Economists who work out of such setups give emphasis to quantities as influenced by changes in relative prices and available resources (Reder, 1999, p. 48), which became the "dominant paradigm" for economics throughout the twentieth century.

Albeit instructive, efforts to interpret everything through the lens of choice have resulted in strange and even wrong-headed constructions. Thinking contractually, especially comparative contractually, about economic organization invites attention to hitherto neglected issues of public and private ordering. The first of these is concerned with the rules of the game and views politics as "a structure of complex exchange among individuals, a structure within which persons seek to secure collectively their own privately defined objectives that cannot be efficiently secured through simple market exchanges" (Buchanan, 1987, p. 298). Private ordering, by contrast, is concerned with the play of the game. Action moves from the level of the polity to that of groups (Greif, 1993) or bilateral traders as they attempt to perfect their trading relations in a self-help way.

Thus, even if the polity has fashioned good rules of the game, transactions of an idiosyncratic kind where the immediate parties have deep and nonverifiable knowledge and for which continuity of the exchange is important are ones for which simple market exchange is poorly suited.[1] Private ordering efforts by the parties, to realign incentives and embed transactions in more protective governance structures, have the purpose and effect of mitigating the contractual problems that would otherwise arise.

---

[1] Differences among mechanism design, agency theory, and incomplete contracting notwithstanding, all take exception with the assumption of the "standard model" that parties to an exchange are price-takers. Upon making provision for opportunism [self-interest-seeking with guile (Makowski and Ostroy, 2001, p. 491)], strategic issues that had been ignored by neoclassical economists from 1870 to 1970 make their appearance (Makowski and Ostroy, 2001, pp. 482–483, 490–491).

This chapter examines economic organization through the lens of contract, with special emphasis on the governance of contractual relations, broadly in the spirit of Common's (1932, p. 4) prescient statement of the economic problem: "the ultimate unit of activity, ... must contain in itself the three principles of conflict, mutuality, and order. This unit is the transaction." Not only does transaction cost economics name the transaction as the basic unit of analysis, but governance is the means by which to infuse order, thereby to relieve conflict and realize mutual gain. Nonstandard and unfamiliar forms of contract and organization that had been condemned when examined through the lens of choice often take on more constructive meaning when the lens of contract is brought to bear; and altogether new phenomena are brought within the ambit.

2. Growing Unease

2.1. *General*

Growing unease within orthodoxy is evident from Hahn's (1991, p. 47) projection that pure theory, "the activity of deducing implications from a small number of fundamental axioms," is giving way to a more veridical description of human actors and their activities: "instead of simple transparent axioms there looms the likelihood of psychological, sociological and historical postulates." Less attention to generalities and more to particularities of information, organization, path dependency, and the like are thus projected (Hahn, 1991, p. 50). Lindbeck raises public-policy concerns. Because young economists lack a feeling for real-world problems, the "role abandoned by economists tends to be taken up by ... other social scientists, including sociologists, political scientists, and economic historians" (Lindbeck, 2001, p. 32). One reaction would be to shrug: If economists are not attending to these issues but other social scientists are, so what? Lindbeck plainly believes, however, that economists have something distinctive to offer and advises that university teachers and researchers of economics should "assume a greater responsibility for transmitting knowledge and understanding of real-world problems, including common sense" rather than dwell on "simple classroom exercises, with oversimplified and often unrealistic assumptions" (Lindbeck, 2001, p. 32). Solow's prescription for doing good economics is set out in three injunctions: keep it simple; get it right; make it plausible (Solow, 2001,

p. 111). He observes with reference to the first that "The very complexity of real life ... [is what] makes simple models so necessary" (Solow, 2001, p. 111). Getting it right "includes translating economic concepts into accurate mathematics (or diagrams, or words) and making sure that further logical operations are correctly performed and verified" (Solow, 2001, p. 112). But there is more: a model can be right mechanically yet be unenlightening because it is "imperfectly suited to the subject matter. It can obscure the key interactions, instead of spotlighting them" (Solow, 2001, p. 112). Maintaining plausible contact with the phenomena of interest (contractual or otherwise) is thus essential.

2.2. *Public-Policy*

Concerns Coase's (1964, p. 195) trenchant critique of the once prevailing (and still lingering) propensity to compare actual with ideal modes of organization in the regulatory arena is pertinent:

> Contemplation of an optimal system may provide techniques of analysis that would otherwise have been missed and, in certain special cases, it may go far to providing a solution. But in general its influence has been pernicious. It has directed economists' attention away from the main question, which is how alternative arrangements will actually work in practice. It has led economists to derive conclusions for economic policy from a study of an abstract of a market situation. It is no accident that in the literature ... we find a category "market failure" but no category "government failure." Until we realize that we are choosing between social arrangements which are all more or less failures, we are not likely to make much headway.

Coase also took issue with the uncritical propensity of antitrust specialists using the lens of choice to invoke monopoly to explain deviations from simple market exchange: "If an economist finds something — a business practice of one sort or another — that he does not understand, he looks for a monopoly explanation" (Coase, 1972, p. 67). But that does not exhaust the possibilities. Upon bringing the lens of contract to bear, such practices and structures are often better understood as private ordering efforts to accomplish economizing purpose and to realize mutual gain.

2.3. *Taken Together*

The lens of contract is less a substitute for than a complement to the ortho-dox lens of choice. Uneasiness with orthodoxy of both general and public-policy kinds is relieved. Previously neglected particularities of information and organization (Hahn) are swept in the process. Real-world problems are addressed in more veridical ways (Lindbeck). A contractual logic of organiza-tion that is both simple and plausible (Solow) and, moreover, yields numer-ous refutable implications that are corroborated by the data is the object.

3. The Lens of Contract: Private Ordering

The overarching argument is that, whatever the rules of the game,[2] be they well developed (as in the United States) or poorly developed [as in Vietnam (McMillan and Woodruff, 1999)], the play of the game is usefully inter-preted as private ordering efforts to infuse order, thereby to mitigate conflict and better realize the "mutuality of advantage from voluntary exchange" to which Buchanan referred. Transaction cost economics is a lens of contract construction that makes additional departures from orthodoxy in the follow-ing ways:

(i)   The human actors who populate the world of contract differ from those of the world of choice in both cognitive and self-interestedness respects. As described above, strategic behavior that had previously been ignored or denied becomes central upon making express allow-ance for opportunism.[3] Bounded rationality (behavior that is intend-edly rational but only limitedly so) is the cognitive assumption. Viewed from the lens of choice, the chief ramification of bounded rationality is

---

[2] Among the reasons why the rules of the game matter is that recourse to reliable courts for purposes of ultimate appeal, should private ordering efforts to resolve conflicts break down, serves to delimit threat positions (hence reduces contractual risks that would otherwise deter exchange). Economies with better rules of the game will thus be able to support more complex and potentially hazardous interim transactions than will economies with less developed rules and/or less-reliable enforcement, ceteris paribus.

[3] Self-interestedness is actually described in a two-part way: whereas a presumption of coopera-tion applies to small disturbances, larger disturbances (exceptions) pose strategic hazards to which opportunism applies, whence the presumption of cooperation is put at risk.

that maximizing should give way to satisficing (Simon, 1957, p. 204). Viewed instead from the lens of contract, the chief lesson is that all complex contracts are unavoidably incomplete. But there is more. Not only are contracts incomplete by reason of bounded rationality, but the readiness with which common knowledge of payoffs is invoked is deeply problematic. Relatedly, the combination of bounded rationality and opportunism is responsible for nonverifiability (Williamson, 1975, pp. 31–33). The upshot is that the manner in which private ordering is implemented turns crucially on the attributes ascribed to human actors.

(ii)   The firm for this purpose is described not as a black box, but as an alternative mode of governance. As Demsetz (1983, p. 377) observes, it is "a mistake to confuse the firm of [orthodox] economic theory with its real-world namesake. The chief mission of neoclassical economics is to understand how the price system coordinates the use of resources, not the inner workings of real firms". Orthodox theory is thus focused on supply and demand and on prices and output. It is well suited to the needs of the resource-allocation paradigm but is poorly suited to work out the comparative contractual differences (in incentive, control, and dispute settlement respects) among alternative modes of governance (markets, hybrids, firms, bureaus).

(iii)   Pertinent in this connection is that adaptation is now taken to be the chief mission of economic organization, of which two kinds are distinguished: autonomous adaptation in response to changes in relative prices for which neoclassical market modes enjoy the advantage (Hayek, 1945), and cooperative adaptation of a "conscious, deliberate, purposeful" kind (Barnard, 1938, p. 4), for which more complex contractual modes (to include hierarchy) enjoy the advantage. There being a need for both spontaneous order and intentional order in a high-performance economy, provision is made for both.

(iv)   Private ordering is accomplished through discriminating alignment, whereby transactions (which differ in their attributes) are aligned with governance structures (which differ in discrete structural ways and display different adaptive capacities) so as to effect an economizing result. Gains from trade are conditional on getting the governance structures right.

(v)   Operationalization entails naming and explicating the critical dimensions with respect to which transactions differ, naming and explicating the critical attributes with respect to which governance structures differ, and working out the logic of efficient alignment. The general argument is this: more complex modes of governance are reserved for more hazardous transactions. Successive moves from neoclassical markets (the textbook ideal) to hybrid modes (into which private-ordering credible commitments have been crafted) to hierarchy (unified ownership) as contractual hazards build up is thus predicted. These (and related predictions that accrue upon studying economic organization through the lens of contract, with emphasis on private ordering) are largely borne out by the data. [Over 600 empirical papers on transaction cost economics have been published and are broadly corroborative (Boemer and Macher, 2001).]

(vi)   Examining economic organization through the lens of contract invites the student of economic organization to entertain the possibility of contract laws (plural) rather than in terms of a single, all-purpose law of contract (as with orthodoxy). Specifically, transaction cost economics holds that the contract law of internal organization is that of forbearance (Williamson, 1991, pp. 97–100). Because the courts forbear (refuse jurisdiction over internal disputes except as "fraud, illegality, or conflict of interest" are shown), the firm, in effect, becomes its own court of ultimate appeal. Firms therefore have access to fiat, and the coordination benefits that accrue thereto, that markets do not.

(vii)   Additional issues, which any would-be theory of firm and market organization should be expected to address, include the following[4]: (a) Does successive application of the basic logic (in this case, of bilateral trade) scale up to describe the boundaries of the firm in the large corporation? (b) Why can a large firm not do everything that a

---

[4] I do not mean to suggest that failure of a would-be theory of economic organization to address these queries is disqualifying. Neither do I mean to suggest that the list of questions posed is exhaustive. I nevertheless regard it a merit of the transaction cost approach to economic organization that it does pose and address (with varying degrees of success) each of these queries. For a brief treatment, see Williamson (1991). For a more encompassing treatment of transaction cost economics, see the articles reprinted in Williamson and Masten (1995).

collection of small firms can do and more? (c) Wherein, if at all, do interim and interim contracting differ in accounting and auditing respects (and what are the ramifications)? (d) Does the logic that informs intermediate product market transactions (vertical integration being the paradigm problem) apply to other transactions as variations on a theme? And (e) Do instructive public policy ramifications accrue?

4. Formal Theories of Contract

Whereas the very idea of incomplete contracts, much less the formal modeling of incomplete contracts, was once apostasy, Grossman and Hart (1986) introduced what has since become the "main formal model" of incomplete contracting (see also Hart and John Moore, 1990). Albeit partly consistent with prior work in transaction cost economics (according to which contracts are incomplete [by reason of bounded rationality], contract as mere promise is not self-enforcing [by reason of opportunism], court ordering is limited [by reason of nonverifiability], and the parties are bilaterally dependent [by reason of transaction specific investments]), there is also a serious disjunction. Specifically, whereas transaction cost economics locates the main analytical action in the *ex post* implementation stage of contract (where inefficiencies due to maladaptation arise), Grossman–Hart–Moore assume away *ex post* maladaptation (by invoking common knowledge of payoffs and costless bargaining), thereby to focus instead on how different configurations of physical asset ownership (to which residual rights of control accrue) are responsible for efficiency differences at the *ex ante* stage of contract.

My concern with this setup is not that it is wrong in a "mechanical sense," but rather that it is "imperfectly suited to the subject matter... [because it obscures] the key interactions instead of spotlighting them" (Solow, 2001, p. 112). As I have discussed elsewhere (Williamson, 2000, pp. 605–607), it makes strange predictions (in that integration does not imply the unified ownership and management of two stages, A and B, but instead integration is "directional": it matters whether A acquires B or B acquires A because unified [coordinated] decision-making is not attempted) and is very nearly untestable (Whinston, 2001). Be that as it may, those who have pioneered this effort to model incomplete contracts deserve great credit; among other things, their work has invited others to follow.

The recent paper by Bajari and Tadelis (2001) on "Incentives Versus Transaction Costs: A Theory of Procurement Contracts" is particularly noteworthy. It starts with the empirical observation that procurement contracts are not menus but take one of the two polar forms: fixed-price or cost-plus. They view the basic trade-off as between high-powered incentives (where fixed-price enjoys the advantage) and *ex post* adaptation (where the advantage accrues to cost-plus). Although the resulting full formalization also requires some strong assumptions, costless bargaining is not one of them.

To be sure, Bajari and Tadelis do not reach the vertical-integration question and therefore do not address the governance structure differences that distinguish markets and hierarchies. Their treatment of outside procurement in terms of fixed-price or cost-plus contracts nevertheless features (spotlights), rather than suppresses, *ex post* maladaptation (key interactions). The paper is not only important as it stands, but it invites follow-on work, both theoretical and empirical, to include vertical integration.

5. Conclusions

Despite the progressive development of a science of contract over the past 30 years, textbook economics remains predominantly a science of choice-undertaking. One reason is inertia. A second reason is that the science of contract is not a unified subject, but has been progressing in a number of (partly rival) research directions. Be that as it may, it is noteworthy that the lens of contract/private ordering yields many refutable implications and has public-policy lessons that go beyond industrial organization to include the making of public policy more broadly (Dixit, 1996). Transition economics is an example of a field where recent errors could have been avoided had the lens of contract been more assiduously applied (Roland, 2001).

More generally, as Sandmo (2000, p. 21) has said, "the economics profession as a whole has been moving towards more attention to institutions and away from the more mechanistic view ... of general equilibrium theory."

Continuing headway, rather than a revolution, is what Sandmo projects. That is what I expect as well.

References

Bajari, Patrick and Tadelis, Steven. 2001. "Incentives Versus Transaction Costs: A Theory of Procurement Contracts." *Rand Journal of Economics*, 32(3), pp. 387–407.

Barnard, Chester I. 1938. *The Functions of the Executive*. Cambridge, MA: Harvard University Press..

Boerner, Christopher and Macher. J. 2001. "Transaction Cost Economics: A Review and Assessment of the Empirical Literature." Unpublished manuscript, University of California-Berkeley.

Buchanan, James. 1975. "A Contractarian Paradigm for Applying Economic Theory." *American Economic Review*, (May) (Papers and Proceedings), 65(2), pp. 225–230.

Buchanan, James M. 1987. "The Constitution of Economic Policy." *American Economic Review*. June, 77.

Buchanan, James. 2001. "Game Theory, Mathematics, and Economics." *Journal of Economic Methodology*, (March) 8(1), pp. 27–32.

Coase, Ronald. 1964. "The Regulated Industries: Discussion." *American Economic Review*, (May) (Papers and Proceedings), 54(2), pp. 194–197.

Coase, Ronald. 1972. "Industrial Organization: A Proposal for Research." In ed. V. R. Fuchs, Policy Issues and Research Opportunities *in Industrial Organization*. New York: National Bureau of Economic Research.

Commons, John R. 1932. "The Problem of Correlating Law, Economics, and Ethics." *Wisconsin Law Review*. (December) 8(8), pp. 3–26.

Demsetz, Harold. 1983. "The Structure of Ownership and the Theory of the Firm." *Journal of Law and Economics*, (June) 26(1), pp. 375–390.

Dixit, Avinash. 1996. *The Making of Economic Policy: A Transaction Cost Politics Perspective*. Cambridge, MA: MIT Press.

Greif, Avner. 1993. "Contract Enforceability and Economic Institutions in Early Trade: The Maghribi Traders' Coalition." *American Economic Review*, (June) 83(3), pp. 525–548.

Grossman, Sanford J. and Hart, Oliver D. 1986. "The Costs and Benefits of Ownership: A Theory of Vertical and Lateral Integration." *Journal of Political Economy*, (August) 94(4), pp. 691–719.

Hahn, Frank. 1991. "The Next Hundred Years." *Economics Journal*, (January) 101(1), pp. 47–50.

Hart, Oliver and Moore, John. 1990. "Property Rights and the Nature of the Firm." *Journal of Political Economy*, (December) 98(6), pp. 1119–1158.

Hayek, Friedrich. 1945. "The Use of Knowledge in Society." *American Economic Review*, (September) 35(4), pp. 519–530.

Lindbeck, Assar. 2001. "Economics in Europe." *CESifo Forum*, pp. 31–32.

Makowski, Louis and Ostroy, Joseph M. 2001. "Perfect Competition and the Creativity of the Market." *Journal of Economic Literature*, (June) 32(2), pp. 479–535.

Mc Millan, John and Woodruff, Christopher. 1999. "Dispute Prevention without Courts in Vietnam." *Journal of Law, Economics, and Organization*, (October) 15(3), pp. 637–658.

Reder, Melvin W. 1999. *The Culture of a Controversial Science*. Chicago: University of Chicago Press.

Robbins, Lionel. 1932. *An Essay on the Nature and Significance of Economic Science*. New York: New York University Press.

Roland, Gerard. 2001. "The Washington Consensus and the Transition Experience." Unpublished manuscript, University of California-Berkeley.

Sandmo, Agnar. 2000. "Neoclassical Economics and Institutions." *Social Okonomen*, (December) 54(9), pp. 19–22.

Simon, Herbert A. 1957. *Models of Man: Social and Rational. Mathematical Essays on Rational Human Behavior in a Social Setting*. New York: Wiley.

Solow, Robert. 2001. "A Native Informant Speaks." *Journal of Economic Methodology*, (March) 8(1), pp. 111–112.

Whinston, Michael. 2001. "Assessing the Property Rights and Transaction Cost Theories of Firm Scope." *American Economic Review*, (May) (Papers and Proceedings), 91(2), pp. 184–188.

Williamson, Oliver E. 1975. *Markets and Hierarchies*. New York: Free Press.

Williamson, Oliver E. 1991. "Comparative Economic Organization: The Analysis of Discrete Structural Alternatives." *Administrative Science Quarterly*, (June) 36(2), pp. 269–296.

Williamson, Oliver E. 2000. "The New Institutional Economics: Taking Stock, Looking Ahead." *Journal of Economic Literature*, (September) 38(3), pp. 595–613.

Williamson, Oliver E. and Masten, Scott E. 1995. *Transaction Cost Economics*, Vols. I and II. Aldershot, U.K.: Elgar.

Chapter 3

Calculativeness, Trust, and Economic Organization*

My main purpose in this article is to explicate what Diego Gambetta has referred to as "the elusive notion of trust."[1] As the literature on trust reveals, and as developed here, "trust" is a term with many meanings. The relentless application of calculative economic reasoning is the principal device that I employ to define and delimit the elusive notion of trust. The calculative approach to economic organization is sketched in Section 1. The concept of "calculative trust," which enjoys widespread and growing acceptance but with which I take exception, is examined in Section 2. Societal trust, which works through the institutional environment and takes a series of hyphenated forms, is briefly treated in Section 3. Nearly noncalculative uses of trust of a personal kind are developed in Section 4. Concluding remarks follow in Section 5.

1. Calculativeness

As compared with the other social sciences, the economic approach to economic organization is decidedly more calculative. That is widely regarded as

---

* Source: *Journal of Law and Economics*, Vol. 36, No. 1, Part 2, Olin Centennial Conference in Law and Economics at the University of Chicago (Apr., 1993), pp. 453–486
[1] Gambetta, Can We Trust Trust? in Trust: Making and Breaking Cooperative Relations, at ix (Gambetta ed., 1988).

both the distinctive strength and the Achilles' heel of economics. A failure to appreciate the limits of calculativeness purportedly gives rise to excesses, as a consequence of which economists are prone to make mistaken assessments of many economic phenomena.

I do not disagree, but I contend that the excesses to which calculativeness is sometimes given are usually remediable. I furthermore contend that the analytical reach of the calculative approach to economic organization is extended rather than diminished by admitting to these limitations. Once the excesses to which calculativeness is given are displayed and understood, the distortions can be anticipated and can thereafter be folded in at the design stage. A (more far-sighted) calculative response to the (myopic) excesses of calculativeness thereby obtains. Provided that bounds on rationality are respected, calculativeness opens the door to a deeper understanding of economic organization.

1.1. *Economics and the Contiguous Disciplines*[2]

Applications of economic analysis and economic reasoning to the contiguous social sciences — principal law, political science, and sociology — have increased considerably in the past thirty years. To be sure, Commons deserves credit for his early recognition that "law and economics" was a combined enterprise (Commons, 1924, 1925). The institutional economics program with which he was involved enjoyed only limited success,[3] however, and the first concerted applications of economics to the law were mainly concentrated on antitrust (Posner, 1979). That quickly changed after 1960 with the publication of Coase's "Social Cost" article (1960) and Calabresi's related work on torts (1961). Economics has since made its way into virtually every field of

---

[2] The heading is borrowed from Coases's article on this subject, Economics and Contiguous Disciplines, 7, *Journal of Legal Studies*, 201, (1978).

[3] The most significant contribution to law and economics stemming from the Commons's tradition is his book *Legal Foundations of Capitalism*, supra note 3. Albeit important, older-style institutional economics became embroiled in methodological controversy and failed to develop a research agenda to rival orthodoxy (see Stigler's remarks appearing in Kitch, The Fire of Truth: A Remembrance of Law and Economics at Chicago, 1932–1970, 26 *Journal of Law and Economics*. 163, 170 [1983]). Some concluded, too harshly I think, that the work of American institutionalists "led to nothing … [since] without a theory, they had nothing to pass on" (Coase, The New Institutional Economics, 140 J. Instituitional and Theoretical Economics. 229, 230 [1984]).

legal scholarship (Posner, 1977). The joinder of economics and political science has also undergone a significant transformation. Arrow's work on social choice (1951), Downs's treatment of an economic theory of democracy,(1957), Olson's logic of collection action(1965) and Buchanan and Tullock's work on constitutions (1964) were all implicated in this transformation. As recent conference volumes in the *Journal of Law, Economics, and Organization* make clear,[4] the use of economic reasoning to examine politics and political institutions has become widespread and, for some issues, even essential.

Economics and sociology bear a more distant relation to each other,[5] although this too has been changing, especially as the "rational choice" approach to sociology has been taking shape (Coleman, 1990; Lindenberg, 1990 and Hecter, 1987). A wide gulf between them nevertheless needed to be bridged. Thus, Samuelson distinguished economics and sociology in terms of their rationality orientations, with rationality being the domain of economics and nonrationality being relegated to sociology (Samuelson, 1947). Duesenberry subsequently quipped that economics was preoccupied with how individuals made choices, whereas sociology maintained that individuals did not have any choices to make (Duesenberry, 1960). Both Homans (1958) and Simon(1978) protested that sociology had a stake in rationality analysis and could not accept this division of labor, but such a division persisted.

What, it might be asked, is behind the successes of economics in moving into law, political science, and sociology? Coase observes that what binds a group of scholars together is "one or more of the following: common techniques of analysis, a common theory, or approach to a subject, or a common subject matter."[6] Although, in the short run, the use of certain techniques or a distinctive approach may provide the means by which economists are able to move successfully into another field,[7] Coase argues that the subject matter is decisive in the long run: "What economists study is the working of the

---

[4] The 1990 conference volume is entitled "The Organization of Political Institutions," while the 1992 conference volume deals with "The Economics and Politics of Administrative Law and Procedures."

[5] Much of the distance between economics and sociology appears to be attributable to the need for sociology, as a new discipline, to define itself in such a way as to avoid confrontation with economics, from which it had been spun off. See Swedberg, *Economic Sociology*: Past and Present, 35 Current Soc. 1 (1987).

[6] Coase, supra note 2, at 204.

[7] Id.

social institutions which bind together the economic system: firms, markets for goods and services, labor markets, capital markets, the banking system, international trade, and so on. It is the common interest in these social institutions which distinguishes the economics profession."[8] He subsequently remarks, however, that it is because economists "study the economic system as a unified whole, ... [that they] are more likely to uncover the basic interrelationships within a social system than is someone less accustomed to looking at the working of a system as a whole. ... [Also, the] study of economics makes it difficult to ignore factors which are clearly important and which play a part in all social systems [such as relative prices]."[9]

These last remarks seem to me to be more an endorsement of the economic approach than of the economic subject matter. Be that as it may, the economic approach, rather than the subject matter, is what I emphasize here. Calculativeness is the general condition that I associate with the economic approach and with the progressive extension of economics into the related social sciences. (I view it as the strategy that Becker (1976) has applied so widely and effectively.)[10] Note in this connection that calculative economic

---

[8] Id. at 206–7

[9] Id. at 209–10

[10] Note that there are real differences between the incomplete contracting approach out of which transaction cost economics works, in which bounded rationality is featured, and the optimality setup out of which Becker works. Simon, however, takes exception with both. Becker is scored for excesses of hyperrationality (Simon, supra note 19, at 2), while I am scored for using an incomplete contracting setup for which empirical support is purportedly lacking (Simon, Organization and Markets, 5 *Journal of Economic Perspective* 25, 26–27 (1991)). Becker is his own best agent. As for myself, I would observe that empirical work in transaction cost economics is much greater than Simon indicates (see Williamson, *The Economic Institutions of Capitalism* (1985), Chapter 5; Joskow, Asset Specificity and the Structure of Vertical Relationships: Empirical Evidence, 4 *J. L. Econ. & Org.* 95 (1988); Joskow, The Role of Transaction Cost Economics in Antitrust and Public Utility Regulatory Policies, 7 *J. L. Econ. & Org.* 53 (1991); and Shelanski, Empirical Research in Transaction Cost Economics: A Survey and Assessment (unpublished manuscript, Univ. California, Berkeley 1991)) and is growing exponentially. Joskow concludes that the empirical research in transaction cost economics "is in much better shape than much of the empirical work in industrial organization generally" (The Role of Transaction Cost Economics, supra, at 81)-to which, however, he quickly adds that more and better theoretical and empirical work is needed: "[T]here is no rest for the weary" (id. at 82). I concur.

reasoning can take several forms-of which price theory, property rights theory, agency theory, and transaction cost economics are all variants.[11]

1.2. Transaction Cost Economics

Institutional Economics. Institutional economics works at two levels of analysis. The macrovariant, which is especially associated with the work of North (1991), deals with the institutional environment. The microvariant deals with the institutions of governance. Davis and North (1971) distinguish between these two as follows (emphasis in original):

> The *institutional environment* is the set of fundamental political, social, and legal ground rules that establishes the basis for production, exchange, and distribution. Rules governing elections, property rights, and the right of contract are examples ...

> An *institutional arrangement* is an arrangement between economic units that governs the ways in which these units can cooperate and/or compete. It ... [can] provide a structure within which its members can cooperate ... or [it can] provide a mechanism that can effect a change in laws or property rights.

The way that I propose to join these two is to treat the institutional environment in which a transaction (or a related set of transactions) is embedded as a set of shift parameters, changes in which elicit shifts in the comparative costs of governance (Williamson, 1991). These issues are

---

[11] Note in this connection is that the massive expansion of economic reasoning out of antitrust law into the law more generally had transaction cost economics origins (Coase, supra note 6). Many of the initial applications of economic reasoning to economic organization also rely, directly and indirectly, on transaction cost arguments (Arrow, supra note 9; Arrow, The Organization of Economic Activity: Issues Pertinent to the Choice of Market Versus Nonmarket Allocation, in 1 U.S. Joint Economic Committee, 91st Cong., 1st Sess., The Analysis and Evaluation of Public Expenditure: The PPB System 59 (1969); Williamson, *Markets and Hierarchies*: Analysis and Antitrust Implications (1975); Alchian & Demsetz, Production, Information Costs, and Economic Organization, *62 American Economic Review* 777 (1972); and Jensen & WilliamMeckling, Theory of the Firm, 3 *Journal of Financial. Economics* 305 (1976)).

developed further in Section 3 below. My main purpose here is to examine the rudiments of governance.

Governance. Although hyperrationality has been responsible for some of the truly deep insights of economics, there is a need, at some stage, to describe "man as he is, acting within the constraints imposed by real institutions."[12] What are the key attributes of economic actors?

Opportunism and bounded rationality are the key behavioral assumptions on which transaction cost economics relies.[13] Bounded rationality is a cognitive assumption, according to which economic agents are "intendedly rational, but only limitedly so (Simon, 1957)." An immediate ramification of bounded rationality is that impossibly complex forms of economic organization (such as complete contingent-claims contracting) are infeasible (Radner, 1968). Standing alone, that is a negative result. But there is more to it than that. If mind is a scarce resource,[14] then economizing on bounded rationality is warranted. This expands, rather than reduces, the range of issues to which the economic approach can be applied. Among other things, the "conscious, deliberate, purposeful" use of organization as a means by which to economize on bounded rationality is made endogenous (Barnard, 1938).

Opportunism is a self-interest-seeking assumption. By contrast with simple self-interest seeking, according to which economic agents will continuously consult their own preferences but will candidly disclose all pertinent information on inquiry and will reliably discharge all covenants, opportunistic agents are given to self-interest seeking with guile. Whether

---

[12] Coase, supra note 4, at 231.

[13] The aspect of bounded rationality that is most frequently emphasized is that of limited cognitive competence, on which account irrationality or satisficing are often thought to be implied. Intended (but limited) rationality, however, is a broader concept. Not only are intendedly rational agents attempting effectively to cope, whence irrationality (except, perhaps, for certain pathological cases) is not implied, but satisficing is merely one manifestation of coping. The satisficing approach, which appeals to psychology and works out of an aspiration level mechanics, has not found wide application within economics (Aumann, What Is Game Theory Trying to Accomplish? in Frontiers of Economics 35 (Arrow & Honkapohja eds. 1985)). Also see Kenneth Arrow, Reflections on the Essays, in Arrow and the Foundations of the Theory of Economic Policy 734 (Feiwel ed. 1987)

[14] Simon, supra note 19, at 12.

economic agents will tell the truth, the whole truth, and nothing but the truth and will reliably self-enforce covenants to behave "responsibly" are therefore problematic. Accordingly, "contract as promise" is fraught with hazards. Although that too is a negative result, again there is a positive research agenda.

The lessons of opportunism can be construed broadly or narrowly. The myopic construction is associated with Machiavelli, who advised his prince that he both could and should breach contracts with impunity (Machiavelli, 1952). By contrast, transaction cost economics advises that, once alerted to the systematic hazards of opportunism, the wise (farsighted) prince will both give and receive credible commitments. That more deeply calculative response permits superior deals to be made than could otherwise be supported.[15] Machiavellian grabbing is not implied if economic agents have a more farsighted understanding of the economic relation of which they are a part than myopic Machiavellianism ascribes to them.

Note, moreover, that the idea of credible commitments is a thoroughly hardheaded one. Contracts that have no need for added support (the "ideal" contracts of both law and economics) will not be provided with them (Macneil, 1974). More generally, contracts will be provided with added supports only in the degree to which these are cost-effective. Calculativeness is thus pervasive.

Taken together, the lessons of bounded rationality and opportunism lead to the following combined result: organize transactions so as to economize on bounded rationality while simultaneously safeguarding them against the hazards

---

[15] See Williamson, Credible Commitments: Using Hostages to Support Exchange, 73 *American. Economic. Review* 519 (1983). The remarks of Dawkins about conscious foresight, expressed in the context of selfish genes, are pertinent (Dawkins, *The Selfish Gene* 215 [1976]):

One unique feature of man ... [is] his capacity for conscious foresight. Selfish genes ... have no foresight.

[Thus] even if we look on the dark side and assume that individual man is fundamentally selfish, our conscious foresight ... could save us from the worst selfish excesses of the blind replicators. We have at least the mental equipment to foster our long-term selfish interests rather than merely our short-term selfish interests. We can see the long-term benefits of participating ..., and we can sit down to discuss ways of making ... [agreements] work.

of opportunism. Not only do credible commitments arise when incomplete contracts are examined in their entirety, but complaints over obsessive calculativeness, truncated calculativeness, and anticalculativeness are mitigated as well.

1.3. *Purported Excesses of Calculativeness*

Obsessive Calculativeness A calculative approach to economic organization can and sometimes does result in obsessive demands for control. One of the prescient lessons of sociology is that demands for control can have both intended and unintended effects and that unintended effects often have dysfunctional consequences (Merton, 1936; March & Simon, 1958).

One possible response to this finding is to argue that the economic approach is flawed because of its preoccupation with intended effects to the neglect of unintended effects. But that assumes that the economic approach is unable or unwilling to take into account all relevant regularities whatsoever. If the deeper lesson is to design control systems with reference to all consequences — both those that are intended and those that were (originally) unanticipated — and if economics can implement this deeper lesson, then the claim that the economic approach is mindlessly given to obsessive calculativeness is overdrawn. The correct view is that a naive application of calculativeness can be and sometimes is given to excesses but that this is often remediable. On being informed about added consequences, these will be factored into the design exercise from the outset. (A calculative response to the excesses of calculativeness thereby obtains.)

Truncated Calculativeness Many models of economic organization work out of truncated logic, according to which economic actors are assumed to be myopic. Aspects of the Keynesian macromodel work out of a myopic logic. The same is true of the cobweb cycle (Coase & Fowler, 1935), barriers to entry arguments(Stigler, 1968), and the resource dependency approach to economic organization (Pfeffer & Salancik, 1978 and Pfeffer, 1981).

Transaction cost economics responds to all of these conditions identically: although complex contracts are unavoidably incomplete, a farsighted approach to contract is often feasible. Many of the problems associated with truncated contracting are relieved in the process.

The differences between the resource dependency and credible commitment approaches to economic organization are illustrative. The resource dependency approach is concerned with power disparities that arise when contractual dependency comes as an unwanted surprise. That occurs frequently if myopic agents are unable to project and make provision for the Fundamental Transformation — according to which a large numbers bidding situation at the outset is (sometimes) transformed into a small numbers supply relation during contract execution and at the contract renewal interval.[16] If this transformation is unforeseen, then one of the parties may find itself at a power disadvantage in relation to the other after the initial contract has been agreed to.

Transaction cost economics employs an efficiency perspective and treats dependency as a (broadly) foreseeable condition. In the degree, therefore, to which asset specificity (which is responsible for bilateral dependency) yields benefits (added revenues and/or production cost savings) that are not more than offset by the added governance costs, added asset specificity is deliberately incurred. Accordingly, farsighted parties purposefully create bilateral dependency and support it with contractual safeguards, but only in the degree to which the associated investments are cost-effective. Because price, asset specificity, and contractual safeguards are all determined simultaneously, calculativeness is the solution to what would otherwise be a problem (unwanted resource dependency).

Anticalculativeness Voice. Yet another view is that the calculative approach to economic organization emphasizes exit (the traditional economic means by which to express dissatisfaction) to the neglect of voice (which is associated with politics and is purportedly less calculative) (Hirschman, 1970). Transaction cost economics is sometimes held to be especially reprehensible (Granovetter, 1985).

My response is two-fold. First, if voice in the absence of an exit option is relatively ineffective, which evidently it is,[17] then voice really does have a calculative aspect. Second, voice works through mechanisms, and those mechanisms are often carefully designed.

Llewellyn's view of contract as framework (1931), as against contract as legal rules, is pertinent: "[The] major importance of legal contract is to provide a framework for well-nigh every type of group organization

---

[16] Williamson, supra note 25, at 61–63.
[17] Hirschman, supra note 44.

and for well-nigh every type of passing or permanent relation between individuals and groups … a framework highly adjustable, a framework which almost never accurately indicates real working relations, but which affords a rough indication around which such relations vary, an occasional guide in cases of doubt, and a norm of ultimate appeal when the relations cease in fact to work."

Plainly, Llewellyn provides for voice: parties to a (bilaterally dependent) contract will try to work things out when confronted by unanticipated disturbances. Within a broad range, the contract serves as framework. Llewellyn nevertheless observes that the contract serves also as a norm of ultimate appeal if the parties are unable to reconcile their differences. An exit option is thereby preserved, but court ordering of the contract serves to delimit threat positions. Bargaining through voice is thus greatly influenced by knowledge that the terms of exit are defined by the contract.

But there is more to it than that. The voice mechanics are often defined by the terms of the contract. Consider the provisions in the 32-year coal supply agreement[18] between the Nevada Power Company and the Northwest Trading Company:

In the event an inequitable condition occurs which adversely affects one Party, it shall be the joint and equal responsibility of both Parties to act promptly and in good faith to determine the action required to cure or adjust for the inequity and effectively to implement such action. Upon written claim of inequity served by one Party upon the other, the Parties shall act jointly to reach an agreement concerning the claimed inequity within sixty (60) days of the date of such written claim. An adjusted base coal price that differs from market price by more than 10% shall constitute a hardship. The Party claiming inequity shall include in its claim such information and data as may be reasonably necessary to substantiate the claim and shall freely and without delay furnish such other information and data as the other Party reasonably may deem relevant and necessary. If the Parties cannot reach agreement within sixty (60) days the matter shall be submitted to arbitration.

---

[18] Reproduced from Williamson, supra note 25, at 164–165.

Plainly, the procedures through which voice is expected to work are laid out in advance. Again, therefore, calculativeness is implicated in the design of *ex post* governance (voice).

As previously remarked, moreover, transaction cost economics maintains that *ex post* governance is aligned with the needs of transactions in a discriminating way. Some, but not all, transactions are provided with voice mechanisms. Specifically, classical transactions in which each party can go its own way without cost to the other will not be supported with voice.

The upshot is that calculativeness, albeit of a much richer and more varied kind than the orthodox exit-without-voice approach contemplates, applies throughout. The importance of voice is not in the least discredited. Instead, voice is encompassed within the extended calculative perspective.

2. Calculative Trust[19]

My purpose in this and the next two sections is to examine the aforementioned "elusive notion of trust."[20] That will be facilitated by examining a series of examples in which the terms trust and risk are used interchangeably-which has come to be standard practice in the social science literature—after which the simple contractual schema out of which transaction cost economics works is sketched. As set out there, transaction cost economics refers to contractual safeguards, or their absence, rather than trust, or its absence. I argue that it is redundant at best and can be misleading to use the term "trust" to describe commercial exchange for which cost-effective safeguards have been devised in support of more efficient exchange. Calculative trust is a contradiction in terms.

2.1. *Trust as Risk*

"Trust" is a good word. So is "risk." Social scientists have begun to describe situations of trust as "a subclass of those involving risk. They are situations in

---

[19] There is an enormous literature on trust. Some of that will be apparent from the discussion. For a more expansive survey, see Craig Thomas, Public Trust in Organizations and Institutions: A Sociological Perspective (1991).

[20] Gambetta, supra note 1, at ix.

which the risk one takes depends on the performance of another actor.""[21] According to this formulation, trust is warranted when the expected gain from placing oneself at risk to another is positive, but not otherwise. Indeed, the decision to accept such a risk is taken to imply trust.[22]

This theme is repeated throughout the influential seminar series organized by Gambetta and published under the title Trust: Making and Breaking Cooperative Relations. That volume closes with the following unifying observation:[23] "[T]here is a degree of convergence in the definition of trust which can be summarized as follows: trust... is a particular level of the subjective probability with which an agent assesses that another agent or group of agents will perform a particular action .... When we say we trust someone or that someone is trustworthy, we implicitly mean that the probability that he will perform an action that is beneficial or at least not detrimental to us is high enough for us to consider engaging in some form of cooperation with him." Bradach and Eccles expressly embrace this view in their recent treatment of "Price, Authority, and Trust" in the Annual Review of Sociology (1989). As discussed below, Kreps (1990) and Dasgupta[24] employ similar notions in their game theoretic treatments of trust. The upshot is that trust is purportedly made more transparent and operational by treating calculated trust as a subset of calculated risk.

Coleman's chapter on "Relations of Trust" develops the rational choice approach to trust through three examples.[25] The first involves a Norwegian shipowner who is urgently seeking a £200,000 loan, thereby to release a ship of his that had undergone repairs in Amsterdam. The second involves the arrival of a farmer to a new area and the unexpected breakdown of his equipment. The third is that of an immigrant high school girl who lacked companionship in her new surroundings.

Confronted by the unwillingness of the Amsterdam shipyard to release his ship, the Norwegian shipowner telephoned his merchant banker, Hambros, in the City of London to arrange a loan. Within three minutes, the Hambros banker had arranged for an Amsterdam bank to deliver the

---

[21] Coleman, supra note 15, at 91.

[22] Id. at 105.

[23] Gambetta, supra note 1, at 217.

[24] Dasgupta, Trust as a Commodity, in Gambetta ed., supra note 1, at 49.

[25] Coleman, supra note 15.

money, whereupon the shipowner was told that his ship would be released. Coleman summarizes this case as follows:[26]

> This case clearly involves trust. The manager of the Norwegian department at Hambros placed trust in the Norwegian shipowner who telephoned him-trust to the extent of £200,000 of Hambros's money. There was no contract signed, no paper involved in the transaction, nothing more substantial than the shipowner's intention to repay the money and the Hambros man's belief in both the shipowner's honesty and his ability to repay. Similarly, the bank in Amsterdam trusted Hambros to the extent of £200,000, again merely on the basis of a verbal request over the telephone. It committed £200,000 of its money on the assumption that Hambros would, on Monday morning, repay the sum.

The farmer example involves the breakdown of a hay baler and the prospect that the crop would be ruined by rain. This was avoided by a neighbor's offer to use his baler and to help bale the hay without charge. When the farmer who had received the assistance asked what was needed in return, he was told "all he wants is the gasoline it took to bale the hay." Coleman interprets this as the "placement of trust by the second farmer in the first-trust that in a situation of need or time of trouble, when he might call on the first farmer, that farmer would provide help, as he had in this case."[27]

The third example begins with the assent by a high school girl to be walked home by a boy. She further assented, at his request, to take a shortcut through the woods. He then made a sexual advance, which she resisted. She was thereupon roughed up and sexually assaulted. Coleman interprets this as "a special case of a special circumstance involving trust" in which weaker women place themselves at hazard where "sometimes, as in this episode, that trust is misplaced."[28]

Another example that is widely believed to reflect trust is that of diamond dealers in New York City. Ben-Porath describes the relationship as one in which major deals are "sealed by a handshake (1980)." Such deals would not be possible were it not for the prevalence of trust within the Jewish community. Interestingly, those conditions of trust are said to be undergoing a

---

[26] Id. at 92.

[27] Id. at 93.

[28] Id. at 94.

change. An elderly Israeli diamond dealer has described the changes as follows: "When I first entered the business, the conception was that truth and trust were simply the way to do business, and nobody decent would consider doing it differently. Although many transactions are still consummated on the basis of trust and truthfulness, this is done because these qualities are viewed as good for business, a way to make a profit."[29]

Henlin's account of the decisions by cab drivers to pick up a fare or not is used by Thomas[30] to illustrate "characteristic-based trust": "Since cabbies do not know anything specific about the prospective passenger based through past experiences with that person, they must make their decision to stop based on what they can infer from the setting, the physical appearance of the person, and the manner in which the person presents himself. Henlin argues that trust consists of an actor offering a definition of herself, and an audience choosing either to interact with (trust) or not to interact with (distrust)."

Recent game theoretic treatments of economic organization routinely refer to trust, usually in the context of parties engaged in sequential, repeated games. Kreps's description of the game is typical. The basic setup is a one-sided version of the Prisoner's Dilemma game in which there is a sequence of two moves on every play of the game. First, Party X decides whether to put himself at hazard ("trust Y") or not ("do not trust Y"). If Party X accepts the hazard, then Party Y decides whether to take advantage of X ("abuse X's trust") or not ("honor X's trust"). The payoffs are such that the joint gain is maximized by the trust/honor outcome. But since Y's immediate gains are maximized if he abuses X's trust, the no-trust/no-play result will obtain if presented as a one-shot game.

Kreps thereupon converts the relation to a repeated game in which there is a high probability that each round will be followed by another. This changes the analysis "dramatically."[31] Say, for example, X tells Y, "I will begin by trusting you, hoping that you will honor that trust. Indeed, I will continue to trust you as long as you do not abuse that trust. But if ever you abuse that trust, I will never again trust you." If Y hears and believes that

[29] Quoted in Bernstein, The Choice between Public and Private Law (Discussion Paper No. 70, Harvard Law School, Program in Law and Economics, 1990), at 38.

[30] Thomas, supra note 49, at 22.

[31] Kreps, supra note 55, at 102.

statement, and if the game is played repeatedly (with high probability), then the honor-trust arrangement is self-enforcing.[32] The commercial context notwithstanding, trust and honor are evidently what this game is all about.

Probably the most expansive treatment of trust in a gaming context is Dasgupta's chapter on "Trust as a Commodity." He begins with the claim that "[t]rust is central to all transactions and yet economists rarely discuss the notion."[33] He elaborates as follows:[34] "For trust to be developed between individuals they must have repeated encounters, and they must have some memory of previous experiences. Moreover, for honesty to have potency as a concept there must be some cost involved in honest behavior. And finally, trust is linked with reputation, and reputation has to be acquired." Dasgupta further remarks that "[i]f the incentives are 'right,' even a trustworthy person can be relied upon to be untrustworthy.'[35]

2.2. *The Simple Contractual Schema*

Risk entails exposure to probabilistic outcomes. If a gamble has two outcomes, good and bad, the utility valuation of each is G and B, respectively, and if the probability of a good outcome is q, then the expected utility of the gamble can be expressed as $V = q G + (1 \ q)B$.

Actions can sometimes be taken to mitigate bad outcomes and/or enhance good outcomes. I will define competent calculativeness as a situation in which the affected parties (1) are aware of the range of possible outcomes and their associated probabilities, (2) take cost-effective actions to mitigate hazards and enhance benefits, (3) proceed with the transaction only if expected net gains can be projected, and, (4) if X can complete the transaction with any of several Ys, the transaction is assigned to that Y for which the largest net gain can be projected.[36]

---

[32] Id. at 103.

[33] Dasgupta, supra note 56, at 49.

[34] Id. at 59.

[35] Id. at 54.

[36] This may appear to be indistinguishable from maximizing-at least if due allowance is made for (1) the incompleteness of contracting, (2) the crude quality of information, and (3) discrete choices. For a discussion of satisficing Versus maximizing, see Williamson, Transaction Cost Economics and Organization Theory, 2 Indus. & Corp. Change 165 (1993).

Parties to such transactions understand a great deal about the contractual relation of which they are a part and manage it in a calculative way.[37] The simple contractual schema to which transaction cost economics makes repeated reference describes exchange as a triple (p, k, s), where p refers to the price at which the trade takes place, k refers to the hazards that are associated with the exchange, and s denotes the safeguards within which the exchange is embedded. The argument is that price, hazards, and safeguards are determined simultaneously.

The schematic and the values that each element in the vector take on are shown in Figure 1. As shown, Node A involves no hazards. The good or service in question is completely generic. Goods or services are exchanged now for prices paid now. This is the classical market exchange that Macneil has described as "sharp in by clear agreement; sharp out by clear performance."[38]

It will facilitate comparisons to assume that suppliers are competitively organized and are risk neutral. The prices at which product will be supplied therefore reflect an expected break-even condition. The break-even price that is associated with Node A is p. There being no hazards, k = 0. And since safeguards are unneeded,[39] s = 0.

Node B is more interesting. The contractual hazard here is $\bar{k}$. If the buyer is unable or unwilling to provide a safeguard, then s = 0. The corresponding break-even price is $\bar{P}$.

Node C poses the same contractual hazard, namely, $\bar{k}$. In this case, however, a safeguard in amount s is provided. The break-even price that is projected under these conditions is 5. It is elementary[40] that $\hat{P} < \bar{P}$.

---

[37] Pervasive calculativeness notwithstanding, the rhetoric of exchange often employs the language of promises, trust, favors, and cooperativeness. That is understandable, in that the artful use of language can produce deals that would be scuttled by abrasive calculativeness. If, however, the basic deal is shaped by objective factors, then calculativeness (credibility, hazards, safeguards, net benefits) is where the crucial action resides.

[38] Macneil, supra note 38, at 738. 72 Another way of putting it is that (transition problems aside) each party can go its own way without cost to the other. Competition provides a safeguard.

[39] Another way of putting it is that (transition problems aside) each party can go its own way without cost to the other. Competition provides a safeguard.

[40] For a more systematic development, see Williamson, supra note 37. For related empirical work, see Masten & Crocker, Efficient Adaptation in Long-Term Contracts: Take or Pay Provisions for Natural Gas, 75 *American Economic Review*. 1085 (1985), and the surveys reported by Joskow, supra note 25.

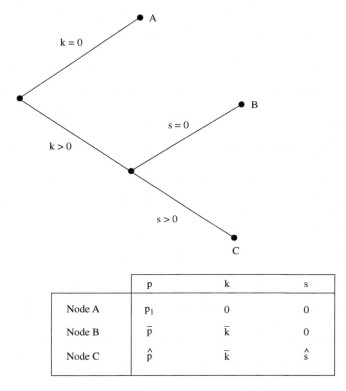

	p	k	s
Node A	p_1	0	0
Node B	$\bar{p}$	$\bar{k}$	0
Node C	$\hat{p}$	$\bar{k}$	$\hat{s}$

Figure 1.   Simple contractual schema

In the language of Section 2.1 above, Node A poses no risk, hence trust is unneeded. Nodes B and C, by contrast, do pose a risk. In the language of trust, Node B is the low-trust and Node C is the high-trust outcome.

Note that Bradach and Eccles contend that "mutual dependence [i.e., k > 0] between exchange partners ... [promotes] trust, [which] contrasts sharply with the argument central to transaction cost economics that ... dependence ... fosters opportunistic behavior."[41] What transaction cost economics says, however, is that because opportunistic agents will not self-enforce open-ended promises to behave responsibly, efficient exchange will be realized only if dependencies are supported by credible commitments.

---

[41] Bradach & Eccles, supra note 54, at 111.

Wherein is trust implicated if parties to an exchange are farsighted and reflect the relevant hazards in the terms of the exchange? (A better price $(\hat{P} < \bar{P})$ will be offered if the hazards $(k > 0)$ are mitigated by cost-effective contractual safeguards $(s > 0)$.) Indeed, I maintain that trust is irrelevant to commercial exchange and that reference to trust in this connection promotes confusion.

Note further that while credible commitments deter breach and support more efficient exchange, breach is not wholly precluded. On the contrary, if it is inefficient to supply under some state realizations, then an optimal contract will project breach for those states. Whereas efficient breach of commercial contract is easy to reconcile with a calculative approach to contract, the notion that trust can be efficiently breached experiences considerable strain. Much of the contract law literature would be clarified if trust were consistently used in a delimited way.

2.3. Applications

If calculative relations are best described in calculative terms, then diffuse terms, of which trust is one, that have mixed meanings should be avoided when possible. As discussed below, all of the above examples save one can be interpreted in terms of efficiency and credibility. (The exception is the assaulted girl, but that, I contend, is not properly described as a condition of trust either.) Were my arguments to prevail, the word "trust" would hereafter be used much more cautiously-at least among social scientists, if not more generally.

The Norwegian Shipowner. The Norwegian shipowner required a loan. Let $q1$, $q2$, and $q3$ be the probabilities of a good outcome (timely loan repayment and profitable future business) that are projected by the shipyard, the Amsterdam bank, and the London merchant banker (Hambros), respectively. Let $G1$, $G2$, and $G3$ be the corresponding gains and $B1$, $B2$, and $B3$ be the corresponding losses that each associates with dealing with the Norwegian shipowner directly. The expected net gains are then given by $Vi = qi\ Gi + (1\ qi)Bi$. As I interpret Coleman, the reason why the Hambros deal went through, while the other two did not, is because $V3 > 0$ (the merchant banker trusts) and $V1 < 0$, $V2 < 0$ (the shipyard and Amsterdam bank distrust). But that is not necessary. As a matter of good business practice, the Hambros deal should go through if $V3 > 0$ and $V3 > V1$ and $V2$.

On my interpretation, (1) all parties were calculative, (2) the loan was made by the party that projected the largest expected net gain, and (3) no trust is implied. That the merchant banker was best suited to bear the risk is, I conjecture, because it had the most knowledge of the shipowner and the best prospect of future business. Indeed, the Amsterdam shipbuilder may have the policy of never releasing ships without payment. That is not because he always projects a net negative outcome. Instead, his policy is one of efficient decision making in the context of the system of which shipbuilding is a part.[42] Shipbuilders know shipbuilding but have much less experience with and knowledge of clients' financial conditions, have less assurance of repeat business, and have less competence to pursue their claims for unpaid debts in court. Since the merchant banker is more well-suited in all of these respects, the shipbuilder adopts a policy whereby production is specialized to one party and financial risk is specialized to another.

Even assuming, *arguendo*, that the merchant banker in London was better suited than the Amsterdam bank or the shipbuilder to bear the risk, might not trust come in through knowledge possessed by the London banker of the personal integrity of the Norwegian shipowner? That is, in addition to the objective features mentioned above, might idiosyncratic knowledge of personal integrity also favor running the transaction through London? Is trust then implicated after all?

I would argue that the London banker's deep knowledge of the personal integrity of the Norwegian shipowner merely permitted him to improve his estimate of integrity. That the London banker has a better estimate, in this sense, does not imply that he has a more favorable estimate of the Norwegian shipowner's integrity. (Indeed, the London banker may refuse the loan because he knows the Norwegian shipowner to be a crook.) More generally, if N shipowners approach Hambros with the same request and only M < N are approved, what are we to infer? I submit that calculativeness is

---

[42] The main systems argument is in the text. But there is another possibility. Shipbuilders (or, more generally, businessmen-as opposed to bankers) are optimistic fellows, on which account they project subjective probabilities for good outcomes that exceed the objective conditions. Refusing to release ships may be a good policy for bringing such excesses of optimism under control. An important but little remarked purpose of having "firm but arbitrary" policies is to protect parties against idiosyncratic appeals.

determinative throughout and that invoking trust merely muddies the (clear) waters of calculativeness.

The Hay Baler The hay baler case is one where issues of informal organization are posed. If accidents occur with stochastic regularity and if there is a great deal of indeterminacy in setting the price for emergency aid, then there are advantages to embedding these transactions in an institutional form in which quick responsiveness on nonexploitative terms will obtain. An informal, reciprocal aid mechanism is one possible institutional response.

Cheating is nevertheless a hazard. Sanctions are needed lest opportunistic farmers abuse informal supports. Thus, although almost all requests for emergency aid elicit quick and favorable responses, failures to reciprocate are not forgotten or forgiven and, if they persist, will elicit moral suasion and, eventually, sanctions — such as ostracism and refusals of assistance. The efficacy of informal organization thus turns on calculative supports. If almost automatic and unpriced assistance is the most efficient response, provided that the practice in question is supported by sanctions and is ultimately made contingent on reciprocity, then calculativeness obtains and appeal to trust adds nothing.

The proviso that "the practice in question is supported by sanctions" is, however, crucial. In regions where informal organization delivers very weak sanctions, deferred payment schemes that rely on a reciprocal sense of responsibility will be less viable. Less "spontaneous" cooperation will therefore be observed and/or immediate payment will be expected (demanded) on providing emergency assistance.

Diamond Dealers. The appearance of trust among diamond dealers is deceptive. As Granovetter observes, these transactions are "embedded in a close knit community of diamond merchants who monitor one another's behavior closely."[43] Bernstein[44] elaborates:

> What is unique about the diamond industry is not the importance of trust and reputation in commercial transactions, but rather the extent to which the industry is able to use reputation/social bonds at a cost low enough to be able to create a system of private law which enables most transactions to be consummated and most contracts enforced completely outside of the

---

[43] Granovetter, Economic Action and Social Structure, supra note 45, at 492.

[44] Bernstein, supra note 62, at 35–36.

legal system. ... This is accomplished in two main ways: (1) through the use of reputation bonds; (2) through a private arbitration system whose damage awards are not bounded by expectancy damages, and whose judgments are enforced by both reputation bonds and social pressure.

Put differently, Node C "trust relations" do not obtain because the diamond industry had the good luck to be organized by an ethnic community in which trust is pervasive. On the contrary, the Jewish ethnic community that organized this market succeeded because it was able to provide cost-effective sanctions more efficiently than rivals. Until recently, moreover, the efficacy of those sanctions[45] depended on restrictive entry: In the past, Jews formed a cohesive geographically concentrated social group in the countries in which they lived. Jewish law provided detailed substantive rules of commercial behavior, and the Jewish community provided an array of extralegal dispute resolution institutions. NonJews to whom the sanctions for rule violation were weak, hence, would follow the rules only if that suited their convenience — could not be admitted without jeopardy to the Node C condition.[46]

---

[45] Id. at 41.

[46] The question of endgames sometimes arises. If Jews do not defect on the last play, does that imply that trust is operative after all? I would respond negatively if retired Jews remain in their community (in which event they would be subject to sanctions) or have active religious consciences. The contrast between a retiring Jew who remains within the community and the illicit deal related by Dostoyevsky in The Brothers Karamozov is instructive. Hardin (Trusting Persons, Trusting Institutions, in Strategy and Choice 185 (Zeckhauser ed. 1991)) retells that event as follows: [A] lieutenant colonel . . . managed substantial sums of money on behalf of the army. Immediately after each periodic audit of his books, he took the available funds to the merchant Trifonov, who soon returned them with interest and a gift. In effect, both the lieutenant colonel and Trifonov benefited from funds that would otherwise have lain idle, producing no benefit for anyone. Because it was highly irregular, theirs was a secret exchange that depended wholly on personal trust not backed by the law of contracts. When the day came that the lieutenant colonel was to be abruptly replaced in his command, he asked Trifonov to return the last sum, 4,500 rubles, entrusted to him. Trifonov replied, "I've never received any money from you, and couldn't possibly have received any." Although Hardin describes the relation between the lieutenant colonel and Trifonov as "personal trust," I submit that Trifonov did view (and the lieutenant colonel should have viewed) the relation calculatively-as a self-enforcing contract to which no legal or social sanctions apply (Telser, A Theory of Self-enforcing Agreements, 53 J. Bus. 27 (1981)).

The organization of this industry has nevertheless been changing in response to new information and monitoring technologies. (Conceivably, the efficacy of ethnic sanctions may be weakening, too.) Despite resistance by "older dealers accustomed to dealing primarily with friends and long standing business acquaintances,"[47] new governance structures[48] are making headway: "Among the proposals currently being considered by the World Federation of Diamond Bourses are: setting up an international computer database with reports of arbitration judgments from all member bourses in an attempt to foster international uniformity in trade customs, and a rule requiring that every bourse be equipped with a fax machine for rapid transmission of credit worthiness information. Also under consideration, although staunchly opposed by many dealers, is the creation of an international computer database describing goods available for sale worldwide."

The change is akin to a new technology, where the need for learning by doing is reduced by the appearance of a standardized machine. In the diamonds case, a new information technology makes it possible to support greater dealer diversity. To be sure, ethnic identity within markets may still have value. But ethnic disparity between markets is now easier to support. To describe the earlier arrangement as a high-trust condition and the emerging arrangement as a low-trust condition confuses rather than illuminates. Both reflect calculativeness.

Put differently, it is a mistake to suppose that commercial trust has supplanted real trust. Rather, the basis for commercial trust has become more transparently calculative as new communication technologies have made inroads into this small trading community by making it possible to track commercial reputation effects in larger trading networks. As a consequence, the diamond market has become larger and more faceless.[49]

Cab Drivers Cab drivers need to decide whether to pick up a fare or not. Although the probability assessment out of which they work is highly

---

[47] Bernstein, supra note 62, at 42.

[48] Id. at 43.

[49] Ethnic groups that greatly prefer continued trading within an identifiable membership, but whose costs are great in comparison with the new alternative, may need to accept lower compensation to be competitively viable, ceteris paribus.

subjective (it reflects risk attitudes, knowledge of particular circumstances, and prior own-and indirect-experience), this is an altogether calculative exercise. There is no obvious value added by describing a decision to accept a risk (pick up a fare) as one of trust.

Game Theory The "dramatic" change in the games described by Kreps comes about on moving from a one-shot game (where refusal to play was the rational choice) to a game that is repeated with high probability. Given the behavioral rules stipulated by Kreps, reputation effects relentlessly track those who breach contracts. Trading hazards are thus mitigated by embedding trades in networks in which reputation effects are known to work well.

Again, that can be interpreted as a Node C outcome. The parties have examined alternative trading scenarios and have opted for one in which the immediate gains of breach are deterred by the prospective loss of future business. To be sure, some markets are better able to support reputation effects than others. Reputation effects can and sometimes do break down[50] and are not therefore a trading panacea. Calculative assessments of the efficacy of reputation effects are, however, properly included within the efficient contracting exercise. Reference to trust adds nothing.

Kreps might agree, but he could argue that this misconstrues his enterprise. What Kreps is really concerned with is the evolution of trading relationships — these being the product of learning, social conditioning, corporate culture, and the like. His use of the word "trust" is merely incidental. The intertemporal mechanisms are the key.

I am not only sympathetic with this line of argument, but I would call attention to the fact that the static schema in Figure 1 oversimplifies, in that it takes these types of intertemporal effects as given. I submit, however, that Kreps's use of the term "trust," especially as stated in the behavioral rules that he employs, obscures rather than illuminates these mechanisms. More

---

[50] See Kreps, supra note 55; Williams, Formal Structure and Social Reality, in Gambetta ed., supra note 1, at 14; Williamson, Economic Institutions: Spontaneous and Intentional Governance, *7 J. L. Econ. & Org.* 159 (1991).

microanalytic attention to the processes through which trading relationships evolve[51] is indeed a rewarding research enterprise.

The Assaulted Girl Consider finally the case of the assaulted girl and suppose that the matter is put to her in the abstract: should she take shortcuts through the woods with ostensibly friendly boys of slight acquaintance? I submit that the girl in question would assign a nontrivial probability to a bad outcome (1 q), and a large negative value to B. Even for large values of G, the expected net gain from such walks would commonly be negative. Posed therefore as an abstract policy decision, the rational choice result is this: do not walk in the woods with strangers.

People, however, often cross bridges when they come to them rather than develop an abstract policy in advance. Still, why did she make the "wrong" decision when faced with the particulars?

One possibility is that she did not have the time to work out the calculus. Another possibility is that she had the time but got rattled. Still another possibility is that there is a dynamics to the situation which complicated matters. She cannot simply say no but needs a reason, otherwise her negative response to a "friendly" invitation will appear to be antisocial. Lacking a previously prepared response such as "I am sorry but I cannot walk in the woods because my hay fever is bothering me," and not wanting to appear unfriendly, she takes a chance.

This last involves a two-stage net benefit calculus. The first stage is as described earlier and, if the expected net gain comes out positive, the person assents and events thereafter unfold. If, however, the first stage comes out net negative, then the issue of tactful refusal must be faced. If a tactful refusal quickly presents itself, then the first stage calculus rules. But if a tactful refusal cannot be devised, then a choice between two net negatives needs to be made. Is a blunt refusal, which gives offense and/or results in a reputation for unfriendliness, more or less negative than the projected net loss from accepting the invitation (taking the risk)? Expressed in this way, the assaulted girl was caught up in a coercive situation. She was confronted with a

---

[51] See Arrow, Uncertainty and the Welfare Economics of Medical Care, 53 *American Economic Review* 941 (1963); Kreps, supra note 55 (and see Section IIIF below); and John Orbell & Robyn Dawes, A "Cognitive Miser" Theory of Cooperators' Advantage, 85 *American Political Science Review*. 515 (1991).

contingency for which she was not prepared, and the social forces coerced her into taking a risky choice.

Situations that are mainly explained by bounded rationality-the risk was taken because the girl did not get the calculus right or because she was not clever enough to devise a contrived but polite refusal on the spot are not illuminated by appealing to trust.[52]

3. Hyphenated Trust

Opportunism and bounded rationality are the key behavioral assumptions on which transaction cost economics relies. That parsimonious description is suitable for some purposes. But if man, after all, is a "social animal," then socialization and social approvals and sanctions are also pertinent. How can these be accommodated?

My response is suggested, if not evident, from my discussions of embeddedness and the institutional environment above. The Norwegian shipowner was part of a network, the farmer and diamond dealers are part of a community, and the assaulted high school girl is presented with a coercive situation. More generally, the argument is that trading hazards vary not only with the attributes of transaction but also with the trading environment of which they are a part.

Although the environment is mainly taken as exogenous, calculativeness is not suspended but remains operative. That is because the need for transaction specific safeguards (governance) varies systematically with the institutional environment within which transactions are located. Changes in the condition of the environment are therefore factored in by adjusting transaction specific governance in cost-effective ways. In effect, institutional environments that provide general purpose safeguards relieve the need for added

---

[52] To be sure, individuals trapped in coercive situations are attempting to cope. Is it really useful, however, to interpret a bad outcome from a coercive event as a bad draw? It is more instructive, I submit, to regard coercive events as a special class of problems that "invite" people to make risky choices from which they should be shielded (for example, by protecting them against exposure to coercive situations-possibly through training, possibly through draconian penalties against those who contrive coercion). Becker's recent treatment of addiction affords a somewhat different perspective — see Gary Becker, Habits, Addictions, and Traditions (unpublished manuscript, Univ. Chicago 1991).

transaction specific supports. Accordingly, transactions that are viable in an institutional environment that provides strong safeguards may be nonviable in institutional environments that are weak-because it is not cost-effective for the parties to craft transaction specific governance in the latter circumstances.

One should not, however, conclude that stronger environmental safeguards are always better than weaker. Not only can added environmental sanctions be pushed to dysfunctional extremes in purely commercial terms, but the environment can be oppressive more generally. My purpose here is merely to describe some of the contextual features with respect to which transaction specific governance is crafted, rather than to prescribe an optimal institutional environment. Embeddedness attributes of six kinds are distinguished: societal culture, politics, regulation, professionalization, networks, and corporate culture.[53] Each can be thought of as institutional trust of a hyphenated kind: "societal-trust," "political-trust," and so forth.

3.1. *Societal Culture*

Culture applies to very large groups, sometimes an entire society, and involves very low levels of intentionality. The degree of trading trust in Japan, for example, is said to be much higher than in Great Britain (Dore, 1983). By contrast, the villages in southern Italy described by Banfield(1958) are characterized by very low trading trust outside of the family.

The main import of culture, for purposes of economic organization, is that it serves as a check on opportunism. Social conditioning into a culture that condones lying and hypocrisy limits the efficacy of contract in three respects. First, social sanctions against strategic behavior (such as contrived breach) are weak. Second, court enforcement is problematic since bribery is widespread. Third, individuals feel slight remorse when they behave in opportunistic ways. Given the added hazards, transactions will tend to be of

---

[53] For more expansive discussions of the institutional environment, see Lynne Zucker, Production of Trust: Institutional Sources of Economic Structure, 1849–1920, 6 *Research in Organizational Behavior.* 53 (1986); Susan Shapiro, The Social Control of Impersonal Trust, *93 American Journal of Sociology 623* (1987); and Thomas, supra note 49.

a more generic (Node A, spot market) kind in societies where cultural checks on opportunism are weak, ceteris paribus.

3.2. *Politics*

Legislative and judicial autonomy serve credibility purposes. As Berman observes, credibility will be enhanced if a monarch who has made the law "may not make it arbitrarily, and until he has remade it-lawfully-he is bound by it (Berman, 1983)." Self-denying ordinances and, even more, inertia that have been crafted into the political process have commitment benefits (North and Weingast, 1989).

That this had not fully registered on Eastern Europe and the Soviet Union is suggested by the following remarks of Gorbachev (advising U.S. firms to invest quickly in the Soviet Union rather than wait): "Those [companies] who are with us now have good prospects of participating in our great country ... [whereas those who wait] will remain observers for years to come — we will see to it."[54] That the leadership of the Soviet Union "will see to it" that early and late movers will be rewarded and punished, respectively, reflects conventional carrot and stick incentive reasoning. What it misses is that ready access to administrative discretion is the source of contractual hazard. The paradox is that fewer degrees of freedom (rules) can have advantages over more (discretion) because added credible commitments can obtain in this way. Effective economic reform thus requires that political reneging options be foreclosed if investor confidence is to be realized.

3.3. *Regulation*

As Goldberg(1976) and Zucker[55] have explained, regulation can serve to infuse trading confidence into otherwise problematic trading relations. The creation and administration of a regulatory agency are both very intentional acts, although that is not to say that regulation does not have a (spontaneous) life of its own (Bernstein, 1955). Provided that the regulation in question is "appropriate," both parties to the transaction — the regulated firm and its

---

[54] Quoted from the International Herald Tribune, June 5, 1990, at 5.

[55] Zucker, supra note 86.

customers — will be prepared to make investments in specialized assets on better terms than they would in the absence of such regulation.

3.4. *Professionalization*

The obligation to fulfill the definition of a role is especially important for professionals — physicians, lawyers, teachers, and so on. Although these roles generally arise in a spontaneous (evolutionary) manner, they are thereafter supported by entry limitations (such as licensing), specific ethical codes, added fiduciary obligations,[56] and professional sanctions. Such support features are highly intentional. They can have the effect of infusing trading confidence into transactions that are characterized by costly information asymmetries, although sometimes the (intentionality) purposes served are strategic.[57]

3.5. *Networks*

The diamond dealers described above are an example of a trading network. So are the network forms of organization that have recently appeared in northern Italy (Mariotti and Cainara,1986). Other ethnic trading groups also qualify(Landa, 1981). Although many of these networks have spontaneous origins, the maintenance of these networks depends on the perfection of intentional trading rules, the enforcement of sanctions, and the like. Credibility turns on whether these reputation effects work well or poorly.

3.6. *Corporate Culture*

The above described features of the institutional environment are population level effects, mainly of a spontaneous kind. Corporate culture displays both spontaneous and intentional features and works mainly within particular

---

[56] Fiduciary obligations arise in the context of information asymmetries where the less informed party is exposed to serious losses by failures of "due care."

[57] Arrow, supra note 84.

organizations. Informal organization[58] is one example; the use of focal points[59] is another.

Barnard argued that formal and informal organization always and everywhere coexist[60] and that informal organization contributes to the viability of formal organization in three significant respects: "One of the indispensable functions of informal organizations in formal organizations . . . [is] that of communication. ... Another function is that of maintaining the cohesiveness in formal organizations through regulating the willingness to serve and the stability of objective authority. A third function is the maintenance of the feeling of personal integrity, of self-respect, and independent choice."[61] That has turned out to be a productive formulation. Economic activity will be better organized where there is an appreciation for and intentional use of informal organization.

Internal effects spill over, moreover, onto external trade if firms take on distinctive trading reputations by reason of the corporate culture through which they come to be known and evaluated.[62] Whether added corporate culture is warranted, however, varies with the circumstance: "In general, it will be crucially important to align culture with the sorts of contingencies that are likely to arise."[63] Accordingly, calculativeness characterizes even such apparently "soft" notions as corporate culture, of which Japanese economic organization is an example (Williamson, 1991).

4. Nearly Noncalculative Trust

Just as it is mind-boggling to contemplate hyperrationality of a comprehensive contracting kind, so is it mind-boggling to contemplate the absence of calculativeness. That is not to say that calculativeness cannot be suppressed or to deny that some actions or individuals are more spontaneous than others. Indeed, I shall argue that it is sometimes desirable to suppress

---

[58] Barnard, supra note 35.
[59] Kreps, supra note 55.
[60] Barnard, supra note 35, at 20.
[61] Id. at 122.
[62] Kreps, supra note 55.
[63] Id. at 128.

calculativeness. If, however, the decision to suppress calculativeness is itself purposive and calculative, then the true absence of calculativeness is rare if not nonexistent.[64]

Unable to foreclose some shred of calculativeness in the personal trust relations described here, I describe personal trust as nearly noncalculative. The argument proceeds in two stages. Discrete structural analysis, with special reference to the economics of atmosphere, is discussed first. Personal trust is then examined.

4.1. *Discrete Structural Analysis*

A colleague noted that the economics of atmosphere plays a larger role in Markets and Hierarchies[65] than in The Economic Institutions of Capitalism[66] and asked about the de-emphasis. I replied that I thought atmosphere at least as important to an understanding of economic organization in 1985 as I had in 1975. Not having made more headway, however, I had little to add.

One of the lessons of the economics of atmosphere is that calculativeness can be taken to dysfunctional extremes. That can show up within governance structures as well as between them. The employment relation is one such context. Suppose that a job can be split into a series of separable functions.

Suppose further that differential metering at the margin is attempted with reference to each. What are the consequences? If functional separability does not imply attitudinal separability, then piecemeal calculativeness can easily be dysfunctional. The risk is that pushing metering at the margin everywhere to the limit will have spillover effects from easy-to-meter onto hard-to-meter activities.

If cooperative attitudes are impaired, then transactions that can be metered only with difficulty, but for which consummate cooperation is important, will be discharged in a more perfunctory manner. The neglect of such interaction effects is encouraged by piecemeal calculativeness, which is to say by an insensitivity to atmosphere.

---

[64] Conceivably, some situations are so complicated that we decide to throw darts or examine entrails. But we are attempting to cope nonetheless. My discussion assumes that noncontingently selfless behavior of a Good Samaritan kind is the exception.

[65] Williamson, supra note 26.

[66] Williamson, supra note 25. 480

A related issue is the matter of externalities. The question may be put as follows: ought all externalities to be metered that, taken separately, can be metered with net gains? Presumably, this turns partly on whether secondary effects obtain when an externality is accorded legitimacy. All kinds of grievances may be "felt," and demands for compensation made accordingly, if what had hitherto been considered to be harmless byproducts of normal social intercourse are suddenly declared to be compensable injuries. The transformation of relationships that will ensue can easily lead to a lower level of felt satisfaction among the parties than prevailed previously at least transitionally and possibly permanently.

Part of the explanation is that filing claims for petty injuries influences attitudes toward other transactions. My insistence on compensation for A leads you to file claims for B, C, and D, which induces me to seek compensation for E and F, and so on. Although an efficiency gain might be realized were it possible to isolate transaction A, the overall impact can easily be negative. Realizing this to be the case, some individuals would be prepared to overlook such injuries. But everyone is not similarly constituted. Society is rearranged to the advantage of those who demand more exacting correspondences between rewards and deeds if metering at the margin is everywhere attempted. Were the issue of compensation to be taken up as a constitutional matter, rather than on a case-by-case basis, a greater tolerance for spillover would commonly obtain (Schelling, 1978).

Also pertinent is that individuals keep informal social accounts and find the exchange of reciprocal favors among parties with whom uncompensated spillovers exist to be satisfying (Goulder, 1954). Transforming these casual social accounts into exact and legal obligations may well be destructive of atmosphere and lead to a net loss of satisfaction between the parties. Put differently, pervasive pecuniary relations impair the quality of "contracting"- even if the metering of the transactions in question were costless.[67]

---

[67] The buying of "rounds" in English pubs is an example. Would a costless meter lead to a superior result? Suppose that everyone privately disclosed a willingness to pay and that successive bids were solicited until a break-even result was projected. Suppose that the results of the final solicitation are either kept secret or posted, depending on preferences, and that rounds are thereafter delivered to the table on request. Monthly bills are sent out in accordance with the break-even condition. How is camaraderie effected?

The argument that emerges from the above is not that metering ought to be prohibited but that the calculative approach to organization that is associated with economics can be taken to extremes. An awareness of attitudinal spillovers and nonpecuniary satisfactions serves to check such excesses of calculativeness. Consider now a more extreme possibility: there are some transactions for which the optimal level of conscious metering is zero.[68]

The idea here is that conscious monitoring, even of a low-grade kind, introduces unwanted calculativeness that is contrary to the spirit of certain very special relations and poses intertemporal threats to their viability. Not only can intendedly noncalculative relations can be upset by Type I error, according to which a true relation is incorrectly classified as false, but calculativeness may be subject to (involuntary) positive feedback. Intendedly noncalculative relations that are continuously subject to being reclassified as calculative are, in effect, calculative.

Issues akin to those examined by Nozick in his discussion of "Love's Bond" " are implicated (Nozick, 1988)." Nozick contends that the idea of "trading up" is inimical to a loving relationship: "The intention in love is to form a 'we' and to identify with it as an extended self, to identify one's fortunes in large part with its fortunes. A willingness to trade up, to destroy the way you largely identify with, would then be a willingness to destroy yourself in the form of your own extended self".[69] If entertaining the possibility of trading up devalues the relation, a discrete structural shift that disallows trading up, which is a variety of calculativeness, is needed.

4.2. Personal Trust

Dunn's recent treatment of "Trust and Political Agency" raises many of the pertinent issues (Dunn, 2000). Thus, Dunn distinguishes between trust as a "human passion" and trust as a "modality of human action," where the

---

[68] Unconscious or subconscious metering is another problem. Observations that are not consciously processed may be processed by the subconscious nonetheless, and their ramifications may insistently intrude on consciousness.

[69] Id. at 78.

latter is "a more or less consciously chosen policy for handling the freedom of other human agents or agencies."[70] He subsequently remarks that "trust as a passion is the confident expectation of benign intentions by another agent," but as a "modality of action, trust is ineluctably strategic."[71]He also contends that "the twin of trust is betrayal"[72] and avers that "human beings need, as far as they can, to economize on trust in persons and confide instead in well-designed political, social, and economic institutions."[73]

Trust as a passion Versus trust as a modality corresponds in my treatment to personal trust and calculative trust, respectfully. Moreover, Dunn's characterization of calculative trust as strategic, whereas personal trust is not, is exactly right. But whereas Dunn contends that the twin of trust is betrayal, I would reserve betrayal for personal trust and would use breach of contract to describe calculative relations. As hitherto remarked, breach of contract is sometimes efficient, even in a commercial contract that is supported by perfect safeguards.[74] By contrast, betrayal of a personal trust can never be efficient. Betrayal is demoralizing.

Also, although I subscribe to the notion of economizing on trust, I would put the issue somewhat differently. Trust, I submit, should be concentrated on those personal relations in which it really matters, which will be facilitated by the use of "political, social, and economic institutions" to govern calculative relations.[75]

If calculativeness is inimical to personal trust, in that a deep and abiding trust relation cannot be created in the face of calculativeness, and if preexisting personal trust is devalued by calculativeness, then the question is how to

---

[70] Id. at 73.

[71] Id. at 74.

[72] Id. at 81.

[73] Id. at 85.

[74] Williamson, supra note 37.

[75] Robertson's remark is pertinent: "[I]f we economists mind our own business, and do that business well, we can, I believe, contribute mightily to the economizing, that is to the full but thrifty utilization, of that scarce resource Love — which we know, just as well as anybody else, to be the most precious thing in the world" (Robertson, What Does the Economist Economize? in Economic Commentaries 154 (1976)).

segregate and preserve relations of personal trust.[76] I will take it that X reposes personal trust in Y if X (1) consciously refuses to monitor Y, (2) is predisposed to ascribe good intentions to Y when things go wrong, and (3) treats Y in a discrete structural way. Conditions 1 and 3 limit calculativeness. Under condition 2, "bad outcomes" are given a favorable construction: they are interpreted by X as stochastic events, or as complexity (Y didn't fully understand the situation), or as peccadillos (Y was inebriated).

To be sure, there are limits. An event where Y unambiguously violates the trust that X reposes in him threatens the relationship. Also (and here is where calculativeness creeps back in), a succession of minor violations may jeopardize the condition of trust. What further distinguishes personal trust, however, is that X insists that Y "reform" rather than merely "do better." That is because experience rating with continuous updating of the trustworthiness of Y places X in a calculative relation to Y. That degrades the relationship. Rather than do that, X elevates the relationship by placing it on all-or-none terms. Should Y refuse to make a discrete structural break with his past, then X will no longer trust him.[77] If instead Y agrees to reform, then trust will be renewed.

Personal trust is therefore characterized by (1) the absence of monitoring, (2) favorable or forgiving predilections, and (3) discreteness. Such relations are clearly very special. Although some individuals may have the natural instincts to behave noncalculatively, others will need to figure it out-to look ahead and recognize that calculativeness will devalue the relation, which is a farsighted view of contract. It does not, moreover, suffice merely to figure it out, in that some of those who do may be unable to shed

---

[76] There is nonetheless a sense in which incomplete contracts are continuously calculative, and that is in relation to reputation effects. If one party cannot make significant commercial moves without notice of the other even moves that have no direct bearing on the immediate contract but involve different contracts with different trading partners then continuous Bayesian updating may "ineluctably" obtain. In that event, reputation effects are pervasive (Kreps, supra note 55).

[77] That does not mean that X will no longer have anything to do with Y. If, however, the relation continues, X will thereafter treat Y in a calculative way.

Note in this connection that any shred of calculativeness does not imply that the relation is calculative. Rather, calculativeness needs to cross some (rather low) threshold before the relation is classified as calculative. The line is drawn —that is, a discrete structural break occurs — where X asks Y to reform.

calculativeness-because calculativeness (or fear) is so deeply etched by their experience.[78] Be that as it may, trust, if it obtains at all, is reserved for very special relations between family, friends, and lovers. Such trust is also the stuff of which tragedy is made. It goes to the essence of the human condition.[79]

5. Concluding Remarks

5.1. *Linguistic and Conceptual Tools*

A case can be made, and I will assume here, that a science of organization is in progress (Williamson and Barnard, 1990). The development of "specialized vocabularies" and "new languages" commonly attend such a project (Kuhn, 1970).

The development of a science of administration,[80] which was Simon's objective in Administrative Behavior,[81] posed exactly those needs. Given the deep insights afforded by Barnard's path-breaking book *The Functions of the Executive*,[82] how could that project be advanced? Simon observed in this connection that "we do not yet have, in this field, adequate linguistic and conceptual tools for realistically and significantly describing even a simple administrative organization-describing it, that is, in a way that will provide the basis for scientific analysis of the effectiveness of its structure and operation."[83] The need, as he saw it, was to "be able to describe, in words, exactly how an administrative organization looks and how it works. I have attempted to construct a vocabulary which will permit such a description."[84]

---

[78] Raz makes a related argument: some people "fail to see that personal relations cannot be valued in terms of commodities" (Raz, The Morality of Freedom 353 (1986)).

[79] See Nozick, supra note 113. Note that to repose trust in someone does not imply confidence in their judgment. Rather, as Dunn (supra note 115) has put it, to trust is to ascribe benign intent. Selective delegation is consistent with trust if the judgment of the trusted delegatee is believed to be better in some contexts than in others.

[80] A science of organization deals with markets, hybrids, hierarchies, bureaucracies, and the like, whereas the science of administration is preoccupied with internal organization.

[81] Simon, supra note 32, at 44, 248–53.

[82] Barnard, supra note 35.

[83] Simon, supra note 32, at xlv.

[84] Id.

5.2. *Calculativeness*

The way in which human actors are described and the processes through which contracting is perceived to work are both crucial to the development of a science of organization. Human actors are described here as boundedly rational and opportunistic, while the contracting process entails "incomplete contracting in its entirety."[85] This last views the governance of contractual relations broadly, including an examination of the systems context within which contracts are embedded. A very calculative orientation to commercial contracting is the result.

Such a farsighted approach to contract (in which credible commitments, or the lack thereof, play a key role) collides with sociological views on power and trust. As March has observed, power is a diffuse and disappointing concept (March, 1988). I contend that the same is true of trust. The recent tendency for sociologists and economists alike to use the terms "trust" and "risk" interchangeably is, on the arguments advanced here, ill-advised.

Not only is "calculated trust" a contradiction in terms, but userfriendly terms, of which "trust" is one, have an additional cost. The world of commerce is reorganized in favor of the cynics, as against the innocents, when social scientists employ userfriendly language that is not descriptively accurate — since only the innocents are taken in. Commercial contracting will be better served if parties are cognizant of the embeddedness conditions of which they are a part and recognize, mitigate, and price out contractual hazards in a discriminating way.[86]

5.3. *Categories of Trust*

Without purporting to be exhaustive, trust differences of three types are distinguished: calculative trust, personal trust, and institutional (or

---

[85] This phrase is my own.

[86] This is not to deny the excesses of calculativeness that sociologists (for example, Merton, supra note 39) and contract law specialists (for example, Macauley, Noncontractual Relations in Business, 28 Am. Soc. Rev. 55 (1963)) have forcefully called to our attention. Transaction cost economics takes a farsighted view of contract in which "feasible" calculativeness is featured.

hyphenated) trust. For the reasons given above, calculative relations should be described in calculative terms, to which the language of risk is exactly suited. The practice of using "trust" and "risk" interchangeably should therefore be discontinued.

Personal trust is made nearly noncalculative by switching out of a regime in which the marginal calculus applies into one of a discrete structural kind. That often requires added effort and is warranted only for very special personal relations that would be seriously degraded if a calculative orientation were "permitted." Commercial relations do not qualify.[87]

Institutional trust refers to the social and organizational context within which contracts are embedded. In the degree to which the relevant institutional features are exogenous, institutional trust has the appearance of being noncalculative. In fact, however, transactions are always organized (governed) with reference to the institutional context (environment) of which they are a part. Calculativeness thus always reappears.[88]

Should these arguments prevail, trust will hereafter be reserved for noncalculative personal relations (and, possibly, in a hyphenated form, to describe differences in the institutional environment). Although this is a long article to reach such a modest result, the literature on trust is truly enormous, and the confusions associated with calculativeness are growing. The incipient science of organization needs common concepts and language as the productive dialogue between law, economics, and organization takes shape. The irony is that the limits on calculativeness are realized by examining userfriendly termsof which "trust" is one in a thoroughly calculative way.

---

[87] I subscribe to the proposition that "[t]he core idea of trust is that it is not based on an expectation of its justification. When trust is justified by expectations of positive reciprocal consequences, it is simply another version of economic exchange" (March & Olsen, Rediscovering Institutions 27 (1989)).

[88] Also, the parties to a transaction sometimes influence the context, the capture (Bernstein, supra note 94) or precapture (Stigler, The Theory of Economic Regulation, 2 *Bell Journal of Economics* 3 (1971)) of regulation being examples.

References

Arrow, Kenneth J. 1951. *Social Choice and Individual Values*.

Banfield, E.C. 1958. *The Moral Basis of a Backward Society*.

Barnard, Chester. 1938. *The Functions of the Executive* 4 (15th printing 1962) (1st printing 1938).

Becker, Gary. 1976. *The Economic Approach to Human Behavior*.

Ben-Porath, Yoram. 1980. *The F-Connection: Families, Friends, and Firms and the Organization of Exchange*. 6 *Population and Development Review*, 1.

Berman, Harold. 1983. *Law and Revolution*.

Bernstein, Marver. 1955. *Regulating Business by Independent Commission*.

Buchanan, James & Tullock, Gordon. 1964. *The Calculus of Consent*.

Bradach, Jeffrey & Eccles, Robert. 1989. "Price, Authority, and Trust." 15 Am. Rev. Social. 97.

Calabresi, Guido. 1961. "Some Thoughts on Risk Distribution and the Law of Torts." 70 *Yale Law Journal*, 499.

Coleman, James. 1990. *Foundations of Social Theory*.

Commons, John R. 1924. *Legal Foundations of Capitalism*.)

Commons, John R. 1925. Law and Economics, 34 *Yale Law Journal*. 371.

Coase, Ronald H. & Fowler, Ronald. 1935. "Bacon Production and the Pig Cycle in Great Britain." 2 *Economica*, 142.

Coase, Ronald H. 1960. "The Problem of Social Cost." 3 *Journal of Law and Economics*, 1.

Davis, Lance E. & North, Douglass C. 1971. *Institutional Change and American Economic Growth*. pp. 6–7.

Dore, Ronald. 1983. "Goodwill and the Spirit of Market Capitalism." 39 *British Journal of Social Psychology*, 459.

Downs, Anthony. 1957. *An Economic Theory of Democracy*.

Duesenberry, James. 1960. An Economic Analysis of Fertility: Comment, In *Demographic and Economic Change in Developed Countries* 233.

Dunn, John. 2000. *Trust and Political Agency*. In ed., Gambetta supra note 1, at 73.

Goldberg, Victor. 1976. "Toward an Expanded Economic Theory of Contract." 10 *Journal of Economic Issues*, 45.

Goulder, A. W. 1954. *Industrial Bureaucracy*.

Granovetter, Mark. 1985."Economic Action and Social Structure: The Problem of Embeddedness." 91 *American Journal of Sociology*, 481.

Granovetter, Mark. 1988. "The Sociological and Economic Approaches to Labor Market Analysis." In *Industries, Firms, and Jobs*, eds.George Farkas & Paula England.

Hirschman, Albert O. 1970. *Exit, Voice and Loyalty*.

Hecter, Michael. 1987. *Principles of Group Solidarity.*

Homans, George. 1958. "Social Behavior as Exchange." 62, *The American Journal of Sociology,* 597.

Kreps, David M. 1990. "Corporate Culture, and Economic Theory." In *Perspectives on Positive Political Economy,* eds.James Alt & Kenneth Shepsle, pp. 90–143.

Kuhn, Thomas S. 1970. *The Structure of Scientific Revolutions.* pp. 203–204.

Landa, Janet T. 1981. "A Theory of the Ethnically Homogeneous Middleman Group: An Institutional Alternative to Contract Law." 10 *Journal of Legal Studies,* 349.

Lindenberg, Siegwart. 1990. Homo Socio-economicus: "The Emergence of a General Model of Man in the Social Sciences." 146 *Journal of Instituitional and Theoretical Economics,* 727.

Llewellyn, Karl N. 1931. "What Price Contract? An Essay in Perspective." 40 *Yale Law Journal,* 704, 736–3.

Macneil, Ian. 1974. "The Many Futures of Contract." 47 *Southern California Law Review,* 691 at 738.

Machiavelli, Niccolo. 1952. *The Prince* pp. 92–93.

March, James G. 1988. *Decisions and Organizations* 6.

March, James G. & Simon, Herbert. 1958. *Organizations.*

Mariotti, Sergio & Cainarca, Gian Carlo. 1986. "The Evolution of Transaction Governance in the Textile Clothing Industry." 7 *Journal of Economic Behavior and Organization,* 351.

Merton, Robert. 1936. "The Unanticipated Consequences of Purposive Social Action." 1 *American Sociology. Review,* 894.

North, Douglass & Weingast, Barry. 1989. "Constitutions and Commitment: The Evolution of Institutions Governing Public Choice in 17th Century England." 49, *Journal of Economic History,* 803.

North, Douglass. 1991. "Institutions." 5 *Journal of Economic Perspective,* 97.

Nozick, Robert. 1988. *An Examined Life.* Chapter 8, Love's Bond.

Olson, Mancur. 1965. *The Logic of Collective Action.*

Pfeffer, Jeffrey & Salancik, Gerald. 1978. *The External Control of Organizations.*

Pfeffer, Jeffrey. 1981. *Power in Organizations.*

Posner, Richard A. 1977. *Economic Analysis of Law.*

Posner, Richard A. 1979. "The Chicago School of Antitrust Analysis."127 *The University of Pennsylvania Law Review,* 925.

Radner, Roy. 1968."Competitive Equilibrium under Uncertainty." 36 *Econometrica,* 31.

Samuelson, Paul. 1947. *Foundations of Economic Analysis.*

Schelling, Thomas. 1978. *Micromotives and Macrobehavior.*

Simon, Herbert. 1957. *Administrative Behavior*, at xxiv, 2nd edn.

Simon, Herbert. 1978. "Rationality as Product and Process of Thought." 68 *American Economic Review*, 1.

Stigler, George. 1968. *The Organization of Industry*.

Williamson, Oliver E. & Barnard, Chester. 1990. "The Incipient Science of Organization." In *Organization Theory.* Williamson. 1991. "supra note 29; and the special issue on The New Science of Organization." 7 *Journal of Law, Economics & Organization*, 1.

Williamson, Oliver E. 1991. "Comparative Economic Organization: The Analysis of Discrete Structural Alternatives." 36 *Administrative Science Quarterly*, 269.

Williamson, Oliver E. 1991. "Strategizing, Economizing, and Economic Organization." 12 *Strategic Management Journal*, 75.

Chapter 4

The Theory of the Firm as Governance Structure: From Choice to Contract*

The propositions that organization matters and that it is susceptible to analysis were long greeted by skepticism by economists. To be sure, there were conspicuous exceptions: Marshall in Industry and Trade (1932), Schumpeter in Capitalism, Socialism, and Democracy (1942) and Hayek (1945) in his writings on knowledge. Institutional economists like Veblen (1904), Commons (1934) and Coase (1937) and organization theorists like Michels (1915, 1962), Barnard (1938), Simon (1957a), March (March and Simon, 1958) and Scott (1992) also made the case that organization deserves greater prominence.

One reason why this message took a long time to register is that it is much easier to say that organization matters than it is to show how and why.[1]

---

* *Journal of Economic Perspectives* — Volume 16, Number 3, Summer 2002, pp. 171–195. The helpful advice of Timothy Taylor and Michael Waldman in revising this manuscript is gratefully acknowledged.
[1] A Behavioral Theory of the Firm (Cyert and March, 1963) was one obvious early candidate for an economic theory of organizations. It deals, however, with more fine-grained phenomena — such as predicting department store prices to the penny — than were of interest to most economists. For a discussion, see Williamson (1999b). The recent and growing interest in behavioral economics — which deals more with the theory of consumer behavior than with the theory of the firm — can be interpreted as a delay response to the lessons of the "Carnegie school" associated with Cyert, March and Simon.

The prevalence of the science of choice approach to economics has also been an obstacle. As developed herein, the lessons of organization theory for economics are both different and more consequential when examined through the lens of contract. This chapter examines economic organization from a science of contract perspective, with special emphasis on the theory of the firm.

1. The Sciences of Choice and Contract

Economics throughout the twentieth century has been developed predominantly as a science of choice. As Robbins famously put it in his book, *An Essay on the Nature and Significance of Economic Science* (Robbins, 1932, p. 16), "Economics is the science which studies human behavior as a relationship between ends and scarce means which have alternative uses." Choice has been developed in two parallel constructions: the theory of consumer behavior, in which consumers maximize utility, and the theory of the firm as a production function, in which firms maximize pro. Economists who work out of such setups emphasize how changes in relative prices and available resources influence quantities, a project that became the "dominant paradigm" for economics throughout the twentieth century (Reder, 1999, p. 48).

But the science of choice is not the only lens for studying complex economic phenomena, nor is it always the most instructive lens. The other main approach is what Buchanan (1964a, 1964b, 1975) refers to as the science of contract. Indeed, Buchanan (1975, p. 225) avers that economics as a discipline went "wrong" in its preoccupation with the science of choice and the optimization apparatus associated therewith. Wrong or not, the parallel development of a science of contract was neglected.

As perceived by Buchanan (1987, p. 296), the principal needs for a science of contract were for the field of public finance and took the form of public ordering: "Politics is a structure of complex exchange among individuals, a structure within which persons seek to secure collectively their own privately defined objectives that cannot be efficiently secured through simple market exchanges." Thinking contractually in the public ordering domain leads into a focus on the rules of the game. Constitutional economics issues are posed (Buchanan and Tullock, 1962; Brennan and Buchanan, 1985).

Whatever the rules of the game, the lens of contract is also usefully brought to bear on the play of the game. This latter is what I refer to as private ordering, which entails efforts by the immediate parties to a transaction to align incentives and to craft governance structures that are better attuned to their exchange needs. The object of such self-help efforts is to realize better the "mutuality of advantage from voluntary exchange ... [that is] the most fundamental of all understandings in economics" (Buchanan, 2001, p. 29), due allowance being made for the mitigation of contractual hazards. Strategic issues — to which the literatures on mechanism design, agency theory and transaction cost economics/incomplete contracting all have a bearing — that had been ignored by neoclassical economists from 1870 to 1970 now make their appearance (Makowski and Ostroy, 2001, pp. 482–483, 490–491).

Figure 1 sets out the main distinctions. The initial divide is between the science of choice (orthodoxy) and the science of contract. The latter then divides into public ordering (constitutional economics) and private ordering parts, where the second is split into two related branches. One branch concentrates on front-end incentive alignment (mechanism design, agency theory, the formal property rights literature), while the second branch features the governance of ongoing contractual relations (contract implementation). This chapter is mainly concerned with governance, especially with reference to the theory of the firm.

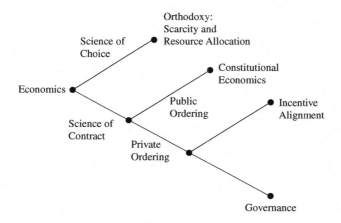

Figure 1. The sciences of choice and contract

2. Organization Theory through the Lens of Contract

Organization theory is a huge subject. Macro and micro parts are commonly distinguished, where the former is closer to sociology and the latter to social psychology. Also, it is common to distinguish among rational, natural and open systems approaches (Scott, 1992). My concern is with macroorganization theory of a rational systems kind (with special reference to the contributions of Simon).

In addition to delimiting organization theory in this way, I also examine the lessons of organization theory for economics not through the lens of choice, but through the lens of contract. Whereas those who work out of the dominant paradigm have sometimes been dismissive of organization theory (Posner, 1993; Reder, 1999, pp. 46–49), the lens of contract/private ordering discloses that lessons of organization theory for economics that the dominant paradigm obscures are sometimes fundamental.

3. Five Lessons from Organization Theory to the Economics of Contracts

A first lesson from organization theory is to describe human actors in more realistic terms. Simon (1985, p. 303) is unequivocal: "Nothing is more fundamental in setting our research agenda and informing our research methods than our view of the nature of the human beings whose behavior we are studying." Social scientists are thus invited (challenged) to name the cognitive, self-interest and other attributes of human actors on which their analyses rest.

Bounded rationality is the cognitive assumption to which Simon (1957a, p. xxiv) refers, by which he has reference to behavior that is intendedly rational, but only limitedly so. In his view, the main lesson for the science of choice is to supplant maximizing by "satisficing" (Simon, 1957b, p. 204) — the quest for an alternative that is "good enough."[2]

---

[2] Although *satisficing* is an intuitively appealing concept, it is very hard to implement. Awaiting further developments, the *satisficing* approach is not broadly applicable (Aumann, 1985, p. 35). Indeed, there is an irony: neoclassical economists who use a mode of analysis (maximizing) that is easy to implement and often is good enough for the purposes at hand are analytical satisficers.

The study of governance also appeals to bounded rationality, but the main lesson for the science of contract is different: ***All complex contracts are unavoidably incomplete***. For this reason, parties will be confronted with the need to adapt to unanticipated disturbances that arise by reason of gaps, errors and omissions in the original contract. Such adaptation needs are especially consequential if, instead of describing self-interest as "frailty of motive" (Simon, 1985, p. 303), which is a comparatively benign condition, strategic considerations are entertained, as well. If human actors are not only confronted with needs to adapt to the unforeseen (by reason of bounded rationality), but are also given to strategic behavior (by reason of opportunism), then costly contractual breakdowns (refusals of cooperation, maladaptation, demands for renegotiation) may be posed. In that event, private ordering efforts to devise supportive governance structures, thereby to mitigate prospective contractual impasses and breakdowns, have merit.

To be sure, such efforts would be unneeded if common knowledge of pay off sand costless bargaining are assumed. Both of these conditions, however, are deeply problematic (Kreps and Wilson, 1982; Williamson, 1985). Moreover, because problems of nonvariability are posed when bounded rationality, opportunism and idiosyncratic knowledge are joined (Williamson, 1975, pp. 31–33), dispute resolution by the courts in such cases is costly and unreliable. Private ordering — that is, efforts to craft governance structure supports for contractual relations during the contract implementation interval — thus makes its appearance.

A second lesson of organization theory is to be alert to all significant behavioral regularities whatsoever. For example, efforts by bosses to impose controls on workers have both intended and unintended consequences. Out of awareness that workers are not passive contractual agents, naive efforts that focus entirely on intended effects will be supplanted by more sophisticated mechanisms where provision is made for consequences of both kinds. More generally, the awareness among sociologists that "organization has a life of its own" (Selznick, 1950, p. 10) serves to uncover a variety of behavioral regularities (of which bureaucratization is one) for which the student of governance should be alerted and thereafter factor into the organizational design calculus.

A third lesson of organization theory is that alternative modes of governance (markets, hybrids, firms, bureaus) differ in discrete structural ways

(Simon, 1978, pp. 6–7). Not only do alternative modes of governance differ in kind, but each generic mode of governance is defined by an internally consistent syndrome of attributes — which is to say that each mode of governance possesses distinctive strengths and weaknesses. As discussed below, the challenge is to enunciate there Levant attributes for describing governance structures and thereafter to align different kinds of transactions with discrete modes of governance in an economizing way.

A fourth lesson of the theory of organizations is that much of the action resides in the microanalytics. Simon (1957a) nominated the "decision premise" as the unit of analysis, which has an obvious bearing on the micro analytics of choice (Newell and Simon, 1972). The unit of analysis proposed by Commons, however, better engages the study of contract. According to Commons (1932, p. 4), "the ultimate unit of activity ... must contain in itself the three principles of conflict, mutuality, and order. This unit is a transaction."

Whatever the unit of analysis, operationalization turns on naming and explicating the critical dimensions with respect to which the unit varies. Three of the key dimensions of transactions that have important ramifications for governance are asset specificity (which takes a variety of forms — physical, human, site, dedicated, brand name — and is a measure of bilateral dependency), the disturbances to which transactions are subject (and to which potential maladaptation accrue) and the frequency with which transactions recur (which bears both on the efficacy of reputation effects in the market and the incentive to incur the cost of specialized internal governance). Given that transactions differ in their attributes and that governance structures differ in their costs and competencies, the aforementioned — that transactions should be aligned with appropriate governance structures — applies.

A fifth lesson of organization theory is the importance of cooperative adaptation. Interestingly, both the economist Hayek (1945) and the organization theorist Barnard (1938) were in agreement that adaptation is the central problem of economic organization. Hayek (1945, pp. 526–527) focused on the adaptations of autonomous economic actors who adjust spontaneously to changes in the market, mainly as signaled by changes in relative prices. The marvel of the market resides in "how little the individual participants need to know to be able to take the right action." By contrast, Barnard featured coordinated adaptation among economic actors working through deep knowledge and the use of administration. In his view, the marvel of hierarchy is that coordinated adaptation is accomplished not spontaneously, but in a "conscious, deliberate, purposeful" way (p. 9).

Because a high-performance economic system will display adaptive properties of both kinds, the problem of economic organization is properly posed not as markets or hierarchies, but rather as markets and hierarchies. A predictive theory of economic organization will recognize how and why transactions differ in their adaptive needs, whence the use of the market to supply some transactions and recourse to hierarchy for others.

4. Follow-on Insights from the Lens of Contract

Examining economic organization through the lens of contract uncovers additional regularities to which governance ramifications accrue. Three such regularities are described here: the Fundamental Transformation, the impossibility of replication/selective intervention and the idea of contract laws (plural).

The Fundamental Transformation applies to that subset of transactions for which large numbers of qualified suppliers at the outset are transformed into what are, in effect, small numbers of actual suppliers during contract execution and at the contract renewal interval. The distinction to be made is between generic transactions where "faceless buyers and sellers . . . meet . . . for an instant to ex-change standardized goods at equilibrium prices" (Ben-Porath, 1980, p. 4) and exchanges where the identities of the parties matter, in that continuity of the relation has significant cost consequences. Transactions for which *a bilateral dependency condition obtains* are those to which the Fundamental Transformation applies.

The key factor here is whether the transaction in question is supported by investments in transaction specific assets. Such specialized investments may take the form of specialized physical assets (such as a die for stamping out distinctive metal shapes), specialized human assets (that arise from firm-specific training or learning by doing), site specificity (specialization by proximity), dedicated assets (large discrete investments made in expectation of continuing business, the premature termination of which business would result in product being sold at distress prices) or brand-name capital. Parties to transactions that are bilaterally dependent are "vulnerable," in that buyers

cannot easily turn to alternative sources of supply, while suppliers can redeploy the specialized assets to their next best use or user only at a loss of
productive value (Klein, Crawford and Alchian, 1978). As a result, value-
preserving governance structures — to infuse order, thereby to mitigate
conflict and to realize mutual gain — are sought.[3] Simple market exchange
thus gives way to credible contracting, which includes penalties for premature termination, mechanisms for information disclosure and verification,
specialized dispute settlement procedures and the like. Unified ownership
(vertical integration) is predicted as bilateral dependency hazards build up.

The impossibility of combining replication with selective intervention is
the transaction cost economics answer to an ancient puzzle: What is responsible for limits to firm size? Diseconomies of large scale is the obvious answer,
but where indo these diseconomies reside? Technology is no answer, since
each plant in a multi plant firm can use the least-cost technology. Might
organization provide the answer? That possibility can be examined by
rephrasing the question in comparative contractual terms: Why can't a large
firm do everything that a collection of small suppliers can do and more?

Were it that large firms could replicate a collection of small firms in all
circumstances where small firms do well, then large firms would never do
worse. If, moreover, large firms could always *selectively intervene* by impos-
ing (hierarchical) order on prospective conflict, but only where expected net
gains could be projected, then large firms would sometimes do better. Taken
together, the combination of replication with selective intervention would
permit large firms to grow without limit. Accordingly, the issue of limits to
firm size turns to an examination of the mechanisms for implementing
replication and selective intervention.

Examining how and why both replication and selective intervention
breakdown is a tedious, microanalytic exercise and is beyond the scope of this
chapter (Williamson, 1985, Chapter 6). Suffice it to observe here that the
move from autonomous supply (by the collection of small firms) to unified
ownership (in one large firm) is *unavoidably attended by changes* in both

---

[3] Bilateral dependency need not result from physical asset specificity if the assets are mobile,
since a buyer who owns and who can repossess the assets can assign them to whichever supplier tenders the lowest bid. Also, site-specific assets can sometimes be owned by a buyer and
leased to a supplier. Nonetheless, such "solutions" will pose user cost problems if suppliers
cannot be relied upon to exercise due care.

incentive intensity (incentives are weaker in the integrated firm) and administrative controls (controls are more extensive). Because the syndromes of attributes that define markets and hierarchies have different strengths and weaknesses, some transactions will benefit from the move from market to hierarchy while others will not.

Yet another organizational dimension that distinguishes alternative modes of governance is the regime of contract laws. Whereas economic orthodoxy often implicitly assumes that there is a single, all-purpose law of contract that is costlessly enforced by well-informed courts, the private ordering approach to governance postulates instead that each generic mode of governance is defined (in part) by a distinctive contract law regime.

The contract law of (ideal) markets is that of classical contracting, according to which disputes are costlessly settled through courts by the award of money damages. Galanter (1981, pp. 1–2) takes issue with this legal centralism tradition and observes that many disputes between firms that could under current rules be brought to a court are resolved instead by avoidance, self-help and the like. That is because in "many instances the participants can devise more satisfactory solutions to their disputes than can professionals constrained to apply general rules on the basis of limited knowledge of the dispute" (p. 4). Such a view is broadly consonant with the concept of "contract as framework" advanced by Llewellyn (1931, pp. 736–737), which holds that the "major importance of legal contract is to provide ... a framework which never accurately indicates real working relations, but which affords a rough indication around which such relations vary, an occasional guide in cases of doubt, and a norm of ultimate appeal when the relations cease in fact to work." This last condition is important, in that recourse to the courts for purposes of ultimate appeal serves to delimit threat positions. The more elastic concept of contract as framework nevertheless supports a (cooperative) exchange relation over a wider range of contractual disturbances.

What is further more noteworthy is that some disputes cannot be brought to a court at all. Specifically, except as "fraud, illegality or conflict of interest" are shown, courts will refuse to hear disputes that arise within firms — with respect, for example, to transfer pricing, overhead, accounting, the costs to be ascribed to interim delays, failures of quality and the like. In effect, the contract law of internal organization is that of forbearance, according to which a firm becomes its own court of ultimate appeal. Firms for this reason are able to exercise at that the markets cannot. This, too, influences the choice of alternative modes of governance.

Not only is each generic mode of governance defined by an internally consistent syndrome of incentive intensity, administrative controls and contract law regime (Williamson, 1991a), but different strengths and weaknesses accrue to each.

5. The Theory of the Firm as Governance Structure

As Demsetz (1983, p. 377) observes, it is "a mistake to confuse the firm of [orthodox] economic theory with its real-world namesake. The chief mission of neoclassical economics is to understand how the price system coordinates the use of resources, not the inner workings of real firms." Suppose instead that the assigned mission of economics is to understand the organization of economic activity. In that event, it will no longer suffice to describe the firm as a black box that transforms inputs into outputs according to the laws of technology. Instead, firms must be described in relation to other modes of governance, all of which have internal structure, which structure "must arise for some reason" (Arrow, 1999, p. vii).

The contract/private ordering/governance (hereafter governance) approach maintains that structure arises mainly in the service of economizing on transaction costs. Note in this connection that the firm as governance structure is a comparative contractual construction. The firm is conceived not as a stand-alone entity, but is always to be compared with alternative modes of governance. By contrast with mechanism design (where a menu of contracts is used to elicit private information), agency theory (where risk aversion and multitasking are featured) and the property rights theory of the firm (where everything rests on asset ownership), the governance approach appeals to law and organization theory in naming incentive intensity, administrative control and contract law regime as three critical attributes.

It will be convenient to illustrate the mechanisms of governance with reference to a specific class of transactions. Because transactions in intermediate product markets avoid some of the more serious conditions of asymmetry — of information, budget, legal talent, risk aversion and the like — that beset some transactions in final product markets, I examine the "make-or-buy" decision.

Should a firm make an input itself, perhaps by acquiring a firm that makes the input, or should it purchase the input from another firm?

6. The Science of Choice Approach to the Make-or-Buy Decision

The main way to examine the make-or-buy decision under the setup of firm as production function is with reference to bilateral monopoly.[4] The neoclassical analysis of bilateral monopoly reached the conclusion that while optimal quantities between the parties might be realized, the division of profits between bilateral monopolists was indeterminate (for example, Machlup and Tabor, 1960, p. 112). Vertical integration might then arise as a means by which to relieve bargaining over the indeterminacy. Alternatively, vertical integration could arise as a means by which to restore efficient factor proportions when an upstream monopolist sold intermediate product to a downstream buyer that used a variable proportions technology (McKenzie, 1951). Vertical integration has since been examined in a combined variable proportions-monopoly power context by Vernon and Graham (1971), Schmalensee (1973), Warren-Boulton (1974), Westfield (1981) and Hart and Tirole (1990).

This literature is instructive, but it is also beset by a number of loose ends or anomalies. First, since preexisting monopoly power of a durable kind is the exception in a large economy rather than the rule, what explains vertical integration for the vast array of transactions where such power is negligible? Second, why don't firms integrate everything, since under a production function setup, an integrated firm can always replicate its unintegrated rivals and can sometimes improve on them? Third, what explains hybrid modes of contracting? More generally, if many of the problems of trading are of an intertemporal kind in which successive adaptations to uncertainty are needed, do the problems of economic organization have to be recast in a larger and different framework?

---

[4] Although the bilateral monopoly explanation is the oldest explanation and the one emphasized in most microeconomics textbooks, three other price-theoretic frameworks have been used to explain the make-or-buy decision: price discrimination, barriers to entry and strategic purposes. For a summary of the arguments on these points, see Williamson (1987, pp. 808– 809). For a more complete discussion, see Perry (1989).

7. Coase and the Make-or-Buy Decision

Coase's (1937, p. 389) classic article opens with a basic puzzle: Why does a firm emerge at all in a specialized exchange economy? If the answer resides in entrepreneurship, why is coordination "the work of the price mechanism in one case and the entrepreneur in the other"? Coase (p. 391) appealed to transaction cost economizing as the hitherto missing factor for explaining why markets were used in some cases and hierarchy in other cases and averred: "The main reason why it is profitable to establish a firm would seem to be that there is a cost of using the price mechanism, the most obvious ... [being] that of discovering what the relevant prices are." This sounds plausible. But how is it that internal procurement by the firm avoids the cost of price discovery?

The "obvious" answer is that sole-source internal supply avoids the need to consult the market about prices, because internal accounting prices of a formulaic kind (say, of a cost-plus kind) can be used to transfer a good or service from one internal stage to another. If, however, that is the source of the advantage of internal organization over market procurement, the obvious lesson is to apply this same practice to outside procurement. The firm simply advises its purchasing office to turn a blind eye to the market by placing orders, period by period, with a qualified sole-source external supplier who agrees to sell on cost-plus terms. In that event, firm and market are put on a parity in price discovery respects — which is to say that the price discovery burden that Coase ascribes to the market does not survive comparative institutional scrutiny.[5]

In the end, Coase's profoundly important challenge to orthodoxy and his insistence on introducing transactional considerations does not lead to refutable implications (Alchian and Demsetz, 1972). Operationalization of these good ideas was missing (Coase, 1992, pp. 716–718). The theory of the firm

---

[5] It does not suffice to argue that vigilance is unneeded for trade within firms because transfer prices are a wash. For one thing, different transfer prices will induce different factor proportions in divisionalized firms where divisions are held accountable for their bottom lines (unless fixed proportions are imposed). Also, because incentives within firms are weaker, ready access to the pass-through of costs can encourage cost excesses. The overarching point is this: to focus on transfer pricing to the neglect of discrete structural differences between firm and market is to miss the forest for the trees.

as governance structure is an effort to infuse operational content. Transaction cost economizing is the unifying concept.[6]

8. A Heuristic Model of Firm as Governance Structure

Expressed in terms of the "Commons triple" — the notion that the transaction incorporates the three aspects of conflict, mutuality and order — governance is the means by which to infuse order, thereby to mitigate conflict and to realize "the most fundamental of all understandings in economics," mutual gain from voluntary exchange. The surprise is that a concept as important as governance should have been so long neglected.

The rudiments of a model of the firm as governance structure are the attributes of transactions, the attributes of alternative modes of governance and the purposes served. Asset specificity (which gives rise to bilateral dependency) and uncertainty (which poses adaptive needs) are especially important attributes of transactions. The attributes that define a governance structure include incentive intensity, administrative control and the contract law regime. In this framework, market and hierarchy syndromes differ as follows: under hierarchy, incentive intensity is less, administrative controls are more numerous and discretionary, and internal dispute resolution supplants court ordering. Adaptation is taken to be the main purpose, where the requisite mix of autonomous adaptations and coordinated adaptations vary among transactions. Specifically, the need for coordinated adaptations builds up as asset specificity deepens.

In a heuristic way, Figure 2 shows the transaction cost consequences of organizing transactions in markets (M) and hierarchies (H) as a function of asset specificity (k). As shown, the bureaucratic burdens of hierarchy place it at an initial disadvantage (k 5 0), but the cost differences between markets $M(k)$ and hierarchy $H(k)$ narrow as asset specificity builds up and eventually reverse as the need for cooperative adaptation becomes especially great ($k...0$). Provision can further be made for the hybrid mode of organization $X(k)$, where hybrids are viewed as market-preserving credible contracting modes that possess adaptive attributes located between classical markets and

---

[6] Other purposes include choice of efficient factor proportions, specialization of labor (in both physical and cognitive respects) and knowledge acquisition and development.

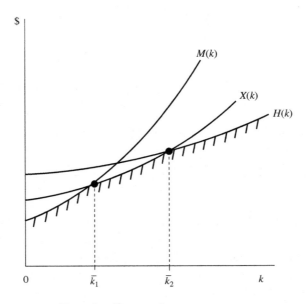

Figure 2.   Comparative cost governance

hierarchies. Incentive intensity and administrative control thus take on intermediate values, and Llewellyn's (1931) concept of contract as framework
applies. As shown in Figure 2, $M(0)$, $X(0)$, $H(0)$ are by reason of bureaucratic
cost differences, while $M9$. $X9$. $H9$ reflect the cost of coordinated
adaptation.

   This rudimentary setup yields refutable implications that are broadly
corroborated by the data. It can be extended to include differential production costs between modes of governance, which mainly preserves the basic
argument that hierarchy is favored as asset specificity builds up, ceteris paribus (Riordan and Williamson, 1985). The foregoing relations among governance structures and transactions can also be replicated with a simple
stochastic model where the needs for adaptation vary with the transaction
and the efficacy of adaptations of autonomous and cooperative kinds vary
with the governance structures. Shift parameters can also be introduced in
such a model (Williamson, 1991a). More fully formal treatments of contracting that are broadly congruent with this setup are in progress.

   Whereas most theories of vertical integration do not invite empirical
testing, the transaction cost theory of vertical integration invites and has been

the subject of considerable empirical analysis. Empirical research in the field of industrial organization is especially noteworthy because the field has been criticized for the absence of such work. Not only did Coase once describe his 1937 article as "much cited and little used" (1972, p. 67), but others have since commented upon the paucity of empirical work on the theory of the firm (Holmstrom and Tirole, 1989, p. 126) and in the field of industrial organization (Peltzman, 1991). By contrast, empirical transaction cost economics has grown exponentially during the past 20 years. For surveys, see Shelanski and Klein (1995), Lyons (1996), Crocker and Masten (1996), Rindfeisch and Heide (1997), Masten and Saussier (2000) and Boerner and Macher (2001).[7] Added to this are numerous applications to public policy, especially antitrust and regulation, but also to economics more generally (Dixit, 1996) and to the contiguous social sciences (especially political science). The upshot is that the theory of the firm as governance structure has become a much used construction.

9. Variations on a Theme

Vertical integration turns out to be a paradigm. Although many of the empirical tests and public policy applications have reference to the make-or-buy decision and vertical market restrictions, this same framework has application to contracting more generally. Specifically, the contractual relation between the firm and its "stakeholders" — customers, suppliers and workers along with financial investors — can be interpreted as variations on a theme.

---

[7] I would note parenthetically that the GM-Fisher Body example (Klein, Crawford and Alchian, 1978) that is widely used to illustrate the contractual strains that attend bilateral dependency has come under criticism (see the exchange in the April 2000 issue of the *Journal of Law and Economics*). My responses are two. First and foremost, even if the GM-Fisher Body anecdote is factually flawed, transaction cost economics remains an empirical success story (see text and Whinston, 2001). Second, the main purpose of an anecdote is pedagogical, to provide intuition. That is what the confectioner and physician cases do for externalities (Coase, 1959), what QWERTY does for path dependency (David, 1985), what the market for lemons does for asymmetric information (Akerlof, 1970) and what the tragedy of the commons does for collective organization (Hardin, 1968). It is better, to be sure, if anecdotes are factually correct. Unless, however, the phenomenon described by the anecdote is trivial or bogus (which conditions may not be evident until an empirical research program is undertaken), an anecdote that helps to bring an abstract condition to life has served its intended purpose.

10. The Contractual Schema

Assume that a firm can make or buy a component, and assume further that the component can be supplied by either a general purpose technology or a special purpose technology. Again, let k be a measure of asset specificity. The transactions in Figure 3 that use the general purpose technology are ones for which $k 5 0$. In this case, no specific assets are involved, and the parties are essentially faceless. If instead, transactions use the special purpose technology, $k. 0$. As hitherto discussed, bilaterally dependent parties have incentives to promote continuity and safeguard their specific investments. Let's denote the magnitude of any such safeguards, which include penalties, information disclosure and verification procedures, specialized dispute resolution (such as arbitration) and, in the limit, integration of the two stages under united ownership. An $s 5 0$ condition is one for which no safeguards are provided; a decision to provide safeguards is reflected by an $s. 0$ result.

Node A in Figure 3 corresponds to the ideal transaction in law and economics: there being an absence of dependency, governance is accomplished through competitive market prices and, in the event of disputes, by court-awarded damages. Node B poses unrelieved contractual hazards, in that specialized investments are exposed ($k. 0$) for which no safeguards ($s 5 0$) have been provided. Such hazards will be recognized by farsighted players, who will price out the implied risks.

Added contractual supports ($s . 0$) are provided at nodes C and D. At node C, these contractual supports take the form of interim contractual

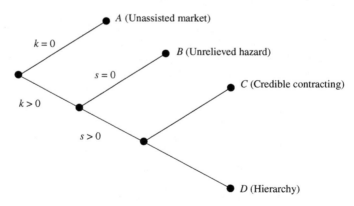

Figure 3.   Simple contracting schema

safeguards. Should, however, costly breakdowns continue in the face of best bilateral efforts to craft safeguards at node C, the transaction may be taken out of the market and organized under united ownership (vertical integration) instead. Because added bureaucratic costs accrue upon taking a transaction out of the market and organizing it internally, internal organization is usefully thought of as the organization form of last resort. That is, try markets, try hybrids and have recourse to the firm only when all else fails. Node D, the united firm, thus comes in only as higher degrees of asset specificity and added uncertainty pose greater needs for cooperative adaptation.

Note that the price that a supplier will bid to supply under node C conditions will be less than the price that will be bid at node B. That is because the added security features serve to reduce the risk at node C, as compared with node B, so Figure 3 Simple Contracting Schema, 'The Theory of the Firm as Governance Structure': From Choice to Contract 183, the contractual hazard premium will be reduced. One implication is that suppliers do not need to petition buyers to provide safeguards. Because buyers will receive product on better terms (lower price) when added security is provided, buyers have the incentive to offer credible commitments. Thus, although such commitments are sometimes thought of as a userfriendly way to contract, the analytical action resides in the hard-headed use of credibility to support those transactions where asset specificity and contractual hazards are an issue. Such supports are without purpose for transactions where the general purpose production technology is employed.

The foregoing schema can be applied to virtually all transactions for which the firm is in a position to own as well as to contract with an adjacent stage — backward into raw materials, laterally into components, forward into distribution.[8] But for some activities, ownership is either impossible or very rare. For example, firms cannot own their workers nor their final customers (although worker cooperatives and consumer cooperatives can be thought of in ownership terms). Also, firms rarely own their suppliers of finance. Node D drops out of the schema in cases where ownership is either prohibited by law or is otherwise rare. I begin with forward integration into

---

[8] Closely complementary activities are commonly relegated to the "core technology" (Thompson, 1967, pp. 19–23) and are effectively exempt from comparative institutional analysis, it being "obvious" that these are done within the firm.

distribution, after which relationships with other stakeholders of the firm, including labor, finance and public utility regulation, are successively considered.

11. Forward Integration into Distribution

I will set aside the case where mass marketers integrate backward into manufacturing and focus on forward integration into distribution by manufacturers of products or owners of brands. Specifically, consider the contractual relation between a manufacturer and large numbers of wholesalers or, especially, of retailers for the good or service in question.

Many such transactions are of a generic kind. Although branded goods and services are more specific, some require only shelf space, since advertising, promotion and any warranties are done by the manufacturer. Since the obvious way to trade with intermediaries for such transactions is through the market, in a node A fashion, what is to be inferred when such transactions are made subject to vertical market restrictions such as customer and territorial restrictions, service restrictions, tied sales and the like?

Price discrimination, to which allocative efficiency benefits were ascribed, was the usual resource allocation (science of choice) explanation for such restrictions. Such benefits, however, were problematic once the transaction costs of discovering customer valuations and deterring arbitrage were taken into account (Williamson, 1975, pp. 11–13). Moreover, price discrimination does not exhaust the possibilities.

Viewed through the lens of contract, vertical market restrictions often have the purpose and effect of infusing order into a transaction where the interests of the system and the interests of the parts are in conflict. For example, the Schwinn bicycle company imposed nonresale restrictions upon franchisees. The concern was that the integrity of the brand, which was a system asset, would be compromised by franchisees who perceived local opportunities to realize individual gain by selling to discounters, who would then sell a "bike in a box" without service or support (Williamson, 1985, pp. 183–189). More generally, the argument is this: In circumstances where market power is small, where simple market exchange (at node A) would compromise the integrity of differentiated products and where forward integration into distribution (at node D) would be especially costly, the use of vertical market restrictions to effect credible commitments (at node C) has much to recommend it.

12. Relationship with Labor

Because the firm is unable to own its labor, node D is irrelevant and the comparison comes down to nodes A, B and C. Node A corresponds to the case where labor is easily redeployed to other uses or users without loss of productive value (k 5 0). Thus, although such labor may be highly skilled (as with many professionals), the lack of firm specificity means that, transition costs aside, neither worker nor firm has an interest in crafting penalties for unwanted quits terminations or otherwise creating costly internal labor markets (ports of entry, promotion ladders), costly information disclosure and verification procedures, and costly firm-specific dispute settlement machinery. The mutual benefits do not warrant the costs.

Conditions change when k. 0, since workers who acquire firm-specific skills will lose value if prematurely terminated (and firms will incur added training costs if such employees quit). Here, as elsewhere, unrelieved hazards (as at node B) will result in demands by workers for a hazard premium, and recurrent contractual impasses, by reason of conflict, will result in inefficiency. Because continuity has value to both firm and worker, governance features that deter termination (severance pay) and quits (no invested benefits) and that address and settle disputes in an orderly way (grievance systems) to which the parties ascribe coincidence have a lotto recommend them. These can, but need not, take the form of "unions." Whatever the name, the object is to craft a collective organizational structure (at node C) in which the parties have mutual coincidence and that enhances efficiency (Baron and Kreps, 1999, pp. 130–138; Williamson, 1975, pp. 27–80, 1985, pp. 250–262).[9]

---

[9] The emphasis on collective organization as a governance response is to be distinguished from the earlier work of Gary Becker, where human asset specificity is responsible for upward-sloping age earnings profiles (Becker, 1962). Becker's treatment is more in the science of choice tradition, whereas mine views asset specificity through the lens of contract. These two are not mutually exclusive. They do, however, point to different empirical research agenda.

13. Relationship with Sources of Finance

Viewed through the lens of contract, the board of directors is interpreted as a security feature that arises in support of the contract for equity finance (Williamson, 1988). More generally, debt and equity are not merely alternative modes of finance, which is the law and economics construction (Easterbrook and Fischel, 1986; Posner, 1986), but are also alternative modes of governance.

Suppose that a firm is seeking cost-effective finance for the following series of projects: general purpose mobile equipment, a general purpose office building located in a population center, a general purpose plant located in a manufacturing center, distribution facilities located somewhat more remotely, special purpose equipment, market and product development expenses and the like. Suppose further that debt is a governance structure that works almost entirely out of a set of rules: (1) stipulated interest payments will be made at regular intervals; (2) the business will continuously meet certain liquidity tests; (3) principal will be repaid at the loan-expiration date; and (4) in the event of default, the debt holders will exercise preemptive claims against the assets in question. In short, debt is unforgiving if things go poorly.

Such rules-based governance is well suited to investments of a generic kind (k 5 0), since the lender can redeploy these to alternative uses and users with little loss of productive value. Debt thus corresponds to market governance at node A. But what about investment projects of more specific (less redeployable) kinds?

Because the value of holding a preemptive claim declines as the degree of assets specificity deepens, rule-based finance of the kind described above will be made on more adverse terms. In effect, using debt to finance such projects would locate the parties at node B, where a hazard premium must be charged. The firm in the circumstances has two choices: sacrifice some of the specialized investment features in favor of greater redeploy ability (move back to node A), or embed the specialized investment in a governance structure to which better terms of finance will be ascribed. What would the latter entail?

Suppose that a financial instrument called equity is invented, and assume that equity has the following governance properties: (1) it bears a residual claimant status to the firm in both earnings and asset liquidation respects; (2) it contracts for the duration of the life of the firm; and (3) a board of directors is created and awarded to equity that (a) is elected by the pro rata votes of those who hold tradable shares, (b) has the power to replace the management, (c) decides on management compensation, (d) has access to internal performance measures on a timely basis, (e) can authorize audits in depth for special follow-up purposes, (f) is apprised of important investment and operating proposals before they are implemented, and (g) in other respects bears a decision-review and monitoring relation to the firm's management (Fama and Jensen, 1983). So construed, the board of directors is awarded to the holders of equity so as to reduce the cost of capital by providing safeguards for projects that have limited redeployability (by moving them from node B to node C). (186 *Journal of Economic Perspectives*)

14. Regulation and Natural Monopoly

The market-oriented approach to natural monopoly is to auction off the franchise to the highest bidder (Demsetz, 1968; Posner, 1972). But whether this works well or poorly depends on the nature of the transaction and the particulars of governance. Whereas some of those who work out of the science of choice setup believe that to "expound the details of particular regulations and proposals ... would serve only to obscure the basic issues" (Posner, 1972, p. 98), the governance structure approach counsels that much of the action resides in the details.

Going beyond the initial bidding competition ("competition for the market"), the governance approach insists upon including the contract implementation stage. Transactions to which the Fundamental Transformation applies — namely, those requiring significant investments in specific assets and that are subject to considerable market and technological uncertainty — are ones for which the efficacy of simple franchise bidding is problematic.

This is not to say that franchise bidding never works. Neither is it to suggest that decisions to regulate ought not to be revisited — as witness the successful deregulation of trucking (which never should have been regulated to begin with) and more recent efforts to deregulate "network industries" (Peltzman and Whinston, 2000). I would nevertheless urge that examining deregulation through the lens of contracting is instructive for both — as it is for assessing efforts to deregulate electricity in California, where too much deference was given to the (assumed) efficacy of smoothly functioning markets and insufficient attention to potential investment and contractual hazards and appropriate governance responses there to. As Joskow (2000, p. 51) observes: "Many policy makers and fellow travelers have been surprised by how difficult it has been to create wholesale electricity markets .... Had policy makers viewed the restructuring challenge using a TCE [transaction cost economics] framework, these potential problems are more likely to have been identified and mechanisms adopted *ex ante* to fix them."

Here as elsewhere, the lesson is to think contractually: Look ahead, recognize potential hazards and fold these back into the design calculus. Paraphrasing Michels [1915, (1962), p. 370] on oligarchy, nothing but a serene and frank examination of the contractual hazards of deregulation will enable us to mitigate these hazards.

15. Recent Criticisms

Many skeptics of orthodoxy have also been critics of transaction cost economics — including organization theorists (especially Simon, 1991, 1997), sociologists (for a recent survey, see Richter, 2001) and the resource-based/core competence/dynamic capabilities perspective. Having responded to these arguments, The Theory of the Firm as Governance Structure: From Choice to Contract 187 elsewhere,[10] I focus here on critiques from within economics — especially those that deal with issues concerning the boundary of the firms.[11]

16. Property Rights Theory

The property rights theory of firm and market organization is unarguably a path-breaking contribution (Grossman and Hart, 1986; Hart and Moore, 1990; Hart, 1995). Prior to this work, the very idea that incomplete contracts could be formally modeled was scorned. That has all changed.

---

[10] On my response to Simon, see Williamson (2002); on sociology, see Williamson (1981, 1993, 1996); on core competence, see Williamson (1999b).

[11] Other criticisms include those of Fudenberg, Holmstrom and Milgrom (1990, p. 21, emphasis omitted) who contend: "If there is an optimal long-term contract, then there is a sequentially optimal contract, which can be implemented via a sequence of short-term contracts." My response is that the proof is elegant, but rests on very strong and implausible assumptions that fail the test of feasible implementation (Williamson, 1991b).

The accomplishments of the property rights theory notwithstanding, I nevertheless take exception in two related respects. First, the view that the property rights theory "builds on and formalizes the intuitions of transaction cost economics, as created by Coase and Williamson" (Salanie', 1997, p. 176) is only partly correct. To be sure, property rights theory does build on (or at least tracks) transaction cost economics in certain respects: complex contracts are incomplete (by reason of bounded rationality), contract as mere promise is not self-enforcing (by reason of opportunism), court ordering of conflicts is limited (by reason of nonverifiability) and the parties are bilaterally dependent (by reason of transaction specific investments). But whereas transaction cost economics locates the main analytical action in the governance of ongoing contractual relations, property rights theory of the firm annihilates governance issues by assuming common knowledge of payoffs and costless bargaining. As a consequence, all of the analytical action is concentrated at the incentive alignment stage of contracting. Since the assumptions of common knowledge of payoffs (Kreps and Wilson, 1982) and costless bargaining are deeply problematic, my interpretation of property rights theory is that it is "imperfectly suited to the subject matter ... [because it] obscures the key interactions instead of spotlighting them" (Solow, 2001, p. 112).

Second, I take exception with the allegation of property rights theory that transaction cost economics offers no explanation why a bilaterally dependent transaction is subject to "less haggling and hold-up behavior in a merged firm." Hart (1995, p. 28), writes that "transaction cost theory, as it stands, does not provide the answer," evidently in the belief that property rights theory does.

Since property rights theory rests only on asset ownership, what Hart and others of this persuasion could say is that they dispute the logic of replication/selective intervention and each of the associated regularities on which transaction cost economics relies to describe why firms and markets differ in discrete structural ways. Specifically, property rights theory disputes all four of the following propositions of transaction cost economics: (1) that firms enjoy advantages over markets in cooperative adaptation respects (it being the case under property rights theory that all ownership configurations costlessly adapt in the contract implementation interval); (2) that incentive intensity is unavoidably compromised by internal organization; (3) that administrative controls are more numerous and more nuanced in firms;[12] and (4) that the implicit contract law of internal organization is that of forbearance, whence the firm is its own court for resolving disputes. Inasmuch as all four of these differences can be examined empirically, the veridicality of property rights theory in relation to transaction cost economics can be established by appealing to the data. What cannot be said is that transaction cost economics is silent or inexplicit on why firms and markets differ.

As it stands, property rights theory makes limited appeal to data, because it yields very few refutable implications and is indeed very nearly untestable (Whinston, 2001). Transaction cost economics, by contrast, yields numerous refutable implications and invites empirical testing.

17. Boundaries of the Firm

Holmstrom and Roberts (1998, p. 91) contend, and I agree, that "the theory of the firm ... has become too narrowly focused on the hold-up problem and the role of asset specificity." Contractual complications of other (possibly related) kinds need to be admitted and the ramifications for governance worked out. But while I agree that more than asset specificity is involved, I hasten to add that asset specificity is an operational and encompassing concept.

Asset specificity is operational in that it serves to breathe content into the idea of transactional "complexity." Thus, although it is intuitively obvious that complex governance structures should be reserved for complex

---

[12] Grossman and Hart (1986, p. 695), for example, assume that "any audits that an employer can have done of his [wholly] owned subsidiary are also feasible when the subsidiary is a separate company." Not only does transaction cost economics hold otherwise (Williamson, 1985, pp. 154–155), but transaction cost economics also recognizes that accounting is not fully objective but can be used as a strategic instrument (Chapter 6). Furthermore, accounting will be used as a strategic instrument if integration is as prescribed by property rights theory (directional) rather than as prescribed by transaction cost economics (united). The upshot is that the high-powered incentives that property rights theory associates with directional integration will be compromised — in that control over accounting by the acquiring stage will be exercised to redistribute profits in its favor by manipulating transfer prices, user-cost charges, overhead rates, depreciation, amortization, inventory rules and the like. Although Hart (1995, pp. 64–66) appears to concede these effects, the basic model of the property rights theory (1995, Chapter 2) disallows them.

transactions, wherein do the contractual complexities reside? Identifying the critical dimensions with respect to which transactions differ, of which asset specificity is especially important, has been crucial for explicating contractual complexity (Williamson, 1971, 1979, p. 239) — which is not to suggest that it is exhaustive.

As for asset specificity being an encompassing concept, consider the Holmstrom and Roberts (1998, p. 87) complaint that multiunit retail businesses (such as franchising) cannot be explained in terms of asset specificity. This complaint ignores brand name capital (Klein, 1980) as a form of asset specificity, the integrity of which can be compromised (as discussed in relation to the Schwinn case, above). Also, asset specificity would be less "overused" if other would-be explanations for complex economic organization (such as technological nonseparability or the idea that agents have different levels of risk aversion) either had wider reach and/or were not contradicted by the data. I would furthermore observe that many of the Holmstrom and Roberts (1998, p. 75) arguments and illustrations for "taking a much broader view of the firm and the determination of its boundaries" are ones with which transaction cost economics not only concurs but has actively discussed, even featured, previously.

I am puzzled, for example, by their claim (Holmstrom and Roberts, 1998, p. 77) that "[i]n transaction cost economics, the functioning market is as much a black box as is the firm in neoclassical economic theory." Plainly, node C in the earlier Figure 3 is a market governance mode supported by conscious efforts by the parties to craft intertemporal contractual safeguards for transactions where identity matters and continuity is important. Node C is a black box only for those who refuse to take a look at the mechanisms through which hybrid governance works. Also, moving beyond the one-size-fits-all view of contract law to ascertain that contract law regimes differ systematically across modes of governance — in that contract as legal rules, contract as framework and forbearance law are the contract laws of market, hybrid and hierarchy, respectively — is not and should not be construed as a black box construction.

Holmstrom and Roberts (1998, p. 81) offer the case of Japanese subcontracting as "directly at odds with transaction cost theory." Relying in part upon the research of Asanuma (1989, 1992), Holmstrom and Roberts (pp. 80–82) report that Japanese subcontracting uses "long-term close relations with a limited number of independent suppliers that mix elements of market and hierarchy ... [to protect] specific assets." These close relations are supported by careful monitoring, a two-supplier system (as at Toyota), rich information sharing and, so as to deter automakers from behaving opportunistically, a "supplier association, which facilitates communication ... and [strengthens] reputation [effects]."

As it turns out, Professor Asanuma and I visited several large Japanese auto firms (Toyota included) in the spring of 1983, and I reported on all of the above previously (Williamson, 1985, pp. 120–123, 1996, pp. 317–318). Interestingly, Baron and Kreps (1999, pp. 542–543) also interpret Toyota contracting practices as consistent with the transaction cost economics perspective.

I would nevertheless concede that the roles of organizational knowledge and learning mentioned by Holmstrom and Roberts (1998, pp. 90–91) are ones with which transaction cost economics deals with in only a limited way. This does not, however, mean that transaction cost economics does not or cannot relate to these issues. I would observe in this connection that transaction cost economics made early provision for firm-specific learning by doing and for tacit knowledge (Williamson, 1971, 1975) and that the organization of "knowledge projects" that differ in their needs for coordination are even now being examined in governance structure respects (Nickerson and Zenger, 2001). Still, the study of these and other issues to which Holmstrom and Roberts refer are usefully examined from several lenses, of which the lens of transaction cost economics is only one.

18. Conclusion

The application of the lens of contract/private ordering/governance leads naturally into the reconceptualization of the firm not as a production function in the science of choice tradition, but instead as a governance structure. The shift from choice to contract is attended by three crucial moves. First, human actors are described in more veridical ways with respect to both cognitive traits and self-interestedness. Second, organization matters. The governance of contractual relations takes seriously the conceptual challenge posed by the "Commons triple" of dealing with issues of conflict, mutuality and order. Third, organization is susceptible to analysis. This last move is accomplished by naming the transaction as the basic unit of analysis, identifying governance structures (which differ in discrete structural ways) as the means by which to manage transactions, and joining these two. Specifically, transactions, which differ in their attributes, are aligned with governance structures, which differ in their cost and competencies, in an economizing way. Implementing this entails working out of the logic of efficient alignment.

Not only does the resulting theory of the firm differ significantly from the neoclassical theory of the firm, but the governance branch of contract also differs from the incentive branch, where more formal mechanism design, agency and property rights theories are located. These latter theories all concentrate the analytical action on the incentive alignment stage of contracting. Differences among governance structures with respect to adaptation in the contract implementation interval are thus suppressed. Intertemporal regularities to which organization theorists call our attention (and to which I selectively appeal) as well as the added contractual complications that I describe — the Fundamental Transformation, the impossibility of replication/selective intervention and contract law regimes — have little or no place in any of these incentive alignment literatures.

Parsimony being a virtue, such added complications need to be justified. I contend that a different and, for many purposes, richer and better understanding of firm and market organization results. Not only does the transaction cost economics theory of firm and market organization afford different interpretations of nonstandard and unfamiliar forms of contract and organization, but it yields many refutable implications. A large and growing empirical research agenda and selective reshaping of public policy toward business have resulted from supplanting the black box conception of the firm by the theory of the firm as governance structure. Dixit (1996), moreover, ascribes public policy benefits to the use of transaction cost The Theory of the Firm as Governance Structure: From Choice to Contract 191 reasoning to open up the black box of public policymaking and explain how decisions are actually made.[13]

---

[13] Kreps's (1999, p. 123) assessment of full formalism also signals precaution: "Most economists, and especially and most critically, new recruits in the form of graduate students, learn transaction cost economics as translated and renamed (incomplete) contract theory … [Awaiting new tools], we should be clear on how (in) complete the translations are, to fight misguided tendencies to put *Markets and Hierarchies* away on that semiaccessible shelf."

Pluralism has much to recommend it in an area like economic organization that is beset with bewildering complexity. Such pluralism notwithstanding, the governance approach has been a productive and liberating way by which to examine economic organization. It has been productive in all of the conceptual and public policy ways described above, with more insights in prospect. It has been liberating in that it has breathed life into the science of contract and, in the process, has served to stimulate other work — part rival, part complementary. A recurrent theme is that recourse to the lens of contract, as against the lens of choice, frequently deepens our understanding of complex economic organization, with a suggestion that this same strategy can inform applied microeconomics and the contiguous social sciences more generally.

References

Akerlof, George A. 1970. "The Market for 'Lemons': Qualitative Uncertainty and the Market Mechanism." *Quarterly Journal of Economics*, August, 84, pp. 488–500.

Alchian, Armen and Harold Demsetz. 1972. "Production, Information Costs, and Economic Organization." *American Economic Review,* December, 62, pp. 777–795.

Arrow, Kenneth. 1999. "Forward." In *Firms, Markets and Hierarchies: The Transaction Cost Economics Perspective.* eds., G. Carroll and D. Teece, pp. vii–viii. New York: New York University Press.

Asanuma, Banri. 1989. "Manufacturer-Supplier Relationships in Japan and the Concept of Relationship-Specific Skills." *Journal of Japanese and International Economies*, 3(1), pp. 1–30.

Asanuma, Banri. 1992. "Manufacturer-Supplier Relationships in International Perspective: The Automobile Case." In *International Adjustment and the Japanese Firm*, ed., Paul Sheard, pp. 99–124. St. Leonards, NSW: Allen and Unwin.

Aumann, Robert J. 1985. "What is Game Theory Trying to Accomplish?" In *Frontiers of Economics*, eds., K. Arrow and S. Hankapohja, pp. 28–78. Oxford: Basil Blackwell.

Bajari, Patrick and Steven Tadelis. 2001. "Incentives Versus Transaction Costs: A Theory of Procurement Contracts." *Rand Journal of Economics*, 32, pp. 387–407.

Barnard, Chester I. 1938. *The Functions of the Executive.* Cambridge: Harvard University Press.

Baron, James N. and David M. Kreps. 1999. *Strategic Human Resources: Frameworks for General Managers.* New York: Wiley.

Becker, Gary. 1962. "Investment in Human Capital: Effects on Earnings." *Journal of Political Economy*, October, 70, pp. 9–49.

Ben-Porath, Yoram. 1980. "The F-Connection: Families, Friends, and Firms and the Organization of Exchange." *Population and Development Review*, March, 6, pp. 1–30.

Boerner, C. S. and J. Macher. 2001. "Transaction Cost Economics: A Review and Assessment of the Empirical Literature." Unpublished Manuscript.

Brennan, Geoffrey and James Buchanan. 1985. *The Reason of Rules*. Cambridge: Cambridge University Press.

Buchanan, James M. 1964(a). "What Should Economists Do?" *Southern Economic Journal*, January, 30, pp. 312–322.

Buchanan, James M. 1964(b). "Is Economics the Science of Choice?" In *Roads to Freedom: Essays in Honor of F. A. Hayek*. ed., E. Streissler, pp. 47–64. London: Routledge & Kegan Paul.

Buchanan, James M. 1975. "A Contractarian Paradigm for Applying Economic Theory." *American Economic Review*, May, 65, pp. 225–230.

Buchanan, James M. 1987. "The Constitution of Economic Policy." *American Economic Review*, June, 77, pp. 243–250.

Buchanan, James M. 2001. "Game Theory, Mathematics, and Economics." *Journal of Economic Methodology*, March, 8, pp. 27–32.

Buchanan, James M. and Gordon Tullock. 1962. *The Calculus of Consent: Logical Foundations of Constitutional Democracy*. Ann Arbor: University of Michigan Press.

Coase, Ronald H. 1937. "The Nature of the Firm." *Economica*, November, 4, pp. 386–405.

Coase, Ronald H. 1959. "The Federal Communications Commission." *Journal of Law and Economics*, October, 3, pp. 1–40.

Coase, Ronald H. 1972. "Industrial Organization: A Proposal for Research." In *Policy Issues and Research Opportunities in Industrial Organization*. ed., V. R. Fuchs, pp. 59–73. New York: National Bureau of Economic Research. Coase, Ronald H. 1992. "The Institutional Structure of Production." *American Economic Review*, September, 82, pp. 713–719.

Commons, John R. 1932. "The Problem of Correlating Law, Economics and Ethics." *Wisconsin Law Review*, 8, pp. 3–26.

Commons, John R. 1934. *Institutional Economics*. Madison: University of Wisconsin Press.

Crocker, Keith and Scott Masten. 1996. "Regulation and Administered Contracts Revisited: Lessons from Transaction-Cost Economics for Public Utility Regulation." *Journal of Regulatory Economics*, January, 9(1), pp. 5–39.

Cyert, Richard and James March. 1963. *A Behavioral Theory of the Firm.* Englewood Cliffs, NJ: Prentice-Hall.

David, Paul. 1985. "Clio in the Economics of QWERTY." *American Economic Review*, May, 75, pp. 332–337.

Demsetz, Harold. 1968. "Why Regulate Utilities?" *Journal of Law and Economics*, April, 11, pp. 55–66.

Demsetz, Harold. 1983. "The Structure of Ownership and the Theory of the Firm." *Journal of Law and Economics*, 26(2), pp. 275–290.

Dixit, Avinash K. 1996. *The Making of Economic Policy: A Transaction-Cost Politics Perspective.* Boston, Mass.: MIT Press.

Easterbrook, Frank and Daniel Fischel. 1986. "Close Corporations and Agency Costs." *Stanford Law Review*, January, 38, pp. 271–301.

Fama, Eugene F. and Michael C. Jensen. 1983. "Separation of Ownership and Control." *Journal of Law and Economics*, June, 26, pp. 301–326.

Fudenberg, Drew, Bengt Holmstrom and Paul Milgrom. 1990. "Short-Term Contracts and Long-Term Agency Relationships." *Journal of Economic Theory*, June, 51, pp. 1–31.

Galanter, Marc. 1981. "Justice in Many Rooms: Courts, Private Ordering, and Indigenous Law." *Journal of Legal Pluralism*, 19:1, pp. 1–47.

Grossman, Sanford J. and Oliver Hart. 1986. "The Costs and Benefits of Ownership: A Theory of Vertical and Lateral Integration." *Journal of Political Economy*, August, 94, pp. 691–719.

Hardin, Garrett. 1968. "The Tragedy of the Commons." *Science*, December, 162, pp. 1243–1248.

Hart, Oliver. 1995. *Firms, Contracts and Financial Structure.* New York: Oxford University Press.

Hart, Oliver and John Moore. 1990. "Property Rights and the Nature of the Firm." *Journal of Political Economy*, December, 98, pp. 1119–1158.

Hart, Oliver and Jean Tirole. 1990. "Vertical Integration and Market Foreclosure," In *Brookings Papers on Economic Activity: Microeconomics.* eds., Martin Neil Baily and Clifford Winston, pp. 205–276. Washington, D.C.: Brookings Institution.

Hayek, Freidrich. 1945. "The Use of Knowledge in Society." *American Economic Review*, September, 35, pp. 519–530.

Holmstrom, Bengt and John Roberts. 1998. "The Boundaries of the Firm Revisited." *Journal of Economic Perspectives*, Fall, 12(3), pp. 73–94.

Holmstrom, Bengt and Jean Tirole. 1989. "The Theory of the Firm." In *Handbook of Industrial Organization*, eds., R. Schmalensee and R. Willig, pp. 61–133. New York: North Holland.

Joskow, Paul L. 2000. "Transaction Cost Economics and Competition Policy." Unpublished Manuscript.

Klein, Benjamin. 1980. "Transaction Cost determinants of 'Unfair' Contractual Arrangements." *American Economic Review*, May, 70, pp. 356–362.

Klein, Benjamin, Robert A. Crawford and Armen A. Alchian. 1978. "Vertical Integration, Appropriable Rents, and the Competitive Contracting Process." *Journal of Law and Economics*, October, 21, pp. 297–326.

Kreps, David M. 1999. "Markets and Hierarchies and (Mathematical) Economic Theory," In *Firms, Markets, and Hierarchies*. eds., G. Carroll and D. Teece, pp. 121–155. New York: Oxford University Press. Kreps, David M. and Robert Wilson. 1982. "Reputation and Imperfect Information." *Journal of Economic Theory*, August, 27(2), pp. 253–279.

Llewellyn, Karl N. 1931. "What Price Contract? An Essay in Perspective." *Yale Law Journal*, May, 40, pp. 704–751.

Lyons, Bruce R. 1996. "Empirical Relevance of Efficient Contract Theory: Inter-Firm Contracts." *Oxford Review of Economic Policy*, 12(4), pp. 27–52.

Machlup, Fritz and M. Tabor. 1960. "Bilateral Monopoly, Successive Monopoly and Vertical Integration." *Economica*, May, 27, pp. 101–119.

Makowski, Louis and Joseph Ostroy. 2001. "Perfect Competition and the Creativity of the Market." *Journal of Economic Literature*, June, 32, pp. 479–535.

March, James and Herbert Simon. 1958. *Organizations*. New York: John Wiley.

Marshall, Alfred. 1932. *Industry and Trade*. London: Macmillan.

Masten, Scott and Stephane Saussier. 2000. "Econometrics of Contracts: An Assessment of Developments in the Empirical Literature on Contracting." *Revue d'Economie Industrielle*, Second and Third Trimesters, 92, pp. 215–236.

McKenzie, L. 1951. "Ideal Output and the Interdependence of Firms." *Economic Journal*, December, 61, pp. 785–803.

Michels, Robert. 1915 [1962]. *Political Parties*. Glencoe, Ill.: Free Press.

Newell, Allen and Herbert Simon. 1972. *Human Problem Solving*. Englewood Cliffs, NJ: Prentice-Hall.

Nickerson, Jackson and Todd Zenger. 2001. "A Knowledge-Based Theory of Governance Choice: A Problem Solving Approach." Unpublished Manuscript.

Peltzman, Sam. 1991. "The Handbook of Industrial Organization: A Review Article." *Journal of Political Economy*, February, 99(1), pp. 201–217.

Peltzman, Sam and Clifford Whinston. 2000. *Deregulation of Network Industries*. Washington, D.C.: Brookings Institution Press.

Perry, Martin. 1989. "Vertical Integration." In *Handbook of Industrial Organization*. eds. R. Schmalensee and R. Willig, pp. 183–255. Amsterdam: North-Holland.

Posner, Richard A. 1972. "The Appropriate Scope of Regulation in the Cable Television Industry." *Bell Journal of Economics*, Spring, 3, pp. 98–129.

Posner, Richard A. 1986. *Economic Analysis of Law, Third Edition*. Boston: Little Brown.

Posner, Richard A. 1993. "The New Institutional Economics Meets Law and Economics." *Journal of Institutional and Theoretical Economics*, March, 149, pp. 73–87.

Reder, Melvin W. 1999. *Economics: The Culture of a Controversial Science*. Chicago: University of Chicago Press.

Richter, Rudolph. 2001. "New Economic Sociology and New Institutional Economics." Unpublished Manuscript. Rindfleisch, Aric and Jan Heide. 1997. "Transaction Cost Analysis: Past, Present and Future Applications." *Journal of Marketing*, October, 61, pp. 30–54.

Riordan, Michael H. and Oliver E. Williamson. 1985. "Asset Specificity and Economic Organization." *International Journal of Industrial Organization*, December, 3(4), pp. 365–378.

Robbins, Lionel. 1932. *An Essay on the Nature and Significance of Economic Science*. New York: New York University Press.

Salanié, Bernard. 1997. *The Economics of Contracts*. Cambridge, Mass.: MIT Press.

Schmalensee, Richard. 1973. "A Note on the Theory of Vertical Integration." *Journal of Political Economy*, March/April, 81, pp. 442–449.

Schumpeter, Joseph A. 1942. *Capitalism, Socialism, and Democracy*. New York: Harper & Row.

Scott, Richard W. 1992. *Organizations*. Englewood Cliffs, NJ: Prentice-Hall.

Selznick, Philip. 1949. *TVA and the Grass Roots*. Berkeley: University of California Press.

Selznick, Philip. 1950. "The Iron Law of Bureaucracy." *Modern Review*, 3, pp. 157–165.

Shelanski, Howard A. and Peter G. Klein. 1995. "Empirical Research in Transaction Cost Economics: A Review and Assessment." *Journal of Law, Economics and Organization*, October, 11, pp. 335–361.

Simon, Herbert. 1957a. *Administrative Behavior, Second Edition*. New York: Macmillan.

Simon, Herbert. 1957b. *Models of Man: Social and Rational; Mathematical Essays on Rational Human Behavior in a Social Setting*. New York: Wiley.

Simon, Herbert. 1978. "Rationality as Process and as Product of Thought." *American Economic Review*, May, 68, pp. 1–16.

Simon, Herbert. 1983. *Reason in Human Affairs*. Stanford: Stanford University Press.

Simon, Herbert. 1985. "Human Nature in Politics: The Dialogue of Psychology with Political Science." *American Political Science Review*, June, 79(2), pp. 293–304.

Simon, Herbert. 1991. "Organizations and Markets." *Journal of Economic Perspectives*, Spring, 5(2), pp. 25–44.

Simon, Herbert. 1997. *An Empirically Based Microeconomics.* New York: Cambridge University Press.

Solow, Robert. 2001. "A Native Informant Speaks." *Journal of Economic Methodology*, March, 8, pp. 111–112.

Stigler, George J. 1951. "The Division of Labor is Limited by the Extent of the Market." *Journal of Political Economy*, June, 59, pp. 185–193.

Thompson, James D. 1967. *Organizations in Action: Social Science Bases of Administrative Theory.* New York: McGraw-Hill.

Veblen, Thorstein. 1904. *The Theory of Business Enterprise.* New York: Charles Scribner's Sons.

Vernon, John M. and Daniel A. Graham. 1971. "Profitability of Monopolization by Vertical Integration." *Journal of Political Economy*, July/August, 79, pp. 924–925.

Warren-Boulton, Frederick. 1974. "Vertical Control With Variable Proportions." *Journal of Political Economy*, July/August, 82(4), pp. 783–802.

Westfield, Fred. 1981. "Vertical Integration: Does Product Price Rise or Fall?" *American Economic Review*, 71(3), pp. 334–346.

Whinston, Michael. 2001. "Assessing Property Rights and Transaction-Cost Theories of the Firm." *American Economic Review*, May, 91(2), pp. 184–199.

Williamson, Oliver E. 1971. "The Vertical Integration of Production: Market Failure Considerations." *American Economic Review*, May, 61(2), pp. 112–123.

Williamson, Oliver E. 1975. *Markets and Hierarchies: Analysis and Antitrust Implications.* New York: Free Press.

Williamson, Oliver E. 1976. "Franchise Bidding: In General and with Respect to CATV." *Bell Journal of Economics*, 7(1), pp. 73–104.

Williamson, Oliver E. 1979. "Transaction Cost Economics: The Governance of Contractual Relations." *Journal of Law and Economics*, October, 22, pp. 233–261.

Williamson, Oliver E. 1981. "The Economics of Organization: The Transaction Cost Approach." *American Journal of Sociology*, November, 87, pp. 548–577.

Williamson, Oliver E. 1983. "Credible Commitments: Using Hostages to Support Exchange." *American Economic Review*, September, 73(4), pp. 519–540.

Williamson, Oliver E. 1985. *The Economic Institutions of Capitalism.* New York: Free Press.

Williamson, Oliver E. 1987. "Vertical Integration." In *The New Palgrave: A Dictionary of Economics, Volume IV.* eds., J. Eatwell *et al.*, pp. 807–812. London: Macmillan.

Williamson, Oliver E. 1988. "Corporate Finance and Corporate Governance." *Journal of Finance*, July, 43, pp. 567–591.

Williamson, Oliver E. 1991(a). "Comparative Economic Organization: The Analysis of Discrete Structural Alternatives." *Administrative Science Quarterly*, June, 36, pp. 269–296.

Williamson, Oliver E. 1991(b). "Economic Institutions: Spontaneous and Intentional Governance." *Journal of Law, Economics and Organization*, (Special Issue), 7, pp. 159 –187.

Williamson, Oliver E. 1993. "Calculativeness, Trust, and Economic Organization." *Journal of Law and Economics*, April, 36, pp. 453– 486.

Williamson, Oliver E. 1996. *The Mechanisms of Governance.* New York: Oxford University Press.

Williamson, Oliver E. 1998. "Transaction Cost Economics: How it Works; Where it is Headed." *De Economist*, April, 146, pp. 23–58.

Williamson, Oliver E. 1999(a). "Public and Private Bureaucracies: A Transaction Cost Economics Perspective." *Journal of Law, Economics and Organization*, April, 15, pp. 306 –342.

Williamson, Oliver E. 1999b. "Strategy Research: Governance and Competence Perspectives." *Strategic Management Journal*, December, 20, pp. 1087–1108.

Williamson, Oliver E. 2000. "The New Institutional Economics: Taking Stock, Looking Ahead." *Journal of Economic Literature*, September, 38(3), pp. 595–613.

Williamson, Oliver E. 2002. "Empirical Microeconomics: Another Perspective." In *The Economics of Choice, Change, and Organization*, eds., Mie Augier and James March, Brookfield, Vt.: EdwardElgar. Forthcoming.

Chapter 5

Pragmatic Methodology: A Sketch with Applications to Transaction Cost Economics

I address the topic of pragmatic methodology as a practitioner in applied microeconomics who has been working in the still nascent field of the "economics of organization." My purpose is both to make explicit the methodology out of which transaction cost economics works and to suggest that other theories of economic organization do the same. Conceivably convergence will develop in the process, may be even a consensus. At a minimum, it will be useful to have each implicit methodology made explicit.

I begin with some contrasting views on methodology. Section 2 sets out the rudiments of pragmatic methodology. Section 3 examines how transaction cost economics responds to the four precepts of pragmatic methodology. Additional methodological considerations that are posed by transaction cost economics are discussed in Section 4. Concluding remarks follow in Section 5.

1. Some Background

Koopmans (1957) chapter on "The Construction of Economic Knowledge" begins with a section titled "The Bad Repute of Methodology," which opens with a quote from Robertson, who finds "it necessary in self-defense to start with a few words on the distasteful subject of methodology" (Koopmans, 1957, p. 129). Koopmans nevertheless perseveres and ends up siding with

Harrod: "My substantial excuse for choosing methodology today is that I find a strong inner urge to say something" (Koopmans, 1957, p. 130).

My strong inner urge is to take exception with the "anything goes" predilection to which Blaug (1997, p. 20) refers — both in general and, especially, with reference to transaction cost economics.

2. Pragmatic Methodology

Describing himself as a native informant rather than as a certified methodologist, Solow's "terse description of what one economist thinks he is doing" (Solow, 2001, p. 111) takes the form of three precepts: keep it simple; get it right; make it plausible. Keeping it simple is accomplished by stripping away inessentials, thereby to focus on first order effects — the main case, as it were — after which qualifications, refinements, and extensions can be introduced. Getting it right entails working out the logic. And making it plausible means to preserve contact with the phenomena and eschew fanciful constructions.

Solow observes with reference to the simplicity precept that "the very complexity of real life ... [is what] makes simple models so necessary" (Solow, 2001, p. 111). Keeping it simple requires the student of complexity to prioritize: "Most phenomena are driven by a very few central forces. What a good theory does is to simplify, it pulls out the central forces and gets rid of the rest" (Friedman, 1997, p. 196). Central features and key regularities are uncovered by the application of a focused lens.

Getting it right "includes translating economic concepts into accurate mathematics (or diagrams, or words) and making sure that further logical operations are correctly performed and verified" (Solow, 2001, p. 112); and plausible simple models of complex phenomena are expected to "make sense for reasonable or plausible" "values of the important parameters" (Solow, 2001, p. 112). Also, because "not everything that is logically consistent is credulous" (Kreps, 1999, p. 125), fanciful constructions that lose contact with the phenomena are suspect – especially if alternative and more veridical models yield refutable implications that are congruent with the data.

This last brings me to a fourth precept: derive refutable implications to which the relevant (often microanalytic) data are brought to bear.

Georgescu-Roegen had a felicitous way of putting it: "The purpose of science in general is not prediction, but knowledge for its own sake," yet prediction is "the touchstone of scientific knowledge" (Georgescu-Roegen, 1971, p. 37). Indeed, most economists know in their bones that theories that are congruent with the data are more influential. Friedman's reflections on a lifetime of work are pertinent: "I believe in every area where I feel that I have had some influence it has occurred less because of the pure analysis than it has because of the empirical evidence that I have been able to organize."[1]

In as much as the social sciences deal with exceptionally complex phenomena (Simon, 1957, p. 89; Wilson, 1999, p.183), "any direction you proceed in has a very high a priori probability of being wrong; so it is good if other people are exploring in other directions" (Simon, 1992, p. 21). Accordingly, we are concerned with theories (plural) rather than a theory (singular). Also pertinent in this connection is that theories rarely appear full blown but undergo a natural progression — from informal to pre-formal, semiformal, and fully formal stages of development — over which interval the relation between the theory and the evidence is interactive (Newell, 1990, p. 14):

Theories cumulate. They are refined and reformulated, corrected and expanded. Thus, we are not living in the world of Popper ... [Theories are not] shot down with a falsification bullet.... Theories are more like graduate students — once admitted you try hard to avoid flunking them out.... Theories are things to be nurtured and changed and built up.

Successive refinements and reformulations of a theory do not, however, go on indefinitely. Sooner or later the time comes for a reckoning when each would-be theory needs to stand up and be counted — which I take to mean that each candidate theory 4 should be examined with reference to the four precepts of pragmatic methodology, with special emphasis on the last.

3. Transaction Cost Economics

The relation of transaction cost economics to each of the four precepts of pragmatic methodology is herein described.

---

[1] Personal communication, February 6, 2006, from Milton Friedman to the author.

3.1. *Keep it Simple*

Of the many purposes served by economic organization, transaction cost economics names transaction cost economizing as the main case — broadly in the spirit of Knight's contention that (Knight, 1941, p. 252):

> Men in general, and within limits, wish to behave economically, to make their activities and their organization "efficient" rather than wasteful. This fact does deserve the utmost emphasis, and an adequate definition of the science of economics ... might well make it explicit that the main relevance of the discussion is found in its relation to social policy, assumed to be directed toward the end indicated, of increasing economic efficiency, of reducing waste.

The more common assumption in 1941 and for the ensuing 30 years was that monopolizing rather than economizing was the main case, but that was conceptually wrong-headed and led to public policy error. Coase spoke to the prevailing misconception as follows: "If an economist finds something — a business practice of one sort or another — that he does not understand, he looks for a monopoly explanation. And as in this field we are very ignorant, the number of un-understandable practices tends to be rather large, and the reliance on a monopoly explanation frequent" (Coase, 1972, p. 67). Public policy errors ensued, as witness the "inhospitality tradition" in antitrust enforcement — according to which nonstandard contractual practices and organizational 5 structures were regarded "not hospitably in the common law tradition, but inhospitably in the tradition of antitrust."[2]

Although monopolizing reasoning is sometimes mesmerizing (as in the business strategy literature, where monopolizing ploys and positioning are commonly the main case), the power and importance of economizing reasoning has made progressive headway.[3] Pertinent in this connection is that economizing can take several forms, of which transaction cost economics focuses principally on adaptation.

---

[2] The quote is attributed to the then head of the Antitrust Division of the U.S. Department of Justice by Stanley Robinson, 1968, N.Y. State Bar Association, Antitrust Symposium, p. 29.
[3] Although the strategic pursuit of monopoly power is analytically interesting, for most firms in large and open economies, such power is negligible or fleeting. For most firms in most industries most of the time, therefore, economy is the best strategy. That sounds mundane and sometimes is. As the study of private ordering reveals, however, many fascinating economizing issues are posed upon examining economic organization through the lens of contract rather than the orthodox lens of choice.

Interestingly, both the economist Hayek and the organization theorist Barnard were in agreement that adaptation is the main problem of economic organization, but they differed as to kind. Autonomous adaptations in response to changes in relative prices were responsible for the "marvel of the market" to which Hayek (1945) referred. Barnard (1938), by contrast, focused on coordinated adaptations of a "conscious, deliberate, purposeful kind" accomplished with the support of hierarchy. Conditional on the attributes of transactions, adaptations of both kinds are important — which is to say that transaction cost economics examines markets and hierarchies in a combined way (rather than persist with the old ideological divide between markets or hierarchies).

3.2. *Get it Right*

The transaction cost economics response to the precept "get it right" is to examine the economizing purposes of economic organization through the lens of contract, where the lens of contract is to be contrasted with the neo-classical resource allocation paradigm — the lens of choice — which focuses on prices and output, supply and demand, and describes the firm as a black box that transforms inputs into outputs according to the laws of technology.

If and as, however, "mutuality of advantage from voluntary exchange ... [is] the most fundamental of all understandings in economics" (Buchanan, 2001, p. 29), then 6 economic organization should be examined through the lens of contract — as well or instead. As applied to the economics of organization, the lens of contract divides into two parts: *ex ante* incentive alignment and *ex post* governance. As between these two, transaction cost economics focuses predominantly on the *ex post* governance of contractual relations, broadly in the spirit of Commons reformulation of the problem of economic organization, namely: "the ultimate unit of activity ... must contain in itself the three principles of conflict, mutuality, and order. This unit is a transaction" (Commons, 1932, p. 4).

Although Commons subsequently recommended that "theories of economics center on transactions and working rules, on problems of organization, and on [how] ... the organization of activity is ... stabilized" (Commons, 1950, p. 21), a coherent theory of organization for implementing these novel ideas eluded Commons and his followers, possibly because the concept of transaction cost had yet to surface and because of the primitive state of organization theory at the time. Be that as it may, TCE subscribes to and aspires to operationalize both parts of the Commons program, in that the transaction is made the basic unit of analysis and governance has the purpose and effect of infusing order, thereby to mitigate conflict and realize mutual gain. This is a recurrent theme. Crucial, moreover, to the operationalization of TCE is that the transaction costs that matter are of a comparative kind. It is neither here nor there, for purposes of organizing a particular transaction, if two alternative modes of governance have high but identical transaction costs. As discussed in 3.4 below, transaction cost differences are where the economizing action resides.

Note with respect to the logic of economic organization that TCE operates at a much more microanalytic level of analysis than does orthodoxy. Rather than deal with composite goods and services, TCE focuses on transactions, the attributes of which matter. The firm, moreover, is described not as a black box but as a mode of 7 governance to be compared with alternative modes or organization, each of which displays distinct attributes. As Arrow observed (Arrow, 1987, p. 734):

> ... the New Institutional Economics movement [of which TCE is a part] ... does not consist primarily of giving new answers to the traditional questions of economics — resource allocation and the degree of utilization. Rather it consists of answering new questions, why economic institutions have emerged as they did and not otherwise ... [and] brings sharper nano-economic ... reasoning to bear.

Although many economists are reluctant to engage the microanalytics and prefer to work at what they regard as the "high ground," it is elementary that the high ground comes at a high cost if the application of textbook reasoning fails to provide good answers to old questions and/or fails to pose new questions that expose core issues, especially those that have public policy significance.

3.3. *Make it Plausible*

Making it plausible poses tensions with both of the first two precepts. When plausibility collides with simplicity and mathematical tractability, what to do?

In the spirit of pluralism to which I referred earlier, different economists will decide that differently. For my purposes here, I merely observe that TCE provides "added plausibility" in the following four respects: (1) the cognitive and self-interestness attributes of human actors are described as bounded rationality and opportunism, respectively;[4] (2) express provision is made for key intertemporal regularities of economic organization (of which the Fundamental Transformation is one and bureaucratization is another);[5] (3) the limits of the courts for contract enforcement purposes are admitted (whereupon much of the burden of contract implementation falls upon private ordering); and (4) as discussed in Section 4, TCE asks that each simple 8 model of economic organization confront the challenge of scaling up, thereby to approximate the real world phenomenon (e.g., the modern corporation) of interest.

3.4. *Predictions and Empirical Testing*

Some social scientists scoff at prediction, evidently in the belief that prediction is easy. Also, since everyone knows that "it is easy to lie with statistics", what useful purpose is served by empirical testing? My experience is different: prediction is a demanding standard and corroboration is not easy but difficult.

The comparison between managerial discretion theory and transaction cost economics is illustrative. Whereas the economics of discretionary behavior (Williamson, 1964, 1970) took exception with the standard assumption that managers in the large corporation were reliably committed to profit maximization and predicted that the managerial firm and the neoclassical firm would differ in their responses to variations in the condition of the environment (as between adverse and munificent) and to lump sum taxes, compelling evidence was difficult to work up and indirect tests were merely suggestive. In the end, few economists were persuaded. The neoclassical theory of the firm remained securely in place.

Neoclassical economics also long resisted the logical lapse to which Coase referred in his famous 1937 paper on "The Nature of the Firm," where

---

[4] These are discussed further in Section 4.
[5] For an elaboration, see Williamson (1985, chaps. 2, 6).

Coase put his finger on a "gap in economic theory." Thus, whereas neoclassical theory took the organization of economic activity as between firm and market as given, Coase advised that firm and market should be viewed as alternative modes for organizing economic activity, the choice between which (the make-or-buy decision) varied among transactions and should be derived (1937, p. 389). Many economists agreed that this lapse should be repaired, yet the 1937 article was "much cited and little used" 35 years later (Coase, 1972, p. 63). The missing ingredient was lack of operationalization. Here as elsewhere, it takes a theory to beat a theory (Kuhn, 1970, p. 77).

Not only did the fiction of zero transaction costs need to give way to positive transaction costs, but also tautological uses of transaction cost reasoning needed to give way to a predictive theory of which transactions would be organized by which modes of governance and why. Naming and explicating the key microanalytic attributes of transactions and of governance was vital. In the spirit of Elster's dictum that "explanations in the social sciences should be organized around (partial) mechanisms rather than (general) theories" (Elster, 1994, p. 75), attention was focused not on economic organization in general but on the intermediate product market transaction in particular.

Interestingly, vertical integration was both the first problem to which transaction cost economics and would become the paradigm problem in relation to which a vast variety of other contractual phenomena would be interpreted as variations on a transaction cost economizing theme.[6] Empirical tests for the relation between the asset attributes of transactions and vertical integration got underway in the 1980s (Monteverde and Teece, 1982; Masten, 1984) and have been continued and refined since — becoming "one of the great success stories in [empirical] industrial organization over the last 25 years" (Whinston, 2001, p. 185). Reaching beyond vertical integration, published empirical transaction cost articles numbered over 900 as of 2005 (Macher and Richman, 2006) and cover a vast range of contractual phenomena (Macher and Richman, 2006, p. 37).

---

[6]The overarching discriminating alignment hypothesis is this (For an elaboration, see Williamson (1985, chaps. 2, 6)): transactions, which differ in their transactional attributes, are aligned with governance structures, which differ in their cost and competence, so as to effect a transaction cost economizing result.

TCE, moreover, has found applications beyond business and economics to include the contiguous social sciences of law, organization theory, and political science. Indeed, transaction cost has become one of the "unifying languages" within economics and more generally. This would not have occurred but for the development of a logic of organization that operated at a more microanalytic level of analysis, an insistent demand for predictive content, and the ensuing empirical research agenda.

4. Supplementary Considerations

Although the four precepts of pragmatic methodology are more basic and universal in their application than are the four supplementary considerations that I introduce here, I contend that all contractual theories to economic organization should be examined with respect to the following: the key attributes of human actors on which they rely; the unit of analysis; the scaling up of simple models to approximate the phenomena of interest, and remediableness.

Human Actors: Whereas, to their credit, economists commonly give meticulous attention to the mechanisms through which their theories work, the implied attributes of the human actors who implement these mechanisms often receive scant attention. Evidently human actors can be expected to rise to the occasion, as defined by "whatever the theory calls for."

That is rather cavalier, yet might be justified by invoking the precepts of simplicity and prediction/testing. Because a "more realistic" theory would be more complex and less tractable, let the predictions and empirical tests thereof speak for the assumptions. But then what are we to make of the many would-be theories that are remiss in prediction/testing respects? Surely there is no harm in unveiling the implied assumptions about human actors. Indeed if, as Simon contends, "Nothing is more fundamental in setting our research agenda and informing our research methods than our view of the nature of the human beings whose behavior we are studying" (Simon, 1985, p. 303), there could be benefits. Especially relevant to the study of contract (and arguably more generally) are the cognitive competence and self-interest attributes that are ascribed to human actors.[7]

---

[7] Note that many phenomena that do not appear to be contractual in nature can often be reformulated in contractual terms, of which Coase"s reformulation of the externality problem (1960) is an early example.

Cognitive competence and self-interest attributes are interactive in the context of contract (Williamson, 1985, pp. 30–32, 43–63). In the face of strong assumptions about 11 cognitive competence (unbounded rationality, or variations, thereon), concerns over contractual defection by reason of opportunism vanish. But similarly, if strong assumptions about benign behavior and/or the reliability of promise are made, the needs to think through complex contingencies and engage in forward planning are vastly reduced.

If, for example, human actors possess the cognitive ability to implement comprehensive contingent claims contracting, then we are in the world of Arrow-Debreu where contracts are ubiquitous, whereupon organization is unneeded for coordination or control purposes. If instead the list of six assumptions that are made by Fudenberg, Holmstrom, and Milgrom (1990) applies, then we are in a world where a sequence of short-term contracts can implement an optimal long-term contract.[8] The latter assumes a slightly weaker condition of rationality than does the former, but the analytical impact of both, as these relate to opportunism, is identical: both vitiate contractual hazards attributable to opportunism. If and as implicit cognitive assumptions made in the service of analytical convenience obscure rather than spotlight key issues, such assumptions should be made explicit.

Transaction cost economics describes both cognition and self-interest in a two part way. Specifically, cognition combines bounded rationality with feasible foresight while self-interest joins benign behavior with opportunism. Thus, all complex contracts are unavoidably incomplete (by reason of bounded rationality), yet human actors are assumed to have the capacity to look ahead, recognize hazards, work out the mechanisms, and, albeit imperfectly, factor the ramifications back into the *ex ante* contractual design (by reason of feasible foresight). Also, most human actors will do what they agree to and some will do more most of the time (benign behavior), but outliers for which the stakes are great will elicit defection and/or posturing with the purpose of inducing renegotiation (which are manifestations of opportunism).

---

[8] The more controversial assumptions made by Fudenberg *et al.* have the effect of annihilating problems of information asymmetry. This is accomplished by 19 assuming three-way costless knowledge of public outcomes (by principal, agent, and arbiter) and common knowledge of both technology and preferences over action-payment streams. These assumptions make strong (but unexamined) demands on limited cognitive competence.

The combination of bounded rationality and state-contingent opportunism transform the world of complete contracting into one where (1) all complex contracts are unavoidably incomplete (by reason of bounded rationality) and (2) contractual hazards await (by reason of opportunism). The assumption of feasible foresight nevertheless affords relief, in that the parties to such incomplete contracts will craft *ex ante* cost effective credible commitments — of which unified ownership of both stages (vertical integration) is an extreme case.

Unit of Analysis: Not all theories of economic organization name the unit of analysis out of which they work, but some do. The "role," the "decision premise," and the "routine" have been variously recommended. The unit of analysis for the behavioral theory of the firm and for evolutionary economics is the routine. The unit of analysis for transaction cost economics is the transaction.

More is needed, however, than merely to nominate a unit of analysis. It has been vital to transaction cost economics and is important more generally, to name the critical dimensions with respect to which the unit of analysis (e.g., the transaction) differs. This in turn depends on how human actors are described in both cognitive and self-interest respects. Given the description of human actors on which transaction cost economics relies, the critical attributes of transactions are asset specificity (which is a measure of bilateral dependency, to which maladaptation hazards accrue), uncertainty (the disturbances, small and great, to which transactions are subject), and the frequency with which transactions recur, which has a bearing on both reputation effects (in the market) and private ordering mechanisms (within firms).[9]

---

[9] Also crucial to the transaction cost economics project is the proposition that governance is the means by which to infuse order, thereby to mitigate conflict and realize mutual gain. Alternative modes of governance — markets, hybrids, and hierarchies are described as discrete structural syndromes of attributes to which adaptive strengths and weaknesses accrue. Incentive intensity, decision and administrative control instruments, and contract law regime are the defining attributes with respect to which governance structures are described. Interestingly, but not surprisingly, market and hierarchy are polar opposites in these three respects — in that markets are characterized by high-powered incentives, negligible administrative control, and a legal rules contract law regime whereas hierarchies display low-powered incentives, considerable administrative control, and settle internal disputes administratively with the support of forbearance law. The discriminating alignment hypothesis provides the predictive link between transactions and governance structures. (See note 6, supra.)

Absent dimensionalization, would-be units of analysis lack predictive content. Appeal to vague units often leads to obscuration.[10]

Scaling Up: Solow observes that "The very complexity of real life ... [is what] makes simple models so necessary" (Solow, 2001, p. 111). The object of a simple model is to capture the essence, thereby to explain hitherto puzzling practices and make predictions that are subjected to empirical testing. But simple models can also be "tested" with respect to scaling up. Does repeated application of the basic mechanism out of which the simple model works yield a result that recognizably describes the phenomenon in question?[11]

The test of scaling up is often ignored, possibly out of awareness that scaling up cannot be done. Sometimes it is scanted, possibly in the belief that scaling up can be accomplished easily. The influential paper by Jensen and Meckling on "Theory of the Firm: Managerial Behavior, Agency Costs, and Capital Structure" (1976) is an exception. The authors work out of a simplified setup where an entrepreneur (100% owner-manager) sells off a fraction of the equity of the firm, as a result of which his incentive intensity is reduced and monitoring and credible contracting issues are posed. What the authors are really interested in, however, is not entrepreneurial firms but in the "modern corporation whose managers own little or no equity" (Meckling, 1976, p. 356). Investigating the latter is beyond the scope of their paper, but they express belief that "our approach can be applied to this case" ... [These issues]

---

[10] Although naming the decision premise as the unit of analysis (Simon, 1957) has been instructive for human problem solving (Newell and Simon, 1972), it has not been similarly useful to the economics of organization. And while naming the routine as the unit of analysis in evolutionary economics seems to be important — "routines play the role [in economic evolutionary theory] that genes play in biological evolutionary theory" (Nelson and Winter, 1982, p. 14) — the critical 20 attributes with respect to which routines differ have yet to be named. Possibly, Geoffrey Hodgson's definition of a routine as "organizational dispositions to energize conditional patterns of behavior within an organized group of individuals, involving sequential response to cues" (2006, p. 208) will be instructive, but that too awaits dimensionalization.

[11] Other examples where scaling up issues are posed include Thomas Schelling's treatment of the evolution of segregation in the "self-forming neighborhood" (Schelling, 1978, pp. 147–155), the expansive claims sometimes made on behalf of the paradox of voting (Williamson and Sargent, 1967), and the move from project financing to composite financing in the modern corporation (Williamson, 1988).

remain to be worked out in detail and will be included in a future paper" (1976, p. 356). The authors deserve credit for recognizing the need for scaling up.

Alas, Jensen and Meckling never produced the follow-up paper, but that is not the end of the story. The fundamental challenges posed by Jensen and Meckling have occupied a place of prominence on the research agenda of finance economics in the years since (Tirole, 2006). Especially noteworthy is what Jean Tirole refers to as the investor activism paradigm, which takes the form of a three-tier hierarchy: "(1) agent 14 (entrepreneur), (2) supervisor (large monitor), (3) principal (other investors). The role of the monitor is ... to reduce the asymmetry of information between the principal [dispersed shareholders] and the agent [entrepreneur]. This role is endangered by the possibility of collusion" between the monitor and the entrepreneur (Tirole, 2006, p. 362). Of the several candidates for monitor that Tirole discusses, the variant that most nearly applies to the separation of ownership from control in the modern corporation is the monitor as compliant board of directors.

Scaling up issues relevant to the modern corporation are also posed by the theory of the firm as team production (Alchian and Demsetz, 1972) and the theory of the firm as governance structure. The theory of team production is grounded in a condition of technological nonseparability, which Alchian and Demsetz illustrate with the example of manual freight loading: "Two men jointly lift heavy cargo into trucks. Solely by observing the total weight loaded per day, it is impossible to determine each person's marginal productivity" (Alchian and Demsetz,1972, p. 779). Accordingly, rather than pay each person according to his (unmeasurable) marginal product, such activities are organized cooperatively (as a team), the members of which are paid as a team and are monitored by a boss lest they engage in shirking. This is instructive, but does technological nonseparability scale up to explain the modern corporation?

One possibility is that the large corporation is an indecomposable whole, in which event everything is connected with everything else and the condition of technological nonseparability is operative throughout the entire enterprise. Another possibility is that, as Simon describes in "*The Architecture of Complexity*" (1962), large hierarchical systems are broken down into nearly decomposable subsystems — within which interactions are extensive and between which they are attenuated.[12] Simon's examination of social, biological, physical, and symbolic systems as well as the logic of 15 complexity supports the proposition that decomposability "is one of the central structural schemes that the architect of complexity uses" (1962, p. 468).

The Alchian and Demsetz model of team production makes no provision for decomposability. Accordingly, the boundary of the firm is defined by the cluster of technologically nonseparable activities within which continuous real time coordination is vital. Manual freight loading qualifies, as do groups as large as the symphony orchestra. Because, however, team production does not extend to the decision to join a series of technologically separable stages such as we observe in the modern corporation, the theory of team production does not scale up to form the modern corporation.

How does that transaction cost economics setup fare in scaling up respects? Does successive application of the make-or-buy decision, as it is applied to individual transactions, scale up to describe something that approximates a multi-stage firm? Note in this connection that transaction cost economics assumes that the transactions of interest are those that take place between technological separable stages. This is the "boundary of the firm" issue as described elsewhere (Williamson, 1985, pp. 96–98). Upon taking the technological "core" as given,[13] attention is focused on a series of separable make-or-buy decisions – backward, forward, and lateral — to ascertain which should be outsourced and which should be incorporated within the ownership boundary of the firm. So described, the firm is the inclusive set of transactions for which the decision is to make rather than buy — which does implement scaling up, or at least is a promising start (Williamson, 1985, pp. 96–98).

More generally, all candidate theories of the firm should be examined in scaling up respects. The public policy ramifications of would-be theories of the modern corporation that do not scale up should be regarded with precaution.

---

[12] "The loose ... coupling of subsystems ... [means that] each subsystem [is] independent of the exact timing of the operation of the others. If subsystem B depends upon subsystem A only for a certain substance, then B can be made independent of fluctuations on A's production by maintaining a buffer inventory" (Simon, 1977, p. 255).

[13] The technological core often rests on site specificity considerations, of which the realization of thermal economics between successive separable stages of production is an example (Williamson, 1996, pp. 15–16).

Remediableness: Dixit's examination of *The Making of Economic Policy* (1996) opens with a discussion of normative public policy analysis in which the government is assumed to maximize a social welfare function. Policymaking, so described, is viewed "as a purely technical problem. The implicit assumption is that once a policy that maximizes or improves social welfare has been found and recommended, it will be implemented as designed, and the desired effects will follow" (Dixit, 1996, pp. 8–9). This is tantamount to doing black box welfare economics in which transaction costs are assumed to be zero.

It is Dixit's judgment (and mine) that applied welfare economics, like the theory of the firm, should open up the black box and examine "the actual workings of the mechanism inside" (Dixit, 1996, p. 9). What I have referred to as the Remediableness Criterion is an effort to restore perspectives.

The Remediableness Criterion holds that an extant practice or mode of organization for which (1) no feasible superior alternative can be described and (2) implemented with expected net gains is (3) presumed to be efficient. The first condition removes hypothetical ideals from the relevant comparison set. The second makes provision for implementation obstacles of both political (real politick) and economic (setup cost) kinds. The Remediableness Criterion thus both disallows pronouncements of inefficiency that rest on a comparison of an actual (hence flawed) practice with a hypothetical (ideal) alternative and asks the public policy analyst to be more respectful of the political process.[14]

As Michels observed early in the twentieth century, we need first to understand deviations from ideals, of which the appearance of oligarchy in systems that were organized with democratic purpose is one, if we are to deal with them effectively: "Nothing but a serene and frank examination of the oligarchical dangers of democracy 17 will enable us to minimize these dangers, even though they can never be entirely avoided" (Michels, 1915, 1962, p. 370). Oligarchy is merely one illustration of path dependent outcomes for which a serene and frank examination of the microanalytic mechanisms is needed if hazard mitigation is to be accomplished.

---

[14] As George Stigler puts it, "government's goals as revealed by actual practice [deserve respect and] are more authoritative than those pronounced by professors of law or economics" (1992, p. 459).

5. Conclusions

A colleague remarked that the four precepts of pragmatic methodology as herein described are uncontroversial. I am pleased if others concur. Pragmatic methodology is concerned first and foremost, however, with practice. Agreement in theory and noncompliance in practice are altogether too common. If and as the demands of logical consistency (in theory) yield infeasibility (in practice), applied economists will understandably question whether the theory is ripe for applications in practice.

Transaction cost economics responsively relates, I think, to each of the four precepts of pragmatic methodology. It furthermore adds four supplementary considerations that are relevant to contractual theories of economic organization and more generally. Both transaction cost economics and pragmatic methodology nevertheless remain works in progress. [15]

References

Alchian, Armen and Demset H. 1972. "Production, Information Costs, and Economic Organization." *American Economic Review*, 62, December, pp. 777–795.
Arrow, Kenneth. 1987. "Reflections on the Essays." In *Arrow and the Foundations of the Theory of Economic Policy*, ed. George Feiwel, pp. 727–734. New York: New York University Press.

---

[15] Probably the most insistent challenge for transaction cost economics has been to move beyond the logic of words and diagrams (as in Williamson 1985, 1991, 21 1996) to include "full formalization" of a mathematical modeling kind. Although recent formalization work has been undertaken (Bajari and Tadelis, 2001; Levin and Tadelis, 2005; Tadelis and Williamson, 2007), full formalization remains a work in progress. Other challenges to transaction cost economics include making provision for (1) the early stage development of high-technology firms (where real-time responsiveness is of the essence); (2) differences in the institutional environment (to which the literatures on Positive Political Theory (Spiller and Tommasi, 2007) and multinational investment (Oxley, 1999; Henisz and Zelner, 2005) are pertinent); (3) applications to "human capital" firms (law firms; consultants) and noncommercial enterprise (Hansmann, 1996; Williamson, 1999); and (4) the enduring puzzles of corporate governance (Williamson, 2007). Also, issues of endogeneity in conjunction with empirical testing have been posed (Masten and Saussier, 2000). Although responses to all of the above have been fashioned, more such work is needed and new challenges can be expected to arise.

Bajari, Patrick and Steven Tadelis. 2001. "Incentives Versus Transaction Costs: A Theory of Procurement Contracts." *RAND Journal of Economics* , 2001, 32(3), pp. 287–307.

Barnard, Chester. 1938. *The Functions of the Executive.* Cambridge: Harvard University Press (fifteenth printing, 1962).

Blaug, Mark. 1997. "Ugly Currents in Modern Economics." unpublished manuscript.

Buchanan, James. 2001. "Game Theory, Mathematics, and Economics." *Journal of Economic Methodology*, 8 (March), pp. 27–32.

Coase, Ronald H. 1937. "The Nature of the Firm." *Economica*, N.S., 4: pp. 386–405. Reprinted In *The Nature of the Firm: Origins, Evolution, Development*, eds. Oliver E. Williamson and Sidney Winter, pp. 18–33. New York: Oxford University Press.

Coase, Ronald H. 1972. "Industrial Organization: A Proposal for Research." In *Policy Issues and Research Opportunities in Industrial Organization*, ed. V.R. Fuchs, pp. 59–73. New York: National Bureau of Economic Research.

Commons, John. 1932. "The Problem of Correlating Law, Economics, and Ethics." *Wisconsin Law Review*, 8(3)-26.23.

Commons, John. 1950. *The Economics of Collective Action*, Madison: University of Wisconsin Press.

Elster, John. 1994. "Arguing and Bargaining in Two Constituent Assemblies." unpublished manuscript, remarks given at the University of California, Berkeley.

Friedman, Milton. 1953. Essays in Positive Economics. Chicago: University of Chicago Press.

Friedman, Milton. 1997. "Modern Macroeconomics and its Evolution from a Monetarist Perspective." eds., Brian Snowdon and Howard Vane, *Journal of Economic Studies*, 24 (4), pp. 192–222.

Georgescu-Roegen, Nicholas. 1971. *The Entropy Law and Economic Process.* Cambridge, MA: Harvard University Press.

Hansmann, Henry. 1996. *The Ownership of Enterprise.* Cambridge, MA: Harvard University Press.

Hart, Oliver. 1995. *Firms, Contracts, and Financial Structure.* New York: Oxford University Press.

Hayek, Friedrich. 1945. "The Use of Knowledge in Society." *American Economic Review*, 35 (September), pp. 519–530.

Henisz, Witold J. and Bennet A. Zelner. 2005. "Legitimacy, Interest Group Pressures and Change in Emergent Institutions: The Case of Foreign Investors and Host Country Governments." *Academy of Management Review*, 30(2), pp. 361–382.

Jensen, Michael and William Meckling. 1976. "Theory of the Firm: Managerial Behavior, Agency Costs, and Capital Structure." *Journal of Financial Economics*, 3 (October), pp. 305–360.

Knight, Frank H. 1941. "Review of Melville J. Herskovits' 'Economic Anthropology'." *Journal of Political Economy*, 49 (April), pp. 247–258.24.

Koopmans, Tjalling. 1957. *Three Essays on the State of Economic Science.* New York: McGraw Hill Book Company.

Kreps, David. 1999. "Markets and Hierarchies and (Mathematical) Economic Theory." In *Firms, Markets, and Hierarchies*, eds. Glenn Carroll and David Teece, New York: Oxford University Press.

Kuhn, Thomas. 1970. *The Structure of Scientific Revolutions.* 2nd edn. Chicago: University of Chicago Press.

Levin, Jonathan and Steven Tadelis. 2005. "Contracting for Government Services: Theory and Evidence from U.S. Cities. " Unpublished manuscript, University of California, Berkeley.

Macher, Jeffrey and Barak Richman. 2006. "Transaction Cost Economics: An Assessment of Empirical Research in the Social Sciences." unpublished manuscript, Georgetown University.

March, James G. and Herbert A. Simon. 1958. *Organizations.* New York: John Wiley & Sons.

Masten, Scott. 1984. "The Organization of Production: Evidence from the Aerospace Industry." *Journal of Law and Economics*, 27 (October), pp. 403–418.

Masten, Scott and Stephane Saussier. 2000. "Econometrics of Contracts: An Assessment of Developments in the Empirical Literature on Contracting." *Revue D'Economie Industrielle*, 92, pp. 215–236.

Michels, R. ([1915] 1962), Political Parties. New York: Collier Books.

Monteverde, Kirk and David Teece. 1982. "Supplier Switching Costs and Vertical Integration in the Automobile Industry." *Bell Journal of Economics*, 13, pp. 206–213.

Newell, Allen. 1990. *Unified Theories of Cognition.* Cambridge, MA: Harvard University Press.

Oxley, Joanne E. 1999. "Institutional Environment and the Mechanisms of Governance: The Impact of Intellectual Property Protection on the Structure of Inter-firm Alliances." *Journal of Economic Behavior and Organization*, 38 (3).

Robinson, Stanley. 1968. 'New York State Bar Association.' Antitrust Symposium. p. 29.

Schelling, Thomas. 1978. *Micromotives and Macrobehavior.* New York: Norton.

Selznick, Philip. 1966. *TVA and the Grass Roots.* Harper Torchbooks.

Simon, Herbert. 1957(a). *Models of Man.* New York: John Wiley & Sons.

Simon, Herbert. 1957(b). *Administrative Behavior*. New York: Macmillan, 2nd edn.

Simon, Herbert. 1962. "The Architecture of Complexity." Proceedings of the American Philosophical Society, 106 (December), pp. 467–482.

Simon, Herbert. 1973. "Applying Information Technology to Organization Design." *Public Administrative Review*, 33 (May, June), pp. 268–278.

Simon, Herbert A. 1985. 'Human Nature in Politics', *American Political Science Review*, 79(2), 293–304.

Simon, Herbert A. 1992. Economics, Bounded Rationality and the Cognitive Revolution, Brookfield, VT: Edward Elgar.

Solow, Robert. 1997. "How Did Economics Get That Way and What Way Did it Get?" Daedulus, 126 (1), pp. 39–58.

Solow, Robert. 2001. "A Native Informant Speaks." *Journal of Economic Methodology*, 8 (March), pp. 111–112.

Spiller, Pablo, and Mariano Tommasi. 2007. "The Institutional Foundations of Public Policy: The Case of Argentina," forthcoming, Cambridge University Press.

Tadelis, Steven, and Oliver E. Williamson. 2007. "Transaction Cost Economics." unpublished manuscript, University of California, Berkeley.

Whinston, Michael. 2001. "Assessing Property Rights and Transaction-Cost Theories of the Firm." *American Economic Review*, 91, pp. 184–199.

Whinston, Michael. 2003. "On the Transaction Cost Determinants of Vertical Integration." *Journal of Law, Economics and Organization*, 19 (1), pp. 1–23.26

Williamson, Oliver E. 1964. *The Economics of Discretionary Behavior: Managerial Objectives in a Theory of the Firm*. Englewood Cliffs, NJ: Prentice Hall.

Williamson, Oliver E. 1970. *Corporate Control and Business Behavior*. Englewood Cliffs, NJ: Prentice Hall.

Williamson, Oliver E. 1975. *Markets and Hierarchies: Analysis and Antitrust Implications*. New York: Free Press.

Williamson, Oliver E. 1985. *The Economic Institutions of Capitalism*. New York: Free Press.

Williamson, Oliver E. 1988. "Corporate Finance and Corporate Governance." *Journal of Finance*, 43 (July), pp. 567–591.

Williamson, Oliver E. 1991. "Comparative Economic Organization: The Analysis of Discrete Structural Alternatives." *Administrative Science Quarterly*, 36 (June), pp. 269–296.

Williamson, Oliver E. 1996. *The Mechanisms of Governance*. New York: Oxford University Press.

Williamson, Oliver E. 1999. "Public and Private Bureaucracies." *Journal of Law, Economics and Organization*, 15 (1).

Williamson, Oliver E. 2007. "Corporate Boards of Directors: A Dual-Purpose (Efficiency) Perspective." unpublished manuscript, University of California, Berkeley.

Williamson, Oliver E. and Thomas J. Sargent. 1967. "Social Choice: A Probabilistic Approach." *Economic Journal*, pp. 77, 797 813.

Wilson, Edward O. 1999. *Consilience*. New York: Alfred Knopf.

Chapter 6

Transaction Cost Economics: How it Works; Where it is Headed

The transaction cost economics program that is described herein is the product of two recent and complementary fields of economic research. The first one is the New Institutional Economics; the second one has been described as the 'new economics of organization' (Moe, 1984, 1990). A key conceptual move for both was to push beyond the theory of the firm as a production function (which is a technological construction) into a theory of the firm as a governance structure (which is an organizational construction).

Work in both of these areas began to take shape in a concerted way in the 1970s and has grown exponentially since. The economics of organization is the more theoretical of the two and more closely relates to public-policy issues traditionally associated with the field of industrial organization. The New Institutional Economics is more interdisciplinary and has applications to the contiguous social sciences.

Although transaction cost economics has a broad reach, any issue that arises as or can be reformulated as a contracting problem is usefully examined through the lens of transaction cost economizing — it does not tell you everything. Moreover, within the ambit of issues to which transaction cost economics is related, it has greater application value in some areas than in others. Transaction cost economics thus takes its place alongside other — partly rival, partly complementary — perspectives on the theory of firm and market organization. Elster's (1994, p. 74) dictum that 'explanations in the social sciences should be organized around (partial) rather than (general) theories' is one to which transaction cost economics subscribes. I begin with a sketch of the New Institutional Economics. Section 2 sets out a series of questions which any theory of economic organization should be expected to address. Section 3 deals with implementation of the transaction cost economics project. Background conceptual moves out of which transaction cost economics works, some of which are still controversial, are examined in Section 4. Extant and potential applications are sketched in Section 5. Concluding remarks follow in Section 6.

1. The New Institutional Economics

1.1. *General*

The New Institutional Economics comes in two parts. Part one deals with the institutional environment — the rules of the game — and traces its origins to Coase's 1960 paper on 'The Problem of Social Cost.' Part two deals with the institutions of governance — the play of the game — and originates with Coase's 1937 paper on '*The Nature of the Firm.*' Both parts got underway in the early 1970s (Davis and North, 1971; Williamson, 1971; Alchian and Demsetz, 1972) and progressively took shape over that decade (North, 1981, Williamson, 1975, 1976, 1979, Klein, Crawford, and Alchian, 1978). Exponential growth occurred in the 1980s and since. Two Nobel Prizes — one to Coase in 1991 and the other to North in 1994 — celebrate its influence.

In addition to major intellectual debts to Coase, both levels of analysis have benefited from interim developments. Especially important to the institutional environment was interim work in economic history during which cliometrics took shape (Fogel and Engerman, 1971, 1974). Related work on property rights (Demsetz, 1969) and path dependence (David, 1985, Arthur, 1989) have also been important. Work on the institutions of governance benefited from the extensive market failure literature, as summarized in Arrow's paper on 'The Organization of Economic Activity: Issues Pertinent to the Choice of Market Versus Nonmarket Allocation' (1969), from research on organization theory, especially that done at Carnegi (March and Simon, 1958, Cyert and March, 1963), and from business history (Chandler, 1962).

The work at Carnegie aside, which took exception with economic orthodoxy but had much more influence on organization theory than on economics, the new economics of organization had no obvious predecessor. By contrast, there definitely was an earlier institutional economics movement — which had fallen on hard times.

Criticisms of the older style of institutional economics in America have been scathing. Unable or unwilling to offer a rival research agenda, the older institutional economics was given over to methodological objections to orthodoxy (Stigler, 1983, p. 70; Coase, 1984, p. 230; Matthews, 1986, p. 903). Like the American Legal Realism movement, with which older style institutional economics shares many common intellectual and public policy attributes, older style institutional economics ran itself into the sand. The problem was not that the economic and legal orthodoxies with which these two movements took exception were beyond legitimate criticism. Orthodoxy always needs good critics. The maxim that it takes a theory to beat a theory (Kuhn, 1970) nevertheless applies. Both older style institutional economics and American Legal Realism were remiss by failing to advance a positive research agenda.

Moreover, it does not suffice to prescribe a general approach — for example, 'study institutions' — or, for that matter, to describe institutions, such as the lumber industry in Wisconsin (Hurst, 1964) in detail. Focus is needed, whence issues of purposefulness and choice of the unit of analysis are important. Of the many purposes served by institutions, what is the 'main purpose'? Going beyond the proposition that institutions matter (with which now almost everyone agrees — although it was not always so) to demonstrate that institutions are susceptible to analysis has been the major challenge. Accepting and responding to that challenge is what distinguishes the NIE from its predecessors (Matthews, 1986, p. 903). Arrow's overview is pertinent (1987, p. 734):

> Why…has the work of Simon, which meant so much to us all, nevertheless had so little direct consequence? Why did the older institutional school fail so miserably, though it contained such able analysts as Veblen, Commons, and Mitchell?… "[One answer is that] in fact there are important specific analyses, particularly in the work of the New Institutional Economics movement. But it does not consist primarily of giving new answers to the traditional questions of economics — resource allocation and the degree of

utilization. Rather it consists of answering new questions, why economic institutions have emerged the way they did and not otherwise; it merges into economic history, but brings sharper [microanalytic]...reasoning to bear than has been customary."

1.2. *Framework*

Four levels of social analysis are distinguished in Figure 1. The solid arrows that connect a higher with a lower level signal that the higher level imposes

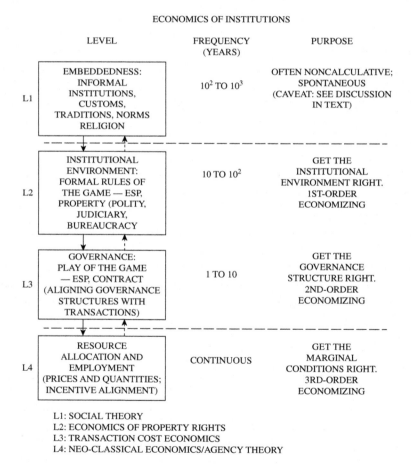

Figure 1.   Economics and Institutions

constraints on the level immediately below. The reverse arrows that connect lower with higher levels are dashed and signal feedback. Although, in the fullness of time, the system is fully interconnected, for my purposes here, these feedbacks are largely neglected. The NIE has mainly concentrated on action at Levels 2 and 3.

The top level is the social embeddedness level. This is where the norms, customs, mores, traditions, etc. are located. Religion plays a large role at this level. Although Level 1 analysis is undertaken by some economic historians and other social scientists (Banfield, 1958, Putnam, 1993, Huntington, 1996; Nee, 1997), Level 1 is taken as given by most economists. Institutions at this level change very slowly — on the order of centuries or millennia — whereupon North (1991, p. 111) poses the query, 'What is it about informal constraints that gives them such a pervasive influence upon the long-run character of economies?'. An answer to this perplexing question is not attempted here, but I conjecture that the mainly spontaneous origin of these practices — deliberative choice of a calculative kind is minimally implicated — is a contributing factor. Be that as it may, the resulting institutions have a lasting grip on the way a society conducts itself. Some societies feel threatened by that and take measures to protect themselves against 'alien values'.

The second level is what I referred to earlier as the institutional environment. The structures observed here are the product of politics and provide the rules of the game within which economic activity is organized. The polity, judiciary, and bureaucracy of government are all located here. The laws regarding property rights — their definition and enforcement — are prominently featured.

According to North (1991, p. 97), institutions are 'the humanly devised constraints that structure political, economic, and social interactions. They consist of both informal constraints (sanctions, taboos, customs, traditions, and codes of conduct), and formal rules (constitutions, laws, property rights)'. Elsewhere he argues that 'institutions consist of a set of constraints on behavior in the form of rules and regulations; and, finally, a set of moral, ethical, behavioral norms which define the contours and that constrain the way in which the rules and regulations are specified and enforcement is carried out' (North, 1984, p. 8). So described, the informal constraints are located at Level 1 and the formal rules — the polity, judiciary, bureaucracy — are located at Level 2. First-order economizing — get the institutional environment right — is featured here. Such choices are vitally important to the economic productivity of an economy (Rosenberg and Birdzell, 1986; Coase, 1992; North, 1994; Levy and Spiller, 1994; Olson, 1996; Henisz, 1996), but cumulative change of a gradual kind is difficult to orchestrate. Massive discontent — civil wars (the Glorious Revolution (North and Weingast, 1989)), or occupations (following World War II), or perceived threats (the Meiji Revolution), or breakdowns (Eastern Europe and the former Soviet Union), or a military coup (Chile), or a financial crisis (New Zealand) — will, however, occasionally produce a sharp break from established procedures. Rare windows of opportunity to effect broad reform are thereby opened. Such 'defining moments' are nevertheless the exception rather than the rule. Otherwise, major changes in the rules of the game occur in the order of decades or centuries.

Of the variety of factors that are brought in through Level 2 analysis, a considerable share of the analytic load is borne by the economics of property rights: 'Modern institutional economics focuses on the institution of property, and on the systems of norms governing the acquisition or transfer of property rights' (Furubotn and Richter, 1991, p. 3). As between the various categories of property rights (Bromley, 1989), the right of ownership — which consists of the right to use an asset, the right to appropriate the returns from an asset, and the right to change its form, substance, or location (Furubotn and Richter, 1991, p. 6) — is the most important.

Work on the economics of property rights flourished in the 1960s. Applications included the study of pollution, allocating the electromagnetic spectrum, dealing with tortious claims, understanding the military draft, defining hunting rights for North American Indians, and interpreting the modern corporation (Demsetz, 1967). A widely held premise was that 'A private-enterprise system cannot function properly unless property rights are created in resources, and, when thesis done, someone wishing to use a resource has to pay the owner to obtain it. Chaos disappears; and so does the government except that a legal system to define property rights and to arbitrate disputes is, of course, necessary' (Coase, 1959, p. 12). Property rights were thus viewed both as the conceptual key that unlocks many of the puzzles of economic organization and as the means to realize superior economic performance.

As it turned out, the study of property further needed to be joined by the study of contract, but that did not register for another decade. As

Furubotn and Richter observe, contract was neglected because, 'In effect, there was faith that…all contracts would be guaranteed perfectly and cost-lessly by the functioning of the legal system' (Furubotn and Richter, 1991, p. 7–8). With the benefit of hindsight, that is implausible and is the opening through which the governance of contractual relations walked in.

The third level is where the institutions of governance are located. Although property remains important, a perfectly functioning legal system in order to enforce contracts is not contemplated. Instead of costless court ordering, a comparison of costly court enforcement with costly private ordering is needed. Much of the relevant governance actions moves to the latter.

Transaction cost economics operates at Level 3. Taking the rules of the game at Level 2 as shift parameters, Level 3 deals with the play of the game. Alternative modes of organization are described as syndromes of attributes that differ indiscrete structural ways. Second-order economizing applies: get the governance structures — markets, hybrids, firms, bureaus — right. The period over which such decisions come up for consideration is of the order of a year to a decade.

Level 4 moves from discrete structural to marginal analysis. This is the level with which neo-classical economics and, more recently, agency theory have been concerned. The neo-classical decision variables are price and out-put; agency theory deals with an efficient incentive alignment in the face of differential risk aversion (Holmstrom, 1979) and/or multi-task factors (Holmstrom and Milgrom, 1991) or multi-principal concerns (Dixit, 1996). Third-order economizing prevails, which entails getting the marginal condi-tions right. Adjustments in price and output are made in a (more or less) continuous way in response to changing market conditions.

The remainder of this chapter predominantly focuses on the discrete structural analysis of governance at Level 3.

2. What are the Questions?

How does transaction cost economics work? First and foremost, it works off of good ideas. Key ideas include comparative economic organization (Coase, 1937), private ordering (Llewellyn, 1931), adaptation as the central problem of economic organization (Barnard, 1938; Hayek, 1945), behavioral attributes of human actors (Simon, 1985), and the distinction between the institutional environment and the institutions of governance (Davis and North, 1971). It will not go unnoticed that many of these good ideas have their origins in the 1930s, which appears to have been an unusually fertile decade for the social sciences.

Although the list of questions set out in this section is not exhaustive, they are, I think, questions that every theory of economic organization should be expected to answer. My response to the observation that the questions are ones to which transaction cost economics easily relates is this: Which questions should be deleted? What questions should be added?

2.1. *What are the Phenomena of Interest?*

'Why are there so many kinds of organization?' (Hannan and Freeman, 1977, p. 936). This is a variant on the earlier Coasian question: Given that there are markets, why are there firms? (Coase, 1937, pp. 387–388). The broader query goes beyond the market and firm dichotomy to include hybrid contracting, regulation, nonprofits, public bureaus, and so on and invites the study of variations within categories (especially hierarchical variants within firms) as well.

In order to answer this question, one needs to start somewhere. Working up an archetypal problem, if such exists, is the obvious place to begin. Vertical integration — or, in more mundane terms, the make-or-buy decision (Coase, 1937; Williamson,1971, 1979, 1991; Klein, Crawford, and Alchian, 1978; Grossman and Hart 1986; Baker, Gibbons, and Murphy, 1997) — has been the archetypal problem for transaction cost economics.

As compared with other interesting contracting issues — for labor, with consumers, or for capital — contracts between firms in intermediate product markets have the advantage that the two parties can be presumed to be risk-neutral and roughly, to be dealing with each other on a parity. Each has extensive business experience and has or can hire specialized legal, technical, managerial, and financial expertise. Attention can therefore be focused on the attributes of the transaction and the properties of alternative modes of governance — rather than be deflected by differential risk aversion or by competence disparities between the parties (as might arise, for example, with contracts between firms and inexperienced consumers). Intermediate product market transactions are simpler in these respects and therefore easier to unpack. Assuming that economic organization works out of variations on a few key themes, working from simple to more complex, in which added complications are folded in, has obvious advantages.

2.2. *How are Human Agents Described?*

Although economists often ascribe analytically tractable attributes (such as hyper-rationality) to human agents, Simon advises social scientists to be more circumspect: 'Nothing is more fundamental in setting our research agenda and informing our research methods than our view of the nature of the human beings whose behavior we are studying' (Simon, 1985, p. 303). The two key attributes to which Simon thereafter refers are the cognitive ability and the self-interestedness of human actors. Bounded rationality — behavior that is intendedly rational but only limitedly so — is the cognitive condition to which Simon refers. 'Frailties of motive' describes the condition of self-interestedness (Simon, 1985, p. 303).

Transaction cost economics subscribes to bounded rationality and urges that the crucial importance of bounded rationality for economic organization resides in the fact that all complex contracts are unavoidably incomplete. Also, transaction cost economics describes self-interestedness not as frailty of motive but as opportunism, whereupon additional contractual complications are posed. Not only does an incomplete contract contain gaps, errors, and omissions (by reason of bounded rationality), but mere promise, unsupported by credible commitments, is not self-enforcing by reason of opportunism.

Although opportunism is an unflattering attribute, it is nonetheless basic to the logic of organization — in that, absent opportunism, there is no contractual reason to supplant market by hierarchy (Williamson, 1985, pp. 30–32, 64–67). Thus, although it is unnecessary to assume that all human agents are identically opportunistic, much less continuously opportunistic, it is truly utopian to presume unfailing stewardship. (Even the saints are known to be fallible, and most of us are better described as mere mortals.)

It is useful in this connection to distinguish between day-to-day routines and occasional disturbances of less familiar or nonstandard kinds. As between frailty of motive and opportunism, which applies where?

I submit that frailty of motive adequately describes day-to-day activity most of the time. People usually will do what they say (and some will do more) without self-consciously asking whether the effort is justified by expected discounted net gains. If they slip, it is a normal friction and often a matter of bemusement.

Suppose, however, we should ask another question: Which assumption better takes us into the deep structure of economic organization? Specifically, if our concern is not with day-to-day affairs but with long-term contractual relations, how should we proceed?

An important part of the exercise now is to look ahead, perceive hazards, and fold these back into the organizational design — in all significant contractual contexts whatsoever (intermediate product market, labor market, capital market, etc.). If candid reference to opportunism alerts us to avoidable dangers, which the more benign reference to frailties of motive would not, then there are real hazards in the more benevolent construction. Attenuating the *ex post* hazards of opportunism through the extant choice of governance is central to the transaction cost economics exercise.

The parallel between the concept of opportunism, as it applies to contract, and that of oligarchy, in relation to democracy, is striking. Michels concluded in his famous book, *Political Parties*, with the observation that 'nothing but a serene and frank examination of the oligarchical dangers of democracy will enable us to minimize these dangers' (Michels, 1966, p. 370). The corresponding proposition on opportunism is this: Nothing but a serene and frank examination of the hazards of opportunism will enable us to mitigate these hazards.

2.3. *How is the Firm Described?*

As Kreps has put it (1990, p. 96):

> The [neo-classical] firm is like individual agents in textbook economics, which finds its highest expression in general equilibrium theory (see Debreu, 1959; Arrow and Hahn, 1971). The firm interacts with other firm sand with individuals in the market. Agents have utility functions, firms have a profit motive; agents have consumption sets, firms have production possibility sets. But in transaction cost economics, firms are more like markets — both are arenas within which individuals can interact.

Thus, whereas neo-classical economics describes the firm as a production function, which is a technological construction, transaction cost economics describes the firm as a governance structure, which is an organizational construction.

Upon describing firms and markets as alternative modes of governance, new answers to old questions can be attempted. Rather than view the efficient boundaries of the firm in terms of technology (economies of scale and scope), the efficient boundaries can be derived by aligning different transactions with governance structures (firm or market) in a discriminating way. Both of the original Coasian questions — Why are there firms? and Why is not all activity organized in one large firm? — can be addressed.

2.4. *What Main Purpose is Served by Economic Organization?*

Economic organization is very complex and services many purposes. It is nonetheless useful to focus on the main purpose, in relation to which other purposes are treated as extensions or refinements. Transaction cost economics concurs with Hayek (1945) and Barnard (1938) that adaptation is the central problem of economic organization.

According to Hayek, 'economic problems arise always and only in consequence of change', whence 'the economic problem of society is mainly one of rapid adaptation in the particular circumstances of time and place' (Hayek, 1945, pp. 523–524). Barnard likewise featured adaptation, albeit of a different kind. On Barnard's reading, 'the survival of an organization depends upon the maintenance of an equilibrium of complex character... [This] calls for readjustment of processes internal to the organization..., [whence] the center of our interest is the processes by which [adaptation] is accomplished' (Barnard, 1938, p. 6). Whereas the adaptations to which Hayek refers are autonomous adaptations in which individual parties respond to market opportunities as signaled by changes in relative prices, the adaptations of concern to Barnard are cooperative adaptations accomplished through administration within the firm.

Transaction cost economics recognizes that a high performance system needs adaptive capacities of both kinds. As described in Section 3, alternative modes of governance are described in terms of their differential competence to deliver adaptations of both kinds. What I should like to emphasize here are that (1) theories of organization that feature adaptations should not be described as 'static, and (2) theories of organization that rely on administration to accomplish cooperative adaptation (sometimes by fiat) are very definitely concerned with 'management.' The upshot is that transaction cost economics is very much an inter-temporal, adaptive, managerial exercise — although this is not to say that more dynamic theories or more prominent provisions for management are unneeded.

2.5. *Does the Theory Scale Up?*

Like other theories of the firm, the transaction cost theory of the firm as governance structure works out of a highly simplified set-up. A key issue for all candidate theories of the firm is how do they explain the boundaries of the firm? One possibility is that successive application of the same underlying mechanism is what defines the boundary. Alternatively, a theory may appeal to other forces or factors to explain the boundary.

Under the firm-as-a-production function set-up, 'the cases of clear economies of integration' were long believed to 'involve a physical or technical integration of the processes in a single plant' (Bain, 1968, p. 381). In that event, what explains the joinder of successive technologically separable stages of production, the multi-plant firm, and/or forward integration out of production into distribution? Appeal to a nontechnological force was needed, of which market power was the obvious candidate. However, as few firms possess market power of a durable kind, integration to effect monopoly purpose (of both price discrimination and strategic entry impeding kinds) has limited explanatory power. Given that narrow technological grounds and the implausible monopoly grounds out of which the neo-classical set-up works provide a very incomplete explanation for the boundary of the firm, there is a need to turn elsewhere.

Consider the more recent property rights theory of the firm associated with Grossman and Hart (1986). According to Grossman and Hart, the integration of a supplier (stage A) and a buyer (stage B) entails directional ownership. Thus, whereas the usual view of vertical integration is that of unified ownership, according to which both stages report to a common peak coordinator who manages the two stages so as to promote coordinated investment and adaptation, that is not an option under Grossman and Hart.

Instead, either A buys B (in which event A has residual rights of control) or B buys A (in which event B has residual rights of control), and it matters which way the ownership goes. Indeed, directional ownership is what most clearly distinguishes Grossman and Hart from other theories of vertical integration.

Inefficiency, in the Grossman and Hart set-up, is entirely attributable to *ex ante* investment distortions that are induced by alternative ownership arrangements. Grossman and Hart further maintain that each stage makes its own investment decision under directional integration that each stage appropriates its own net receipts, and that management is never called upon to manage. Except as they grant that all contracts are unavoidably incomplete, theirs is a theory of property rights and of property rights only (Holmstrom, 1996).

Whether or how this management-free firm would scale up from two stages to include the directional integration over many has never been addressed — although Hart (1995) makes frequent references to the modern corporation, the suggestion being that these fall within the ambit. Given that the logic out of which this set-up works is implausible (Kreps, 1996) or mistaken (Maskin and Tirole, 1997), scaling up from two to N stages only compounds the difficulties. (To date, no such attempt has been made.)

The transaction cost economics approach to the boundary of the firm begins with a 'core technology' (Thompson, 1967), within which integration is treated as unproblematic. Forward, lateral, and backward integration in relation to the core (Williamson, 1985, pp. 96–98) are then examined. Will the firm integrate backward into raw material (e.g., plastics and chemical feed stocks) or will it pro-cure raw materials from others? Will the firm produce its own components (e.g., electrical switches) or will it buy these in the market? Will the firm integrate forward into distribution or will it rely on the wholesale and retail capacities of others? The transaction in each case is between technologically separable stages — which is to say that a buffer inventory could be introduced to effect temporal separation between an ascent stages in the transaction.

Sometimes economies of scale and scope will be such that the decision will be easy: if the firm is too small to produce efficiently to its own needs, the make-or-buy decision is obvious. For many transactions, however, either market procurement or own-production is technologically feasible and the choice is predominantly decided by comparative transaction cost considerations. This is the microanalytic exercise described in Section 3 below, in which the action resides in the attributes of transactions in relation to the cost on the one hand and competencies of alternative modes of governance on the other.

With respect to intermediate product market transactions, the boundary of the firm is the inclusive set of stages for which the make-or-buy calculus is resolved by supplanting market by hierarchy (Williamson, 1985, pp. 96–98). Within the firm so described, the ownership of all stages is unified (as against directional), investments and strategic decisions are coordinated by hierarchy, and those disputes for which adjacent stages are unable to reach agreement are decided by fiat (the firm is its own court of ultimate appeal). This same contractual calculus, moreover, extends to the organization of labor within the firm and to the choice between debt and equity — where debt is the more market-like instrument and equity is more akin to hierarchy. The upshot is that something resembling the modern corporation unfolds from the successive application of transaction cost economics to the series of comparative contractual choices that the firm is required to make. So, repeated application of the same contractual calculus does, as it were, scale up.

Consider finally the agency theory set-up. Agency theory is predominantly a theory of the employment relation in which output is jointly determined by the state realization and the effort expended by the agent. Complications arise by reason of asymmetric information and risk aversion (where the agent has better information about effort expenditure and is normally assumed to be more risk-averse), whereupon a trade-off between incentive intensity and efficient risk-bearing is posed, and/or by the need to induce efficient effort expenditure across multiple tasks. Although Holmstrom (1996) contends that boundary of the firm issues are usefully informed by this framework, applications to date are limited. Forward integration into distribution — choice of an inhouse sales office or an independent distributor — as a function of the difficulty of measuring a salesperson's performance, especially with multiple brands, is one example whereas agency theory fits (Holmstrom, 1996, p. 32). Integration into stages for which quality is difficult to measure is another possibility (Holmstrom, 1996, pp. 32–33), although quality can often be interpreted as a hazard to brand name capital and can be folded into the asset specificity set-up.

Indeed, as Holmstrom observes, agency theory and transaction cost economics are not mutually exclusive (Holmstrom, 1996, p. 32). Be that as it may, it is noteworthy that the agency theory approach needs to move away from its long preoccupation with efficient risk-bearing in favor of interim contractual hazards (which has been the transaction cost economics focus from the outset) in order to engage the make-or-buy issue in an interesting way. Awaiting further developments, these two approaches can be regarded as complementary — each applying to different circumstances.

3. How is it Implemented?

Many would-be theories of economic organization are primarily retrospective, in that they offer an *ex post* explanation for what has transpired. Although such rationalizations can be interesting and informative, plausible theories proliferate and there is a need to sort the wheat from the chaff. As Roegen has put it, even though the 'purpose of science in general is not prediction, but knowledge for its own sake,' prediction is nevertheless 'the touchstone of scientific knowledge' (Roegen, 1971, p. 37). Sooner or later, candidate theories of economic organization must go beyond *ex post* rationalization and offer predictions.

Although the concept of transaction cost is attractive — it has obvious relevance and is connected with a huge number of phenomena — it is also an elastic concept and, unless delimited, could be and was invoked as an *ex post* rationalization: for every anomaly there is an easy transaction cost explanation (Alchian and Demsetz, 1972; Fischer, 1977; p. 322, n. 5). Predictive content required operationalization. As herein described, this entailed (1) naming and dimensionalizing the unit for which organization was needed, (2) naming and dimensionalizing the structures through with organization was realized, (3) effecting a dis-criminating alignment between the two, after which (4) empirical testing could be done (and rapidly followed).

3.1. *Unit of Analysis*

According to Commons, 'the ultimate unit of activity... must contain in itself the three principles of conflict, mutuality, and order. This unit is the transaction' (Commons, 1932, p. 4). Not only does transaction cost economics subscribe to the idea that the transaction is the basic unit of analysis, but the triple to which Commons refers — conflict, mutuality, order — is very much what governance is all about.

Declaring that the transaction is the basic unit of analysis usefully moves economics in the direction of being a science of contract, as against a science of choice (Buchanan, 1975, p. 229), but the transaction takes on operational significance as a unit of analysis only when the factors that distinguish transactions from one another are identified. Given that all complex contracts are incomplete, by reason of bounded rationality, and that many pose maladaptation hazards, by reason of opportunism, what are the attributes of transactions to which contractual hazards accrue and how can they be mitigated?

Of the many attributes for describing transactions, the three dimensions that have been especially instructive to the study of commercial transactions are the frequency with which transactions recur, the uncertainty (disturbances) to which they are subject, and the condition of asset specificity. The last dimension gives rise to a condition of bilateral dependency, whereupon what may have been a large numbers supply condition at the outset gets transformed into a small numbers exchange relation thereafter. Asset specificity takes a variety of forms — physical assets, human assets, site specificity, dedicated assets, brand name capital, and temporal specificity — to which individuated governance structure responses accrue. It is the big locomotive to which transaction cost economics owes much of it predictive content.

3.2. *Governance*

Transaction cost economics regards the firm not as a production function but as a governance structure. Indeed, the concept of governance is precisely responsive to the triple to which Commons referred: governance is the means by which *order* is accomplished in a relation in which potential *conflict* threatens to undo or upset opportunities to realize mutual gains.

Engaged, as it is, in comparative institutional analysis, the firm is but one of several alternative modes of governance. Others include market, hybrid contracting, and public bureau modes of governance. The question which then presents itself is what are the critical dimensions with respect to which alternative modes of governance are described?

As discussed in Section 4, transaction cost economics maintains that each generic mode of governance is supported by a distinctive form of contract law. In that event, the pertinent law of contract needs to be addressed. Additionally, if adaptation (of both autonomous and cooperative kinds) is the central purpose of economic organization, then the comparative efficacy of alternative modes of governance in both adaptive respects needs to be described. Further, since governance works through instruments, of which incentive intensity and administrative controls are basic, then governance structure differences of these two kinds need to be developed. The ways and reasons whereby alternative generic modes of governance differ in these five respects are developed elsewhere (Williamson, 1991, 1997). With reference to markets and firms, the salient differences are these:

(1) incentive intensity: the high-powered incentives of markets give way to low powered incentives in firms;
(2) administrative controls: firms are supported by a more extensive array of administrative rules and procedures;
(3) adaptation: markets enjoy the advantage in effecting autonomous adaptation in response to changes in relative prices, but the advantage accrues to firms as more cooperative adaptations are needed; and
(4) contract law: the contract law of markets is legalistic and relies on court or Bering whereas the firm supplants court ordering by private ordering and settles disputes by fiat (in effect, the firm is its own court of ultimate appeal).

3.3. *Predictions*

Transaction cost economics invokes the discriminating alignment hypothesis, according to which transactions, which differ in their attributes, are aligned with governance structures, which differ in their cost and competence, so as to effect a (mainly) transaction cost economizing result. The simple

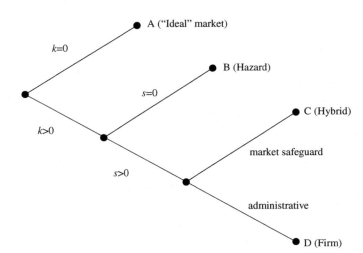

Figure 2. Simple contracting schema

contractual scheme set out in Figure 2 invites comparative contractual reasoning in which differences in technology give rise to different contractual hazards which in turn elicit safeguards, the effects of which are priced out. Price, technology, and governance are thus all determined simultaneously.

Assume that a good service can be supplied by either of two alternative technologies. One is a general purpose technology, the other a special purpose technology. The special purpose technology requires greater investment in transaction specific durable assets and is more efficient for servicing steady-state demands. Contractual complications, however, arise when there is a need to adapt to disturbances.

Using k as a measure of transaction specific assets, transactions that use the general purpose technology are ones for which $k = 0$. If instead transactions use the special purpose technology, a $k > 0$ condition exists. Assets here are specialized to the particular needs of the parties. Productive values would therefore be sacrificed if transactions of this kind were to be prematurely terminated. A bilateral dependency condition applies to such transactions. Parties have an incentive to devise safeguards to protect investments for transactions of the latter kind. Let's denote the magnitude of any such safeguards. An $s = 0$ condition is one in which no safeguards are provided; a decision to provide safeguards is reflected by an $s > 0$ result.

Safeguards can take either of two forms. One would be to craft added supports into the contract, whereby penalties to deter breach are introduced, added in formation disclosure is provided, and specialized dispute settlement machinery (e.g., arbitration) is devised. This is the credible interim commitment option. A second be to take transactions out of markets and organize them under unified ownership within which hierarchy (to include fiat) is used to effect coordination.

Node A corresponds to the ideal transaction in law and economics: there is both an absence of dependency ($k = 0$) and such transactions benefit from the safeguard of competition. Node B presents contractual hazards, in that specialized investments are exposed ($k > 0$) for which there are no safeguards ($s = 0$).Such hazards will be recognized by farsighted players, who will price out the risk in the contract. Nodes C and D are nodes to which additional contractual support has been provided, either in the form of contractual safeguards (node C) or unified ownership (Node D).

Because of the added bureaucratic costs that accrue upon taking a transaction out of the market and organizing it internally, internal organization is usefully thought of as the organization form of last resort: try markets, try hybrids, and have recourse to the firm only when all else fails. Node D, the firm, thus comes in only as transactions have especially high degrees of asset specificity and as added uncertainty pose greater needs for cooperative adaptation. Also, as discussed in Section 5, the schema can be extended to include regulation and public bureaus. As heretofore remarked, the study of contract involves variation on a few key themes.

3.4. *Empirical Testing*

Some theories of economic organization make little effort to advance refutable implications. Among those that do, few believes that transaction cost economics are empirically tested. Simon evidently is remiss in empirical respects: empirical testing, 'the new institutional economics and related approaches of faith, or perhaps of piety' (Simon, 1991, p. 27).

Coase had registered similar concerns about the dearth of empirical work on contract and organization twenty years earlier (Coase, 1972), but that was before the operationalization of transaction cost economics had begun and predicted alignments were advanced. Empirical applications of transaction cost economics got under way in the US in the 1980s and have grown exponentially since: the number of published studies exceeds 400 and involves scientists in Europe, Japan, India, Mexico, South America, New Zealand, and the list goes on.

Although the empirical phenomena with which transaction cost economics is concerned are often of a simple, discrete structural kind — such as vertical integration (whether to make or buy), vertical market restrictions (when contracts re-quire nonstandard — and hitherto suspect — contractual supports), the differential efficacy to be expected of deregulation (as between natural monopoly industries within a country) and of privatization (of a common industry, such as telecommunications, between countries), when to use debt and equity, and so on — transaction cost economics does generate many refutable implications. It could have been otherwise, but the theory and evidence display a remarkable congruity (Masten, 1995, p. 11). Recent empirical surveys include Shelanski and PeterKlein (1995), Bruceons (1996), and Crocker and Masten (1996).

Not only has this research been broadly corroborative of the predictions of transaction cost economics, but the importance of risk aversion to commercial contracting has been placed in doubt. To be sure, transaction cost economics, like very thing else, will benefit from more and better empirical work. I have no hesitation, however, in declaring that transaction cost economics is an empirical success story. Joskow concurs: 'this empirical work is in much better shape than much of the empirical work in industrial organization generally' (1991, p. 81).

4. Supporting Conceptual Concepts

4.1. *From Property to Contract*

The economics of property rights hold that the central problem of economic organization is one of defining and enforcing property rights. Because the court ordering of contracts was assumed to be costless and efficacious, problems of contracting vanished.

Transaction cost economics proceeds differently. Especially in developed economies, where property rights can be assumed to be reasonably well defined and secure against expropriation by the state, the principal problem of organization is that of aligning transactions with governance structures so as to support a high performance result. This does not in the least dispute that property is important everywhere. Much of the analytical action, however, moves from property to contract as development progresses. As Farnsworth observes, 'ex-change of promises did not become important in practice until a relatively advanced level of economic development had been attained... Indeed, a general theory of contract would have been something of a luxury in a society concerned with the basic protection of life and property' (Farnsworth ,1990, p. 10). Scott concurs (1996, p. 57):

> In primitive societies... there would be a role for the principles of tort law, but not much of a role for contract principles. Cooperation and ex-change would be very immediate and short-term... With the Industrial Revolution, production becomes, by orders of magnitude, more complex and interdependent... Long-range planning and coordination require the ability to rely on long-term promises.

A greater need to examine contract, in the context of property rights, thus takes shape as development progresses. The study of economic organization moves to Level 3, taking Level 2 institutions as a constraint.

Transaction cost economics makes that move by studying contract laws (plural) rather than contract law (singular). This entails going beyond legal rules and legal centralism to include private ordering. Llewellyn's concept of contract as a framework, as opposed to legal rules, is pertinent (Llewellyn, 1931, pp. 736–737):

> ...the major importance of legal contract is to provide a framework for well-nigh every type of group organization and for well-nigh every type of passing or permanent relation between individuals and groups. — a framework highly adjustable, a framework which almost never accurately indicates real working relations but which affords a rough indication around which such relations vary, an occasional guide in cases of doubt, and a norm of ultimate appeal when the relations cease in fact to work.

Ultimate appeal is important, in that it delimits threat positions, but the main contractual action nevertheless takes place in the context of private ordering. Most disputes, including many that under current rules could be brought to a court, are resolved by avoidance, self-help, and the like (Galanter, 1981, p. 2). That is because in 'many instances the participants can devise more satisfactory solutions to their disputes than can professionals constrained to apply general rules on the basis of limited knowledge of the dispute' (Galanter, 1981, p. 4). The assumption that 'the courts will get it right' is a convenient but overweening simplification (Tullock, 1996, p. 5). The study of economic organization needs to make provisions for governance in all of its forms.

Such a project is facilitated by moving beyond the convenient idea of a single, all-purpose law of contract to consider contract laws plural (Summers, 1969). Macneil's distinctions between classical, neo-classical, and relational contract law (Macneil, 1974, 1978) are pertinent. The first of these refers to the ideal transaction in law and economics, according to which the identity of the parties is irrelevant (asset specificity is zero) and a legal rules approach prevails. What he refers to classical contract law moves from spot market to long-term contracting in which continuity is valued and is closer in spirit to Llewellyn's concept to 'contract as framework.'

Although the third type of contract law to which Macneil refers — relational contracting — has attracted wide support and has considerable intuitive appeal, Macneil concedes that 'no such system as yet exists in American contract law' (Macneil, 1978, p. 889). In as much as the object is to support more efficacious modes of contracting/organization, rather than devise an ever more elastic form of contract law, the apparent failure of relational contracting is not necessarily to be regret-ted. As Macneil goes on to observe, 'the spin-off of many subject areas from the classical, and later the neo-classical, contract law system, e.g., much on corporate law and collective bargaining' (Macneil, 1978, p. 885) can and has afforded relief from the incapacity of contract law (narrowly conceived) to respond to the felt needs. Corporate law and collective bargaining can thus be regarded as extensions upon the contractual approach (broadly conceived) to deal with governance more broadly. If contract really is the seminal and classical subject of American legal education (Rubin, 1996), we ought to be able to build out from that foundation.

Transaction cost economics advances the argument that each generic mode of governance is supported by a distinctive form of contract law and holds that the implicit law of hierarchy is that of forbearance. Thus, whereas courts routinely grant standing to firms should there be disputes over prices, the damages to be ascribed to delays, failures of quality, and the like, courts will refuse to hear disputes between one internal division and another over identical technical issues. The firm becomes its own court of ultimate appeal in this way, which explains why markets and hierarchies differ significantly in dispute settlement (fiat) respects.

4.2. *Far-sighted Contracting*

Although transaction cost economics maintains that all complex contracts are unavoidably incomplete by reason of bounded rationality, such incompleteness should not be confused with myopia. On the contrary, transaction cost economics maintains that intendedly rational economic agents are far-sighted — in that they will look ahead, perceive hazards, and fold these back into the contractual calculus. As Hennipman has put it, 'the general characteristic of economic efficacy is seen to lie in the fact that the decisions are taken on the basis of [informed] insight into the economic phenomena and their interrelationships'(Hennipman, 1995, p. 29). Schultz's reflection on the importance of his training in economics is pertinent: 'my training in economics has had a major influence on the way I think about public policy tasks, even when they have no particular relationship to economics. Our discipline makes one think ahead, ask about indirect consequences, take note of variables that may not be directly under consideration' (Schultz ,1995, p. 1). That is an exercise in far-sighted contracting — according to which incomplete contracts are examined in their entirety.

The contrast between Machiavelli's advice to his Prince to breach contracts with impunity and the concept of credible commitment out of which transaction cost economics works illustrates the differences. Whereas the former is my concept of contract — get them before they get us — the latter is a far-sighted construction. Rather than reply to opportunism in kind, the wise prince is advised to give and receive credible commitments. Order is thereby realized, potential conflict is mitigated, and expected mutual gain results.

4.3. *Efficiency/Remediableness*

The analytical ease of working out of a hypothetical set-up (zero dead weight losses, zero transaction costs, benign governance) notwithstanding, the pressing need, always and everywhere, is to 'study the world of positive transaction costs' (Coase, 1992, p. 717). Thus, although contemplation (Coase, 1964, p. 195):

> ...of an optimal system may provide techniques of analysis that would otherwise have been missed,... in general its influence has been pernicious. It has directed economists' attention away from the main question, which is how alternative arrangements will actually work in practice. It has led economists to derive conclusions for economic policy from a study of an abstract of a market situation. It is no accident that in the literature... we find a category 'market failure' but no category 'government failure.' Until we realize that we are choosing between social arrange-ment which are all more or less failures, we are not likely to make much headway.

Nirvana economics (Demsetz, 1969) carries a similar message.

As against a hypothetical ideal, transaction cost economics advances the remediableness criterion, according to which an extant mode of organization for which no superior feasible alternative can be described and implemented with expected net gains is presumed to be efficient. Note with respect to this criterion that, except when comparisons are made between de novo alternatives, remediableness makes reference to an extant alternative, which, in effect, is privileged in relation to rival alternatives that arrive later. This has major ramifications for reinterpreting the purported inefficiencies that accrue to 'path dependency.' Relatedly, even if a proposed alternative is superior to an extant alternative on a side-by-side comparison, there is a further need to examine implementation obstacles. If it is very costly to overcome pre-existing conditions, of either economic or political kinds, then implementation with net gains may not be possible (Hennipman, 1995, p. 37). In effect, the remediableness criterion treats the efficiency of the extant mode as a rebuttable presumption (Williamson, 1996, Chapter 8).

The readiness with which economists ascribe welfare gains to proposed re-forms is thereby questioned. As against the usual practice of 'claiming' that al-locative efficiency will be enhanced 'upon supplanting price supports with lump-sum subsidies and taxes,' remediableness in addition requires that (1) the requisite information upon which to base the lump-sum taxes be displayed, (2) the pay-out mechanisms be described, and (3) political resistance be factored in if the political purposes served by ongoing price supports cannot be replicated. This does not deny that economic reforms that ignore practicalities and politics can be informative; but they can also be misleading. Economics rarely trumps but operates in the service of politics (Stigler, 1992).

4.4 *Selective Intervention*

Why cannot a large firm do everything that a collection of small firms can and more? It is widely believed, for example, that large, established firms have advantages over smaller potential entrants because (Lewis, 1983, p. 1092):

> ...the leader can at least use [inputs] exactly as the entrant would have..., and earn the same profit as the entrant. But typically, the leader can improve on this by coordinating production from his new and existing inputs. Hence the same inputs will be valued more by the dominant firm.

A similar argument can be applied to vertical integration with the following result: if large firms can, in all respects, do as well as a collection of smaller firms, through replication, and can sometimes do better, through selective intervention, then large firms ought to grow without limit.

Working this through is tedious and is reported elsewhere (Williamson, 1985, Chapter 6). The core arguments are these: (1) internal organization (the large firm) cannot replicate small firms (market procurement) in incentive intensity respects, and (2) the agreement to always intervene but only for good cause (selective intervention) is fatuous because it is unenforceable. The upshot is that the hypothetical advantages of combining replication with selective intervention cannot be realized, on which account the move from market to hierarchy (and the reverse) is always attended with a trade-off between the benefits of added coordination/cooperation on the one hand and the costs of added bureaucracy on the other. Which way that trade-off goes depends on the attributes of transactions in relation to the costs and competencies of alternative modes of governance. This is an exercise in discrete structural analysis, whereby alternative modes of organization are described as syndromes of related attributes — distinctive strengths and weaknesses — that cannot be replicated.

5. Applications and Extensions

5.1. *Successive Developments*

From its origins in the archetypal problem of vertical integration, transaction cost economics has successively examined the organization of labor (in teams and peer groups and unions), dominant firms and the oligopoly problem, technical and organizational innovation, the organization of work, the modern corporation (of multidivisional, conglomerate, multinational, and Japanese kinds), problems of contracting for natural monopoly (especially in relation to the efficacy of franchise bidding), various nonstandard forms of contracting in which issues of credibility are posed (to include quality assurance, franchising, customer and territorial restrictions, reciprocity and exchange relations, take-or-pay purchase agreements, two part pricing schemes, and the like), corporate governance and corporate finance, the use and limits of reputation effect mechanisms and corporate culture, and the ramifications of all of the above for public policy toward business (virtually all of antitrust and much of regulation). Still more recent applications combine both parts of the New Institutional Economics — the institutions of governance and the institutional environment — to examine the efficacy of privatization and reform in relation to credible commitments. As Levy and Spiller put it, examining privatization 'through the lens of transaction cost economics — with its microeconomical perspective, its emphasis on discriminating alignment and remediableness, and its view of regulation as a contracting problem — provides an understanding of the determinants of performance of privatized utilities in different political and social circumstances' (1994, p. 202). Much more work of this kind is in progress and more is in prospect. Applications to public bureaus and strategic management are sketched here.

(a) Public bureaus

The public bureau has had a mixed reputation within economics. At the one extreme is the older (now discredited) public finance tradition, where the public bureau (and the government to which it reported) was treated as an 'omnipotent, omniscient, and benevolent' actor (Dixit, 1996, p. 8). Condemnation from the other extreme comes from the property rights view that the public bureau is a haven for inefficiency, relief from which will be realized only if property rights are correctly assigned and the activity in question privatized.

Transaction cost economics views the public bureau instrumentally, as an alternative mode of governance that is well-suited for some purposes, poorly suited for others. For which transactions is the public bureau well-suited and why? Where does the public bureau fit into the overall scheme of economic organization? Several moves are needed to answer these questions, the first of which is to supplant the idea of the public bureau as a benign, technical entity (in which production costs are featured) with the concept of the public bureau as a flawed, organizational entity (in which transaction costs are featured). Just as the study of business organization benefited from recognizing 'the inadequacy of the neo-classical view of the firm and [developing] richer paradigms and models based on the concepts of various kinds of transaction costs..., [so does] policy analysis... stand to benefit from... opening up the black box and examining the actual working of the mechanism inside' (Dixit,1996, p. 9).

The second move is to entertain the possibility that transactions to which public sector governance is assigned pose added complications to which the attributes of the public bureau afford a (comparatively) efficacious response. The attributes that distinguish public sector transactions thus need to be identified and explicated.

Third, the discrete structural attributes that define and distinguish the public bureau and are responsible for its powers and limitations need to be identified and explicated. Relatedly, the puzzle of why a private firm is unable to replicate the public bureau needs to be addressed.

Some of the pertinent issues have been addressed in conjunction with regulation (Williamson, 1976, Goldberg, 1976, and Priest, 1993). Others arise in relation to redistribution (Krueger, 1990, Williamson, 1996, Chapter 8). And still others arise for transactions where the integrity of the state is at risk (Williamson,1997). Transactions of the last kind are sometimes described as 'sovereign,' of which the foreign affairs transaction is an example. Such transactions are in especially great need of probity, for which very low-powered incentives and social conditioning to the mission of the bureau are responsive governance attributes. Because private bureaus are unable to replicate the attributes of public bureaus in these respects,'2 the putative gains of privatization would, for such transactions, come at a great cost.

It bears repeating that there is no one, all-purpose, superior form of organization. Transactions vary in their attributes; governance structures vary in costs and competencies; efficient alignment is where the predictive action resides. The unchanging lesson of transaction cost economics for all feasible forms of organization, of which the public bureau is one, is this: a place needs to be made for each generic form, but each form needs to be kept in its place.

Note that the common practice of condemning public bureaus because they have lower-powered incentives, more rules and regulations, and greater job security than are associated with a counterpart private bureau completely misses the point. Those features have been deliberately crafted into the public bureau, thereby giving it the desired governance result. The appropriate concern is not that public bureaus have these properties but that public bureaus will overreach — in that they will be used to govern both those transactions for which they are well-suited and those for which they are poorly suited. Vigilance in this latter respect is continuously needed — lest those with planning predilections will over-prescribe use of the public bureau. As shown in Figure 3, the public bureau is usefully thought of as the organization form of very last resort: try markets, try hybrids, try firms, try regulation, and resort to public bureaus only when all else fails (comparatively).

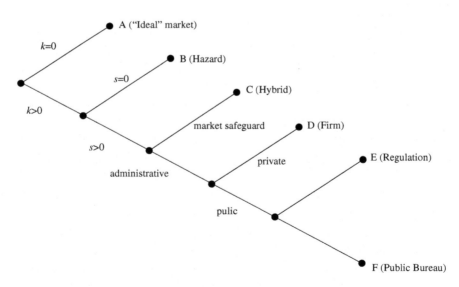

Figure 3. Simple contracting scheme extended

(b) Strategic management

'The fundamental question in the field of strategic management is how firms achieve and sustain competitive advantage' (Teece, Pisano, and Shuen (1996)). That is an ambitious undertaking and a huge literature — on competitive forces, strategic conflict, the resource-based perspective, and dynamic capabilities — has taken shape over the past decade.

Much of this literature is preoccupied with *ex post* rationalizations of 'successes' (the object being to uncover what explains 'excellence'). Although this can be informative, efforts to predict success are rarely made. Empirical work on success management rarely gets beyond cases and anecdotes.

Transactions cost economics views strategic ploys and positioning as of second order of importance. Clever gambits will rarely save a firm in which serious governance misalignments are observed (Williamson, 1996, chapter 12). Because, however, the economizing/discriminating alignment hypothesis operates at the generic level, it does not engage the strategic concerns of individual firms. Can transaction cost economics be brought into greater contact with strategic management issues? Applications to the resource-based perspective are sketched here.

According to the resource-based perspective, firms are described by their 'resources /capabilities/endowments' and 'at least in the short run, firms are to some degree stuck with what they have and may have to live without what they lack' (Teece, Pisano, and Shuen 1996, p. 6). But how are these resource capabilities described? What strategic lessons accrue?

The strategic management literature responds to the first of these by developing a long list of 'isolating mechanisms' — which, predominantly, are barriers to imitation (Mahoney, and Pandian1992, pp. 371–373). That is an important step, but the long list needs to be prioritized and its key features uncovered and explicated. The crucial question put by Mahoney and Pandianis (1992, p. 371), 'What is the generalizable insight?'. Their response is that 'isolating mechanisms exist because of asset specificity and bounded rationality.' In the language of strategic management, these two transaction cost concepts translate into 'uniqueness and causal ambiguity,' respectively (Mahoney and Pandian,1992, p. 373).

A key move, if transaction cost economics is to more fully engage strategy, is to push beyond the generic level at which it now operates and to consider paroculars. Thus rather than ask the question 'What is the best generic mode (market, hybrid, firm, or bureau) to organize X?,' which is the traditional transaction cost query, the question to be put instead is 'How should firm A — which has preexisting strengths and weaknesses (core competencies and disabilities) — organize X?'

Not only does this latter question focus explicitly on firm A, but it requires that we describe both the strengths (competencies) and weaknesses (disabilities) of firm A. This last is typically neglected in the usual inventory of firm attributes.

Further, because transaction cost economics is relentlessly comparative and because a strategy is being devised in relation to a market in which current and potential competition need to be taken into account, transaction cost economics counsels that these assessments be done comparatively. How does firm A compare with extant and potential rivals with reference to the market niche (X) in question?

Note, moreover, as shown in Table 1, that niches other than X can be considered. What I describe in the table as 'resource-based perspective: level II' exam rose a variety of niches — to be assessed both in relation to rivals and between one another. The question therefore becomes 'How should firm A, with its pre-existing strengths and weaknesses, proceed with respect to market niches described by (X, X2; Y,Y3; }'? Repositioning the firm to

Table 1. Transaction cost economics and strategy

---

generic level

How do alternate generic modes (markets, hybrids, firms, bureaus) compare for purposes of organizing transaction X?

resource-based: level I

How should firm A, with its pre-existing strengths and weaknesses (core competencies and disabilities), organize transaction X?

resource-based: level II

How should firm A, with its pre-existing strength and weaknessnes, proceed with respect to market niches described by (X_1, X_2, Y_3, Z)?

resource-based: level II

How should firm A, with its pre-existing strength and weaknessnes, reposition for the future in relation to the strategic situation (actual and potential rivalry; actual and potential market niches) of wich it is a part or to which it can relate?

---

build up core competencies and/or relieve disabilities is what level III contemplates. The question at this level is 'How should firm A, with its preexisting strengths and weaknesses, reposition for the future in relation to the strategic situation (actual and potential rivalry; actual and potential market niches) of which it is a part or to which it can relate'?

Each of the moves shown in Table 1 pushes transaction cost economics to orient more fully to the needs of strategic management. Level III analysis is especially ambitious and may often be implemented piecemeal rather than as a comprehensive plan (in which mergers and acquisitions, investments, contracting, finance, marketing, etc. are all considered simultaneously). Be that as it may, transaction cost economics has an important role to play in taking an inventory of a firm's assets (and those of its rivals) and in assessing the hazards associated with alternative planning scenarios.

5.2. *Future Challenges*

(a) Fully-formal analysis

A continuing challenge to transaction cost economics is to move beyond semiformal analysis of a reduced-form kind to do fully-formal analysis — in the spirit of the work by Grossman and Hart (1986), but to place greater emphasis on plausible constructions. As hitherto remarked, the leading formal models of an incomplete contracting kind work out of implausible assumptions (Kreps, 1996) and/or have logical lapses (Maskin and Tirole, 1997). Be that as it may, the formal modeling of incomplete contracts is a difficult undertaking for which those who have pioneered the formal study of incomplete contracts deserve enormous credit.

(b) Real-time responsiveness

Aoki's (1990) distinction between H-form (Western hierarchy) and J-form (Japanese hierarchy) invites attention to a third form of organization, the T-form, where T denotes temporary or transitional or, especially, timely. This last, timeliness, plays a huge role in the success and failure of firms that are operating in newly developing markets where technology and rivalry are undergoing rapid change. Chance — being in the right place at the right time — is important in these circumstances, but not to the exclusion of foresight. Firms that are flexibly positioned and responsive have the edge. Best efforts notwithstanding, large, mature and diffusely owned firms are at a disadvantage to smaller, younger and more entrepreneurial (concentrated ownership) firms in these respects (Williamson, 1975, pp. 196–207).

Also, what may be thought of as disequilibrium forms of organization can be important in real-time responsiveness respects. Joint ventures and alliances should sometimes be thought of as T-forms of organization that permit the parties to remain players in a fast-moving environment. Each party being unable, by itself, to assemble and deploy the requisite resources in a timely way, the requisite re-sources are instead assembled by pooling. Thus construed, both successful and unsuccessful joint ventures will commonly be terminated when contracts expire. Successful joint ventures will be terminated because the combined effort has permuted each to remain viable and learn enough and/or buy time to go alone. Unsuccessful joint ventures will be terminated because the opportunity to participate will have passed them by.

Our understanding of T-forms of organization is not good but is steadily improving (Nelson and Winter, 1982, Dose, 1988, Teece, 1992, Barnett and Carroll, 1993, and Teece, Rumelt, Dosi, and Winter, 1993) — which is good news to the study of strategy.

(c) Intractable transactions

Intractable transactions are complex transactions for which there are no good solutions. Upon adopting a comparative orientation, however, the absence of good solutions is neither here nor there. It suffices that there are better and worse solutions. Choice of the best from the feasible lot, all of which are flawed, is a significant accomplishment.

What I refer to as intractable transactions are transactions for which one of the parties enjoys a significant strategic information advantage. They are also transactions which often, but not always, are dimensionally complex (hard to describe). Third, at least for several of the transactions referred to here, intractable transactions are ones for which it is relatively easy to recover costs by passing them through (in a cost-plus or related way) or otherwise shedding legal responsibility (possibly through bankruptcy).

The governance of natural monopoly is one such transaction (Williamson,1976, Goldberg, 1976). Regulatory transactions of a health and safety kind are also troublesome — especially transactions where consumers or workers are poorly informed, hazards have long-latency, and reputation effects are weak (Thalidomide and PCBs and gypsum are candidates).

Defense procurement often poses similar problems. One option is for the government to produce to its own needs. However, with the exception of very special circumstances (the 'Manhattan Project' in World War II), that option is rare. The incentive deficits of the government in managing production (as against early-stage research) are simply overwhelming. And phasing out a government facility (e.g., an arsenal) is a tortured political exercise.

Although outside procurement yields comparative advantages, specialized weapons procurement is often beset by problems akin to natural monopoly: competition among large numbers of qualified suppliers is impossible. The specialized investments in question and associated learning by doing (human asset specificity) quickly convert these relations into ones of bilateral dependency. Further, the contracting officers who manage these contracts often develop a sympathetic relation with the defense contractor. Moreover, cost-plus contracting (de facto if not de jure) often occurs as changes are made (and renegotiated) and because auditing problems are severe. A quasi-regulatory relation develops; something akin to capture often results.

Many health care transactions also have the *indicia* of an intractable transaction — in that such transactions (1) are embedded in a contractual relation in which physicians enjoy a huge information advantage over patients (Arrow (1963)), (2) are complex, and (3) can be subverted by pass-through.

Regarding this last, Robinson describes the relation between physicians and hospitals in the period from 1920 through 1980 as being that of a 'doctor's workshop' in which effective 'control of the community hospital rested with physicians' (Robinson, 1996, p. 5). That worked for a long time but contained the seeds of its own demise: 'The clinical autonomy and de facto budgetary control exerted byte procedure-oriented physicians who dominated the medical staffs produced a feeding frenzy [in the United States] when the Medicare and Medicaid programs loosened the pecuniary limits of what could be done and at what price' (Robinson,1996, p. 6). Given the resulting ease of pass-through, the cost of medical care spiraled. Attempting to craft a superior governance structure response to this condition explains much of what is going on in health care organization presently.

The nonprofit mode of organization is yet another form that is often complex, is beset by information asymmetries, and is sometimes subverted by pass-through. Many of the issues have been examined by Hangman (1980), James (1987), and Rose-Ackerman (1996). A thorough transaction cost economics treatment of the nonprofit form has yet to be attempted — in part because that is a difficult undertaking.

(d) Informal organization

The study of 'informal organization' poses a continuing challenge to students of organization. Thus, although Barnard (1938) made early and prominent reference to the importance of informal organization and discussed some of the mechanisms through which it worked, our understanding of informal organization is still primitive (Kreps, 1990, Simon, 1991) avers that considerations of identity and docility are important, but these arguments need to be worked out more fully. The economics of atmosphere (Williamson, 1996, pp. 270–272) is similarly underdeveloped.

6. Concluding Remarks

The current level of interest in the New Institutional Economics and the economics of organization represents a sea of change. As of 1970, institutional economics had been relegated to the field of economic thought and, except at the level of nation-states (comparative economic systems), the study of comparative economic organization was something for other social scientists — sociologists or political scientists or organization theorists. The 1974 conference on 'The Economics of Internal Organization' helped to secure a place for organization on the economics research agenda from which it has continued to grow. Moreover, the revival of interest in institutional economics has been such that R.C.O. Matthews, is his 1986 presidential address to the Royal Economic Society, declared that the New Institutional Economics had become 'one of the liveliest areas in our discipline' (1986, p. 903). Transaction cost economics relates to both of these projects. As herein described, transaction cost economics (1) is an interdisciplinary joiner of law, economics, and organization in which economics is the first among equals, (2) is a comparative institutional exercise in which economizing is the main case and the action resides in the details of transactions and governance, (3) generates numerous refutable implications in relation to which the data are broadly corroborative, and (4) has many public policy ramifications. Much of transaction cost economics can be digested by orthodoxy, and this has been happening. New problems and challenges appear, however, to be unending. A healthy tension between transaction costs economics and each of the parts on which it stands — law, economics, and organization — can be safely projected into the future (Kreps, 1996; Williamson, 1993a, 1993b, 1996b).

References

Alchian, Armen, and Harold Demsetz. 1972. "Production, Information Costs, and Economic Organization." *American Economic Review*, 62, pp. 777–795.

Aoki, Masahiko. 1990. "Toward an Economic Model of the Japanese Firm." *Journal of Economic Literature*, 28, pp. 1–27.

Arrow, Kenneth J. 1963. "Uncertainty and the Welfare Economics of Medical Care." *American Economic Review*, 53, pp. 941–973.

Arrow, Kenneth J. 1969. "The Organization of Economic Activity: Issues Pertinent to the Choice of Market Versus Nonmarket Allocation,." In *The Analysis and Evaluation of Public Expenditure: The PPB System.* 1, pp. 59–73. Washington, DC: US Government Printing Office.

Arrow, Kenneth J. 1987. "Reflections on the Essays." In *Arrow and the Foundations of the Theory of Economic Policy*, ed. George Feiwel, pp. 727–734. New York: New York University Press.

Arrow, Kenneth J. 1989. "Competing Technologies, Increasing Returns, and Lock-in by Historical Events." *Economic Journal*, 99, pp. 116–131.

Arrow, Kenneth J., and F. Hahn. General competitive analysis [M]. North-Holland, 1971.

Arthur, Brian. 1989. "Competing Technologies, Increasing Returns, and Lock-in by Historical Events." *Economic Journal*, 99 (March): 116–131.

Bain, Joe. 1968. *Industrial Organization.* New York: Wiley.

Baker, George, Robert Gibbons, and Kevin Murphy. 1997. "Implicit Contracts and the Theory of the Firm." unpublished manuscript.

Barnard, Chester. 1938. *The Functions of the Executive.* Cambridge, MA: Harvard University Press.

Barnett, W. and G. Carroll. 1993, "How Institutional Constraints Affected the Organization of the Early American Telephone Industry." *Journal of Law, Economics, and Organization*, 9, pp. 98–126.

Ben-Ner, Avner, and Theresa Van Hoomissen. 1991. "Nonprofit Organizations in the Mixed Economy." *Annals of Public and Cooperative Economics*, 62, pp. 519–550.

Bromley, Daniel. 1989. *Economic Interest and Institutions*. New York: Basil Blackwell.

Buchanan, James. 1975. "A Contractarian Paradigm for Applying Economic Theory." *American Economic Review*, 65, pp. 225–230. See also Claude Menard 996@beta/een/CLS_kap/GRP_201/JOB_008/DIV_198-3P53 Transaction Cost Economics 53.

Chandler, Alfred D. Jr. 1962. *Strategy and Structure*. Cambridge, MA: MIT Press.

Coase, Ronald H.1937. "The Nature of the Firm." *Economica, N.S.*, 4, pp. 386–405. (Reprinted in G.J. Stigler and K.E. Boulding eds., *Readings in Price Theory*, Homewood, IL, Richard D. Irwin).

Coase, Ronald H. 1959. "The Federal Communications Commission." *Journal of Law and Economics*, 2, pp. 1–40.

Coase, Ronald H. 1960. "The Problem of Social Cost." *Journal of Law and Economics*, 3, pp. 1–44.

Coase, Ronald H. 1964. "The Regulated Industries: Discussion." *American Economic Review*, 54, pp. 194–197.

Coase, Ronald H. 1972. "Industrial Organization: A Proposal for Research." In: *Policy Issues and Research Opportunities in Industrial Organization*, ed. V.R. Fuchs, pp. 59–73. New York: National Bureau of Economic Research.

Coase, Ronald H. 1978. "Economics and Contiguous Disciplines." *Journal of Legal Studies*, 7, pp. 201–211.

Coase, Ronald H. 1984. "The New Institutional Economics." *Journal of Institutional and Theoretical Economics*, 140, pp. 229–231.

Coase, Ronald H. 1992. "The Institutional Structure of Production." *American Economic Review*, 82, pp. 713–719.

Commons, John, R. 1932. "The Problem of Correlating Law, Economics and Ethics." *Wisconsin Law Review*, 8, pp. 3–26.

Cosmides, Leda, and John Tooby. 1996. "Are Humans Good Intuitive Statisticians After All?." *Cognition*, 58, pp. 1–73.

Crocker, Keith, and Scott Masten.1996, "Regulation and Administered Contracts Revisited: Lessons from Transaction Cost Economics for Public Utility Regulation." *Journal of Regulatory Economics*, 8, pp. 5–39.

Cyert, Richard, and James March. 1963. *A Behavioral Theory of the Firm*. Englewood Cliffs, NJ: Prentice-Hall.

David, Paul.1985. 'Clio in the Economics of QWERTY." *American Economic Review*, 75, pp. 332–337.

Davis, Lance, and Douglass North. 1971. *Institutional Change and American Economic Growth.* Cambridge: Cambridge University Press.

Debreu, Gerard. 1959. *Theory of Value.* New York: John Wiley and Sons.

Demsetz, Harold. 1967. "Toward a Theory of Property Rights." *American Economic Review,* 57, pp. 347–359.

Demsetz, Harold. 1969. "Information and Efficiency: Another Viewpoint." *Journal of Law and Economics,* 12, pp. 1–22.

Dixit, Avinash. 1996. *The Making of Economic Policy: A Transaction Cost Politics Perspective.* Cambridge: MIT Press.

Dosi, Giovanni. 1988. "Sources, Procedures, and Microeconomic Effects of Innovation." *Journal of Economic Literature,* 26, pp. 1120–1171.

Elster, Jon. 1994. "Arguing and Bargaining in Two Constituent Assemblies." unpublished manuscript.

Farnsworth, E. Allan. 1990. *Farnsworth on Contracts.* Vol. 1, Boston: Little-Brown.

Fischer, Stanley. 1977. "Long-term Contracting, Sticky Prices, and Monetary Policy: Comment." *Journal of Monetary Economics,* 3, pp. 317–324.

Fogel, Robert William and Stanley L. Engerman. 1971. *The Reinterpretation of American Economic History.* New York: Harper and Row. @beta/een/CLS_kap/GRP_201/JOB_008/DIV_198-3P54

O.E. WILLIAMSON, Fogel, Robert William, and Stanley L. Engerman, 1974, *Time on the Cross: The Economics of American Negro Slavery,* Boston: Little-Brown.

Fogel, Robert William, and Stanley L. Engerman. 1992. *Without Consent or Contract: The Rise and Fall of American Slavery.* New York: Norton.

Furubotn, Eirik, and Rudolf Richter. 1991. "The New Institutional Economics: An Assessment." In: *The New Institutional Economics,* eds., E. Furubotn and R. Richter,, pp. 1–32.College Station, TX: Texas A&M University Press.

Galanter, Marc. 1981. "Justice in Many Rooms: Courts, Private Ordering, and Indigenous Law." *Journal of Legal Pluralism,* 19, pp. 1–47.

Georgescu-Roegen, N. 1971. *The Entropy Law and Economic Process.* Cambridge, MA: Harvard University Press.

Goldberg, Victor. 1976. "Regulation and Administered Contracts." *Bell Journal of Economics,* 7, pp. 426–452.

Granovetter, Mark. 1985. "Economic Action and Social Structure: The Problem of Embeddedness." *American Journal of Sociology,* 91, pp. 481–501.

Grossman, Sanford, and Oliver Hart. 1986. "The Costs and Benefits of Ownership: A Theory of Vertical and Leteral Integration." *Journal of Political Economy,* 94, pp. 691–719.

Hannan, Michael T., and John Freeman. 1977. "The Population Ecology of Organizations." *American Journal of Sociology*, 82, pp. 929–964.

Hansmann, Henry. 1980. "The Role of Nonprofit Enterprise." *Yale Law Journal*, 89, pp. 835–901.

Hart, Oliver. 1995. *Firms, Contracts, and Financial Structure*. New York: Oxford University Press.

Hayek, Friedrich. 1945. "The Use of Knowledge in Society." *American Economic Review*, 35, pp. 519–530.

Henisz, Witold. 1996. "A Case Study of the Institutions and Governance of Economic Reform: New Zealand's State Owned Enterprises." unpublished manuscript.

Hennipman, Pieter. 1995. *Welfare Economics and the Theory of Economic Policy*, Brookfield, VT: Edward Elgar.

Holmstrom, Bengt. 1979. "Moral Hazard and Observability." *Bell Journal of Economics*, 10, pp. 74–91.

Holmstrom, Bengt. 1996. The Firm as a Subeconomy. -unpublished manuscript.

Holmstrom, Bengt, and Paul Milgrom. 1991. "Multi-task Principal-Agent Analysis." *Journal of Law, Economics, and Organization*, 7, pp. 24–52.

Huntington, Samuel. P. 1996. *The Clash of Civilizations and the Remaking of World Order*, New York: Simon and Schuster.

Hurst, J.W. 1964. *Law and Economic Growth: The Legal History of the Lumber Industry in Wisconsin, 1836–1915*, Madison: University of Wisconsin Press.

James, Estelle. 1987. "The Nonprofit Sector in Comparative Perspective." In: *The Nonprofit Sector*, ed., Walter Powell, pp. 397–415. New Haven: Yale University Press.

Joskow, Paul. 1991. "The Role of Transaction Cost Economics in Antitrust and Public Utility Regulatory Policies." *Journal of Law, Economics, and Organization*, 7, pp. 53–83.

Klein, Benjamin, R.A. Crawford, and A.A. Alchian. 1978. "Vertical Integration, Appropriable Rents, and the Competitive Contracting Process." *Journal of Law and Economics*, 21, pp. 297–326.

Kreps, David. 1990. "Corporate Culture and Economic Theory", In: *Perspectives on Positive Political Economy*, eds., James Alt and Kenneth Shepsle, pp. 90–143. Cambridge: Cambridge University Press. @beta/een/CLS_kap/GRP_201/JOB_008/DIV_198-3P55 Transaction Cost Economics 55.

Kreps, David. 1996. "Markets and Hierarchies and Mathematical Economic Theory." *Industrial and Corporate Change*, 5, pp. 561–596.

Kuhn, Thomas S. 1970. *The Structure of Scientific Revolutions*, 2nd edn., Chicago: University of Chicago Press.

Levy, Brian, and Pablo Spiller. 1994. "The Institutional Foundations of Regulatory Commitment." *Journal of Law, Economics, and Organization*, 10, pp. 201–246.

Lewis, Tracy. 1983. "Preemption, Divestiture, and Forward Contracting in a Market Dominated by a Single Firm." *American Economic Review*, 73, pp. 1092–1101.

Llewellyn, Karl N. 1931. "What Price Contract? An Essay in Perspective." *Yale Law Journal*, 40, pp. 704–751.

Lyons, Bruce. 1996. "Empirical Relevance of Efficient Contract Theory: Inter-firm Contracts." *Oxford Review of Economic Policy*, 12, pp. 27–52.

Macneil, Ian R. 1974. "The Many Futures of Contracts." *Southern California Law Review*, 47, pp. 691–816.

Macneil, Ian R. 1978. "Contracts, Adjustments of Long-term Economic Relations Under Classical, Neo-classical, and Relational Contract Law." *Northwestern University Law Review*, 72, pp. 854–906.

Mahoney, Joseph, and Rajendran Pandian. 1992. "The Resource-based view within the Conversation of Strategic Management." *Strategic Management Journal*, 13, pp. 363–380.

March, James G., and Herbert A. Simon. 1958. *Organizations*. New York: John Wiley and Sons.

Maskin, Eric, and Jean Tirole. 1997. "Unforeseen Contingencies, Property Rights, and Incomplete Contracts." Unpublished manuscript.

Masten, Scott. 1995. "Introduction to Vol. II." In: *Transaction Cost Economics*, eds., Oliver Williamson and Scott Masten, Brookfield, VT: Edward Elgar.

Matthews, R.C.O. 1986. "The Economics of Institutions and the Sources of Economic Growth." *Economic Journal*, 96, pp. 903–918.

Michels, Robert. 1966. *Political Parties*. Glencoe, IL: Free Press.

Moe, Terry. 1984. "The New Economics of Organization." *American Journal of Political Science*, 28, pp. 739–777.

Moe, Terry. 1990. "The Politics of Structural Choice: Toward a Theory of Public Bureaucracy." In: *Organization Theory*, ed., Oliver Williamson, pp. 116–153. New York: Oxford University Press.

Nee, Victor. 1997. "Embeddedness and Beyond." In: *The New Institutionalism in Sociology*, eds., Mary Brinton and Victor Nee, New York: Russell Sage.

Nelson, Richard, and Sidney Winter. 1982. *An Evolutionary Theory of Economic Change*. Cambridge, MA: Harvard University Press.

Nickerson, Jackson A. 1997. "Toward and Economizing Theory of Strategy: The Choice of Strategic Position, Assets, and Organizational Form." University of California, Berkeley, unpublished Ph.D. dissertation.

North, Douglass. 1981. *Structure and Change in Economic History*. New York: Norton.

North, Douglass. 1984. "Transaction Costs, Institutions, and Economic History." *Journal of Institutional and Theoretical Economics*, 140, pp. 7–17.

North, Douglass. 1990. "A Transaction Cost Theory of Politics." *Journal of Theoretical Politics*, 2, pp. 355–367.

North, Douglass. 1991. "Institutions." *Journal of Economic Perspectives*, 5, pp. 97–112.

North, Douglass. 1994. "Economic Performance Through Time." *American Economic Review*, 84, pp. 357–368. @beta/een/CLS_kap/GRP_201/JOB_008/ DIV_198-3P5656 O.E. WILLIAMSON

North, Douglass. and Barry Weingast. 1989. "Constitutions and Commitment: The Evolution of Institutions Governing Public Choice in 17th Century England." *Journal of Economic History*, 49, pp. 803–832.

Olson, Mancur. 1996. "Big Bills Left on the Sidewalk: Why Some Nations Are Rich, and Others Are Poor." *Journal of Economic Perspectives*, 10, pp. 3–24.

Priest, George. 1993. "The Origins of Utility Regulation and the "Theories of Regulation" Debate." *Journal of Law and Economics*, 36, pp. 289–323.

Putnam, Robert. D, Robert Leonardi, and Rafaella Y. Nanetti. 1993. *Making Democracy Work: Civic Traditions in Modern Italy*, Princeton, NJ: Princeton University Press.

Robinson, James. 1996. "Physician-Hospital Integration and the Economic Theory of the Firm." unpublished manuscript, School of Public Health, University of California, Berkeley.

Rose-Ackerman, Susan. 1996. "Altruism, Nonprofits, and Economic Theory." *Journal of Economic Literature*, 34, pp. 701–728.

Rosenberg, Nathan, and L.E. Birdzell. 1986. *How the West Grew Rich: The Transformation of the Industrial World*, New York: Basic Books.

Rubin, Edward. 1996. "The Phenomenology of Contract." *Journal of Institutional and Theoretical Economics*, 152, pp. 123–139.

Samuels, Warren J. 1988. *Institutional Economics* Vol. 3, Aldershot: Edward Elgar.

Schlegel, John Henry. 1979. "American Legal Realism and Empirical Science: From The Yale Experience." *Buffalo Law Review*, 29, pp. 195–323.

Schultz, George. 1995. "Economics in Action." *American Economic Review*, 85, pp. 1–8.

Scott, Kenneth. 1996. "The Evolving Roles of Contract Law." *Journal of Institutional and Theoretical Economics*, 152, pp. 55–58.

Shelanski, Howard, and Peter Klein. 1995. "Empirical Research in Transaction Cost Economics: A Review and Assessment." *Journal of Law, Economics, and Organization*, 11, pp. 335–361.

Simon, Herbert. 1985. "Human Nature in Politics: The Dialogue of Psychology with Political Science." *American Political Science Review*, 79, pp. 293–304.

Simon, Herbert. 1991. "Organizations and Markets." *Journal of Economic Perspectives*, 5, pp. 25–44.

Smith, Vernon. 1994. "Economics in the Laboratory." *Journal of Economic Perspectives*, 8, pp. 113–131.

Stigler, George J. 1983. Comments in: "The Fire of Truth: A Remembrance of Law and Economics at Chicago." ed., Edmund W. Kitch, *Journal of Law & Economics*, pp. 163–234.

Stigler, George J. 1988. "Palgrave's Dictionary of Economics." *Journal of Economic Literature*, 26, pp. 1729–1736.

Stigler, George J. 1992. "Law or Economics?." *Journal of Law and Economics*, 35, pp. 455–468.

Summers, Clyde. 1969. "Collective Agreements and the Law of Contracts." *Yale Law Journal*, 78, pp. 537–575.

Teece, David J. Gary Pisano and Amy Shuen. 1996. "Dynamic Capabilities and Strategic Management." *Strategic Management Journal*, 17, pp. xx–yy.

Teece, David J; Gary Pisano and Amy Shuen; Richard Rumelt; Giovanni Dosi and Sidney Winter. 1993. "Understanding Corporate Coherence." *Journal of Economic Behavior and Organization*, 22, pp. 1–30.

Thompson, James D.1967. *Organizations in Action*. New York: McGraw-Hill.

Tullock, Gordon. 1996. "Legal Heresy: President's Address to the Western Economic Association." *Economic Inquiry*, 34, pp. 1–9. @beta/een/CLS_kap/GRP_201/ JOB_008/DIV_198-3P57 Transaction Cost Economics 57

Williamson, Oliver. 1971. "The Vertical Integration of Production: Market Failure Considerations." *American Economic Review*, 61, pp. 112–123.

Williamson, Oliver. 1975. *Markets and Hierarchies: Analysis and Antitrust Implications*. New York: Free Press.

Williamson, Oliver. 1976. "Franchise Bidding for Natural Monopolies – In General and with Respect to CATV." *Bell Journal of Economics*, 7, pp. 73–104.

Williamson, Oliver. 1979. "Transaction Cost Economics: The Governance of Contractual Relations." *Journal of Law and Economics*, 22, pp. 233–261.

Williamson, Oliver. 1985. *The Economics Institutions of Capitalism*. New York: Free Press.

Williamson, Oliver. 1991(a). "Comparative Economic Organization: The Analysis of Discrete Structural Alternatives." *Administrative Science Quarterly*, 36, pp. 269–296.

Williamson, Oliver. 1991(b). "Strategizing, Economizing, and Economic Organization." *Strategic Management Journal*, 12, pp. 75–94.

Williamson, Oliver. 1993(a). "Calculativeness, Trust, and Economic Organization." *Journal of Law and Economics*, 36, pp. 453–486.

Williamson, Oliver. 1993(b). "Transaction Cost Economics Meets Posnerian Law and Economics." *Journal of Institutional and Theoretical Economics*, 149, pp. 99–118.

Williamson, Oliver. 1996(a). *The Mechanisms of Governance.* New York: Oxford University Press.

Williamson, Oliver. 1996(b). "Revisiting Legal Realism: The Law, Economics, and Organization Perspective." *Industrial and Corporate Change*, 5, pp. 383–420.

Williamson, Oliver. 1997. "Public and Private Bureaus." unpublished manuscript.

Williamson, Oliver, and Scott Masten. 1995. *Transaction Cost Economics*, Brookfield, VT: Edward Elgar.

Wilson, James Q. 1989. *Bureaucracy.* New York: Basic Books.

Chapter 7

The New Institutional Economics: Taking Stock, Looking Ahead

1. Introduction

I open my discussion of the new institutional economics with a confession, an assertion, and a recommendation. The confession is that we are still very ignorant about institutions. The assertion is that the past quarter century has witnessed enormous progress in the study of institutions. The recommendation is that, awaiting a unified theory, we should be accepting of pluralism.

Chief among the causes of ignorance is that institutions are very complex. That neoclassical economics was dismissive of institutions and that much of organization theory lacked scientific ambitions have also been contributing factors. As to progress, that is what most of this paper is about. There being many instructive lenses for studying complex institutions, pluralism is what holds promise for overcoming our ignorance.

Speaking for myself, I subscribe to Elster's view that we work predominantly on partial mechanisms rather than general theories at this stage of development (Elster, 1994, p. 75). In consideration, however, of the "splendid plausibility of error" to which Lord Acton refers, we need to sort the sheep from the goats. That is accomplished by asking each would-be theory to advance refutable implications to which the data are applied.

Matthews, in his presidential address to the Royal Economic Society in 1986, pronounced that "the economics of institutions has become one of the liveliest areas in our discipline" (Matthews, 1986, p. 903). Such a pronouncement was a surprise to most of the profession. Hadn't institutional economics long since been relegated to the history of economic thought? Whence the vitality to which Matthews made reference?

Matthews' response was that the New Institutional Economics (NIE) turned on two propositions. First, "institutions do matter"; and second, "the determinants of institutions are susceptible to analysis by the tools of economic theory" (Matthews, 1986, p. 903). The second of these is what distinguishes the NIE, it being the case that institutional economists of all kinds — old and new — are unanimous in the view that institutions matter.

Indeed, although both the older and newer styles of institutional economics subscribe to many of the same good ideas, a progressive research program requires more. Arrow speaks to the transformation as follows (Arrow, 1987, p. 734):

> Why did the older institutionalism school fail so miserably, though it contained such able analysts as Torstein Veblen, J. R. Commons, and W. C. Mitchell? I now think that ... [one of the answers is in the] important specific analyses ... of the New Institutional Economics movement. But it does not consist of giving new answers to the traditional questions of economics resource allocation and the degree of utilization. Rather, it consists of answering new questions, why economic institutions emerged the way they did and not otherwise; it merges into economic history, but brings sharper [microanalytic] ... reasoning to bear than had been customary.

There is no question that the NIE has grown in stature and influence over the fourteen years since Matthews' pronouncement. Initial skepticism has gradually given way to respect — it being the case that economists are very pragmatic people. Tell them something different and consequential about phenomena that are of interest to them and demonstrate that the data are corroborative: that will get their attention. The NIE has progressed not by advancing an overarching theory but by uncovering and explicating the microanalytic features to which Arrow refers and by piling block upon block until the cumulative value added cannot be denied.

The NIE, moreover, will not stand still. Even as institutional economics is being incorporated within orthodoxy, new opportunities, and challenges await. Both unfinished business and new projects yet to be undertaken await the new millennium.

I begin with a sketch of four levels of social analysis, next turn to some of the good ideas out of which the NIE works, and then examine some of the applications to which the NIE has been put. Concluding remarks follow in Section 4.

2. Four Levels of Social Analysis

It will be useful for purposes of perspective to consider the four levels of social analysis that are distinguished in Figure 1. The solid arrows that connect a higher with a lower level signify that the higher level imposes constraints on the level immediately below. The reverse arrows that connect lower with higher levels are dashed and signal feedback. Although, in the fullness of time, the system is fully interconnected, I mainly neglect these feedbacks. The NIE has been concerned principally with levels 2 and 3.

The top level is the social embeddedness level. This is where the norms, customs, mores, traditions, etc. are located. Religion plays a large role at this level. Although Level 1 analysis is undertaken by some economic historians and other social scientists (Banfield, 1958; Putnam, Leonardi, and Nanetti, 1993; Huntington, 1996; Nee, 1998), Level 1 is taken as given by most institutional economists. Institutions at this level change very slowly — on the order of centuries or millennia — whereupon North poses the query, "What is it about informal constraints that gives them such a pervasive influence upon the long-run character of economies?" (North, 1991, p. 111).

North does not have an answer to that perplexing question, nor do I. The concept of "embeddedness," both at the level of society and in the context of ongoing network relations, has been advanced to help explicate these issues (Granovetter, 1985). The vast literature on culture (DiMaggio, 1994) is also pertinent. Smelser and Swedberg discuss these and related issues in their introduction to the Handbook of Economic Sociology, where they observe that different kinds of embeddedness — cognitive, cultural,

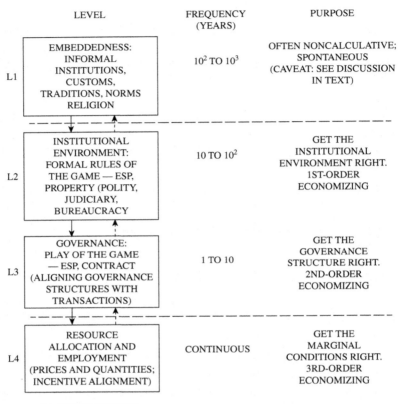

Figure 1.   Economics of Institutions

structural, and political — should be distinguished, and conclude that "the concept of embeddedness remains in need of greater theoretical specification" (Smelser and Swedberg, 1994, p. 18).

An identification and explication of the mechanisms through which informal institutions arise and are maintained would especially help to understand the slow change in Level 1 institutions. I conjecture in this connection that many of these informal institutions have mainly spontaneous origins — which is to say that deliberative choice of a calculative kind is minimally implicated. Given these evolutionary origins, they are "adopted" and thereafter display a great deal of inertia — some because they are functional (as with conventions); others take on symbolic value with a coterie of true believers; many are pervasively linked with complementary institutions (formal and informal), etc. Be that as it may, the resulting institutions have a lasting grip on the way a society conducts itself. Insular societies often take Williamson: The New Institutional Economics 597 measures to protect themselves against "alien values."

The second level is referred to as the institutional environment. The structures observed here are partly the product of evolutionary processes, but design opportunities are also posed. Going beyond the "informal constraints (sanctions, taboos, customs, traditions, and codes of conduct)" of a Level 1 kind, we now introduce "formal rules (constitutions, laws, property rights)" (North, 1991, p. 97). This opens up the opportunity for first-order economizing: get the formal rules of the game right.

Constrained by the shadow of the past, the design instruments at Level 2 include the executive, legislative, judicial, and bureaucratic functions of government as well as the distribution of powers across different levels of government (federalism). The definition and enforcement of property rights and of contract laws are important features.

Although such first-order choices are unarguably important to the economic productivity of an economy (Rosenberg and Birdzell, 1986; Coase, 1992; North, 1994; Levy and Spiller, 1994; Olson, 1996; Henisz, 1998) cumulative change of a progressive kind is very difficult to orchestrate. Massive discontent — civil wars (the Glorious Revolution; see North, and Weingast, 1989), or occupations (following World War II), perceived threats (the Meiji Revolution), breakdowns (Eastern Europe and the former Soviet Union), a military coup (Chile), or a financial crisis (New Zealand) — will, however, occasionally produce a sharp break from established procedures. Rare windows of opportunity to effect broad reform are thereby opened. Such "defining moments" are nevertheless the exception rather than the rule. At least partly because of our primitive understanding, the response to such opportunities is often one of "failure." Absent such a window, major changes in the rules of the game occur on the order of decades or centuries. The European Union, for example, has been "in progress" for fifty years and is still in early stages of development.

What is often referred to as Positive Political Theory (PPT) is concerned with working out the economic and political ramifications of Level 2 features. To be sure, such research also has lessons for the normative design of better polities. Like the NIE of which it is a part, however, PPT is predominantly an exercise in positive analysis. The object is to better understand how things work — warts and all. The research product of PPT scholarship has been nothing less than auspicious, which has been good for both political science and the NIE.

Much of the economics of property rights is of a Level 2 kind. Such research flourished in the 1960s. A strong version of the argument is that "a private-enterprise system cannot function properly unless property rights are created in resources, and, when this is done, someone wishing to use a resource has to pay the owner to obtain it. Chaos disappears; and so does the government except that a legal system to define property rights and to arbitrate disputes is, of course, necessary" (Coase 1959, p. 12). Once property rights have been defined and their enforcement assured, the government steps aside. Resources are allocated to their highest value as the marvel of the market works its wonders.

This compact statement illustrates both the strength and the weakness of the property rights literature. The great strength of this literature is that it brings property rights to the forefront, where they belong, whereupon novel 598 *Journal of Economic Literature*, Vol. 38 (September, 2000) property rights reasoning could be brought to bear in informative ways (Alchian, 1961, 1965; Coase, 1959, 1960; Demsetz, 1967). The weakness is that it overplayed its hand. The claim, for example, that the legal system will eliminate chaos upon defining and enforcing property rights assumes that the definition and enforcement of such rights is easy (costless). Plainly, many transactions do not qualify (Coase, 1960). Going beyond the rules of the game (property) to include the play of the game (contract) was needed. That is the opening through which the governance of contractual relations walked in during the 1970s.

This brings me to the third level, which is where the institutions of governance are located. Although property remains important, a perfectly functioning legal system for defining contract laws and enforcing contracts is not contemplated. Costless court ordering being a fiction, much of the contract management and dispute settlement action is dealt with directly by the parties — through private ordering. The need to come to terms with contract laws (plural), rather than an all-purpose law of contract (singular), is posed (Summers, 1969; Macneil, 1974). The governance of contractual relations becomes the focus of analysis.

Commons prefigured this work with his observation that "the ultimate unit of activity . . . must contain in itself the three principles of conflict, mutuality, and order. This unit is a transaction" (Commons, 1932, p. 4). Not only does transaction cost economics subscribe to the idea that the transaction is the basic unit of analysis, but governance is an effort to craft order, thereby to mitigate conflict and realize mutual gains.

So conceived, a governance structure obviously reshapes incentives. To focus entirely on *ex ante* incentive alignment, however, is a truncated way to study organization — especially if all complex contracts are unavoidably incomplete and if adaptation is the central problem of economic organization (Barnard, 1938; Hayek, 1945). Moving beyond the agency theory tradition of *ex ante* incentive alignment, transaction cost economics turns its attention — additionally and predominantly — to the *ex post* stage of contract.

This entails four moves: (1) to name and explicate the principal dimensions with respect to which transactions differ (thereby to uncover differential adaptive needs); (2) to name and explicate the principal attributes for describing governance structures (where each is defined by a distinctive syndrome of related attributes, whence markets, hybrids, firms, regulation, bureaus, nonprofits, etc. differ in discrete structural ways); (3) to effect a discriminating match, according to which transactions are aligned with governance structures so as to promote adaptation of autonomous and cooperative kinds; and (4) to ascertain whether the predicted alignments are corroborated by the data.

The canonical problem for dealing with these issues is that of vertical integration, which is the issue posed by Coase in his classic 1937 article on "The Nature of the Firm." As it turns out, any issue that arises as or can be reformulated as a contracting issue can be examined to advantage in transaction cost economizing terms. A huge number of phenomena turn out to be contractual variations on a common theme. What I refer to as second-order economizing — get the governance structures right — is realized at Level 3. The possible reorganization of transactions among governance structures is re-examined periodically, on the order of a year to a decade, often at contract renewal or equipment renewal intervals. Williamson: The New Institutional Economics 599 Such discrete structural analysis of governance is to be distinguished from the fourth level, which is the level at which neoclassical analysis works. Optimality apparatus, often marginal analysis, is employed, and the firm, for these purposes, is typically described as a production function. Adjustments to prices and output occur more or less continuously. Agency theory, which emphasizes *ex ante* incentive alignment and efficient risk bearing, rather than *ex post* governance, nonetheless makes provision for nonneoclassical complications, of which multi-tasking is one (Holmstrom and Milgrom, 1991).

Indeed, a still earlier (zero level) of analysis warrants remark: an evolutionary level in which the mechanisms of the mind take shape (Pinker, 1997). The application of these ideas to economics even now is beginning to reshape our understanding of human actors. Our evolutionary psychologist and cognitive science colleagues are vital to the exercise.

Finally, I should call attention to technology. As compared with technological innovation, the study of organizational innovation has been comparatively neglected. The NIE has attempted to rectify that — the idea being that "truly among man's innovations, the use of organization to accomplish his ends is among both his greatest and his earliest" (Arrow, 1971, p. 224). We cannot fail, however, to be awed by the profound importance of technological innovation (Fogel, 1999). Inasmuch as these two work in tandem, we need to find ways to treat technical and organizational innovation in a combined manner.

3. Good Ideas

The new institutional economics had its origins in good critics of orthodoxy who believed that institutions were both important and susceptible to analysis. Feeling expansive, I would include six Nobel Laureates among the key figures: Kenneth Arrow, Friedrich Hayek, Gunnar Myrdal, Herbert Simon, Ronald Coase, and Douglass North — the last two being the first two presidents of ISNIE. But there are others. Alchian has been an influential figure. So too has been research on organization theory, especially at Carnegie (some of it prefigured by earlier work by Barnard) — where the names of Cyert and

March join that of Simon. Chandler's pioneering work in business history was also path-breaking. Thoughtful contributors from the law, especially contract law, include Llewellyn, Macaulay, Fuller, and Macneil. Commons also brought original and important ideas to the study of institutional economics. The German Historical School was also concerned with related ideas (Furubotn and Richter, 1997, pp. 34–35).

Among the key good ideas that I associate with the NIE are these:

Human Actors. If "nothing is more fundamental in setting our research agenda and informing our research methods than our view of the nature of the human beings whose behavior we are studying" (Simon, 1985, p. 303), then social scientists should be prepared to name the key attributes of human actors. Both the condition of cognition and self-interestedness need to be addressed. There is close to unanimity within the NIE on the idea of limited cognitive competence — often referred to as bounded rationality. Mind being a scarce resource, cognitive specialization has economizing consequences. Also, given cognitive limits, the complex contracts to which I referred earlier are 600 *Journal of Economic Literature*, Vol. 38 (September 2000) unavoidably incomplete. But while there is near-unanimity that complete contingent claims contracting is impossible, the appropriate way to model incomplete contracts remains controversial. Lack of agreement on the definition and operational import of bounded rationality is a major obstacle (Rubinstein, 1998; Kreps, 1999).

Contractual incompleteness poses added problems when paired with the condition of opportunism — which manifests itself as adverse selection, moral hazard, shirking, subgoal pursuit, and other forms of strategic behavior. Because human actors will not reliably disclose true conditions upon request or self-fulfill all promises, contract as mere promise, unsupported by credible commitments, will not be self-enforcing.

But for opportunism, the courts would simply ask witnesses to "tell us what you know that is germane to our decision." That is not, however, the way that testimony is taken. Witnesses are required to take an oath to "tell the truth, the whole truth, and nothing but the truth": don't lie; don't conceal; don't mislead. In as much, moreover, as oaths are not self-enforcing, penalties for perjury remind witnesses that prevarication has consequences.

Still a third attribute of human actors warrants remark, and that is the capacity for conscious foresight. Indeed, as Dawkins observes, it is the "capacity to simulate the future in imagination ... [that saves] us from the worst consequences of the blind replicators" (Dawkins, 1976, p. 200). Parties to a contract who look ahead, recognize potential hazards, work out the contractual ramifications, and fold these into the exalted contractual agreement obviously enjoy advantages over those who are myopic or take their chances and knock on wood. The governance of contractual relations — the Commons triple of conflict, mutuality, and order to which I referred earlier — is centrally implicated.

Feasibility. Students of the NIE eschew hypothetical ideals — which work off of omniscience, benevolence, zero transaction costs, full credibility, and the like — and deal instead with feasible organizational alternatives, all of which are flawed. Coase (1964) and Demsetz (1969) were among the first to take exception with the asymmetric standards that were once used in the "market failure" literature — according to which markets are beset with failures whereas "omniscient, omnipotent, benevolent" governments (Dixit, 1996, p. 8) would reliably administer efficacious remedies. As we all should have recognized (but needed to be told), all feasible forms of organization — government included — are flawed.

What I have referred to as the remediableness criterion is intended to rectify this asymmetric state of affairs. This criterion holds that an extant mode of organization for which no superior feasible alternative can be described and implemented with expected net gains is presumed to be efficient.

To be sure, public policy analysis becomes more complicated when analysts can no longer condemn extant modes because they deviate from a hypothetical ideal, full stop. The remediableness criterion presses the public policy analyst to display a superior feasible alternative. If, moreover, a proposed feasible alternative cannot be costlessly implemented, then the costs of implementation are appropriately included in the net benefit calculus — which has major ramifications for the path dependency literature. Finally, grounds for rebutting the efficiency presumption need to be addressed — which brings in politics (Williamson, 1996, 1999). Absent rebuttal, the remediableness criterion stands as a reminder of the obvious: it is impossible to do better than one's best.

Firms and Bureaus. In addition to the nature of the human beings to which Simon referred, we need also to be self-conscious about the "Nature of the Firm," which was the title of Coase's classic 1937 article from which the NIE draws much of its inspiration. Arrow speaks to the fundamental importance of the theory of the firm, and to long-standing misconceptions thereof, as follows: "Any standard economic theory, not just neoclassical, starts from the existence of firms. Usually, the firm is a point or at any rate a black box. . . . But firms are palpably not points. They have internal structure. This internal structure must arise for some reason" (Arrow, 1999, p. vii).

The need was to get beyond the analytically convenient (and sometimes adequate) conception of the firm-as production function (which is a technological construction) to consider the firm as a governance structure (which is an organizational construction) in which internal structure has economic purpose and effect. More generally, the need was to identify and explicate the properties of alternative modes of governance — spot markets, incomplete long term contracts, firms, bureaus, etc.— which differ in discrete structural ways. Because each generic mode of governance possesses distinctive strengths and weaknesses, there is a place for each yet each needs to be kept in its place. The logic of discriminating alignment to which I referred earlier applies.

In a heuristic way, the choice of governance structure moves from market to hierarchy through the sequence of moves shown in Figure 2 (where h denotes contractual hazards and s denotes safeguards). This can be interpreted

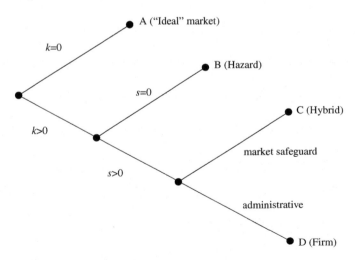

Figure 2.   Simple contracting Schema

as a move from simple to complex. We thus begin with autonomous contracting, which is the ideal transaction in both law and economics: "sharp in by clear agreement; sharp out by clear performance" (Macneil, 1974, p. 738). This discrete transaction paradigm comes under strain as contractual hazards appear. The inability of courts, for example, to verify what is common knowledge between the parties to an exchange (Williamson, 1975, p. 30) could induce a move from interim to interim organization. Other sources of contractual hazard include bilateral dependency (by reason of nonredeployable assets), weak property rights (especially intellectual property rights), undisclosed quality, health, and safety hazards, failures of probity, and the like. Such hazards compromise contractual integrity and give rise to contractual impasses, maladaptations, and investment distortions. Here, as elsewhere, inefficiency invites relief. Cost-effective hazard mitigation through added governance ensues.

Moving from less to more complex governance entails introducing added security features, reducing incentive intensity, and incurring added bureaucratic costs. Moving from simple (discrete) contracts to complex (incomplete long term) contracts is thus attended by a whole series of features: the length of the contract increases, penalties to deter breach are introduced, provision is made for added information disclosure and processing, and specialized dispute settlement mechanisms appear.

Additional mechanisms, to include the use of hierarchy to effect coordination and decide disputes by fiat, are introduced when transactions are removed from the market and placed under unified ownership (the firm). Because added compliance and security features always come at a cost, more complex modes of governance are reserved for those transactions for which contractual hazards are especially difficult.

The public bureau, in this scheme of things, can be thought of as the organization form of last resort: try spot markets, try incomplete long-term contracts, try firms, try regulation, and reserve recourse to public bureaus for when all else fails (comparatively). Note that the common practice of condemning public bureaus because they have lower-powered incentives, more rules and regulations, and greater job security than a counterpart firm completely misses the point. These features have been deliberately crafted into the public bureau, thereby to make it better suited to govern some (especially difficult) transactions. Vigilance is nonetheless needed — lest the public bureau be "overused."

If transaction cost economics works out of variations on a few key themes, then this schema, which was initially devised to help explicate the governance of contractual relations in intermediate product market transactions, should also apply, with variation, to other classes of transactions. It does.

The four nodes are interpreted with reference to intermediate product transactions above. Consider final goods markets and government procurement transactions.

Transactions in final goods markets, where individual consumers are the buyers, are similar but different. Node A transactions are generic and competitively organized. Node B transactions are rare. These correspond to "P. T. Barnum" — there's a sucker born every minute — and other fly-by-night transactions. Node C is the credible commitment node. Branding in combination with reputation effects and product warranties appear. Also, for some natural monopoly transactions, public utility regulation serves credibility purposes. Node D is a nearly empty set. Economies of scale and of specialization are impediments to own-supply by consumers, although collective organization (consumer cooperatives) can be used to manage some transactions. (Many household services can be thought of as own-supply, but few fit comfortably within the schema.)

Government procurement transactions are also similar but different. Node A describes generic transactions to which, often, tedious technical specifications apply. Very few government transactions are of a Node B kind. Credibility mechanisms at Node C include the elaborate machinery of "administered contracting," as with defense procurement (which transactions, however, are sometimes compromised by the shared interests of the government agency and the private supplier). And Node D is the public bureau, where for probity or political reasons the government chooses to manage the transaction itself.

Other applications of the schema include the employment relation (Baron and Kreps, 1999, Chapter 4) and corporate finance (the choice between debt and equity). Some transactions, such as alliances and joint ventures, pose complications of a disequilibrium contracting kind (Williamson, 1991) that are beyond the reach of the schema.

Operationalization Many good ideas are initially expressed as tautologies, which Coase (1988, p. 19) has wryly defined as "a proposition that is clearly right." Because good tautologies expand the mind and are hard to come by, they deserve respect. Lest, however, we slip into the speculations to which Mitchell once referred — which is a fate that beset the older style institutional economics as well as the American Legal Realism movement — we need to ask what are the mechanisms through which a proposed theory operates and what are the refutable implications.

The effort to operationalize promising ideas has both theoretical and empirical parts. The theoretical often takes the form of a progression from informal to preformal, semiformal, and fully formal modes of analysis — ideally acquiring value added in the process. Such an effort helps to sort the sheep from the goats. Georgescu-Roegen (1971, p. 37) had a felicitous way of putting it: although the "purpose of science is not prediction, but knowledge for its own sake," prediction is nevertheless "the touchstone of scientific knowledge." Would-be theories for which predictive content is lacking must eventually step aside (be set aside) for those for which the hard work of formalization and empirical testing are undertaken.

Theory Development, Formalization is vital to a progressive research agenda, but it sometimes comes at a cost. Thus although Simon once argued that "mathematical translation is itself a substantive contribution to theory ... because it permits clear and rigorous reasoning about phenomena too complex to be handled in words" (Simon, 1957, p. 89) and subsequently asserted that the "poverty of mathematics is an honest poverty that does not parade imaginary riches before the world" (Simon,1957, p. 90), provision also needs to be made for the possibility that core features of the theory are left out or obscured by the translation. There is, after all, such a thing as prematurely formal theory. Kreps speaks to the issues as follows (Kreps, 1999, p. 122):

> If Markets and Hierarchies has been translated into game theory using notions of information economics, it is a very poor translation ... In particular, mathematics-based theory still lacks the language needed to capture essential ideas of bounded rationality, which are central to ... transaction costs and contractual form. Anyone who relies on the translations alone misses large and valuable chunks of the original.

What is referred to as the "property rights theory of the firm," which had its origins with Grossman and Hart (1986) and has subsequently been developed by Hart and Moore (hence the reference to the GHM model), relates to but differs significantly from the transaction cost economics setup (as presented, for example, in Williamson, 1985, 1991). It is similar in that it deals with the make-or-buy decision through a setup where contracts are incomplete (by reason of bounded rationality), mere promise cannot be used to overcome noncontractibility (by reason of opportunism), and parties to the contract are bilaterally dependent (by reason of asset specificity). These commonalities notwithstanding, there are also major differences.

Some of these differences are attributable to simplifications that invariably attend formal modelling. Ideally, core features of the verbal argument and the mechanisms through which they work are made more precise in the process of formalization. Such a case can be made for the property rights theory of the firm, which is a major intellectual achievement that has spawned a growing literature on the formal modelling of incomplete contracts. As Kreps suggests, however, valuable chunks are missing. In the spirit of full disclosure (honest poverty), I focus on these.

The most consequential difference between the TCE and GHM setups is that the former holds that maladaptation in the contract execution interval is the principal source of inefficiency, whereas GHM vaporize *ex post* maladaptation by their assumptions of common knowledge and costless ex post bargaining. The upshot is that all of the inefficiency in GHM is concentrated in the *ex ante* investments in human assets (which are conditional on the ownership of physical assets).

This shift from *ex post* maladaptation (the hazards from which vary with the condition of asset specificity and the disturbances to which a transaction is subject) to *ex ante* investment distortions matters. For one thing, GHM makes very limited contact with the data whereas (as discussed below) TCE is an empirical success story. Related (*ex post*) governance and (exalted) investment differences are as follows:

(1) The TCE rendition of the maker-buy decision between successive stages (A and B) asks whether A and B should be separately owned and operated or if the ownership and operation of these two stages should be unified. If independent, then each stage appropriates its net receipts

(high-powered incentives obtain) but maladaptation problems can arise during contract execution. If unified, then the two stages are managed coordinately through hierarchy. (Maladaptation problems are thereby relieved; incentives are lower-powered; and added bureaucratic costs arise.) By contrast, GHM view vertical integration in a directional way: either A buys B or B buys A, and it matters which way this is done. That is because common ownership under GHM does not imply unified management. Instead, each stage (in all configurations — A and B are independent; A buys B; B buys A) appropriates its net receipts. This last is a very unusual condition, in that unified ownership is normally thought of as a means by which to effect cooperation.

(2) TCE maintains that each generic mode of governance — spot market, incomplete long-term contract, firm, bureau, etc. — is defined by a syndrome of attributes to which distinctive strengths and weaknesses accrue. Specifically, TCE holds that alternative modes differ in incentive intensity, administrative controls (to include auditing, accounting, and transfer pricing), access to the courts, and informal organization (to include politicking). GHM assume that incentive intensity, administrative controls, and informal organization are unchanged by ownership and that courts are irrelevant (because of costless renegotiation). None of the physical asset utilization and transfer pricing distortions that I associate with the "impossibility of selective intervention" (Williamson, 1985, pp. 135–140) thus occur under the GHM setup.

(3) TCE examines a wide range of *ex post* devices for infusing credible commitments into contracts and applies this reasoning to a wide set of transactions. Variations on this theme include hybrid modes of organization (Masten, 1996, Part III), exchange agreements and other uses of hostages to support exchange, the organization of work, the organization of labor and human resources more generally, corporate governance, regulation (and deregulation), public bureaus, and project financing. Because GHM is a property rights and property rights only construction (Holmstrom, 1999), it relates to some of these issues not at all and others very selectively (Hart, 1995; Hart, Shleifer, and Vishny, 1997).

GHM is nonetheless a path-breaking contribution and has set the formal modelling of incomplete contracting in motion. New formal models of incomplete contracts which are closer in spirit to TCE include the treatment of procurement by Bajari and Tadelis (1999), which focuses on the incentive and *ex post* adaptation differences between fixed price and cost plus contracting. Also, the recent paper by Wang and Zhu (2000) employs the idea that alternative modes of governance work out of different contract law regimes (Williamson, 1991). And Grossman and Helpman (1999) appeal to the added bureaucratic costs of unified as compared with market governance in their assessment of alternative modes for producing differentiated consumer products. More veridical treatments of incomplete contracting are thus in progress and still more are in prospect.

Empirical. Some scoff at prediction, evidently in the belief that prediction is easy. Also, since everyone knows that "it is easy to lie with statistics," what useful purpose is served by empirical testing? My experience is different: prediction is a demanding standard, which is why so many would-be theories remain excogitated speculations; and corroboration is difficult, which explains why few predictions are tested.

Because, however, good theories are rarely fully developed at the outset, the theory and the evidence are often interactive. As Newell observes (Newell, 1990, p. 14):

> Theories cumulate. They are refined and reformulated, corrected and expanded. Thus, we are not living in the world of Popper. ... [Theories are not] shot down with a falsification bullet. ... Theories are more like graduate students — once admitted you try hard to avoid flunking them out. ... Theories are things to be nurtured and changed and built up.

Good but underdeveloped ideas are evidently like good but underdeveloped minds: both are precious things. Because development is costly, promising theories, like promising graduate students, are admitted only if they cross a threshold. Once admitted, theories (and graduate students) are progressively built up — moving from less formal to more formal stages of development. Finally, as with promising graduate students, we do not hold on to cherished theories indefinitely: some do flunk out. Specifically, theories that remain tautological or yield predictions that are contradicted by the data must make way for theories that yield predictions for which the data are corroborative.

Empirical applications of transaction cost economics got under way in the U.S. in the 1980s and have grown exponentially since: the number of published studies exceeds 500 and involves social scientists in Europe, Japan, India, China, Mexico, South America, Australia, New Zealand, and the list goes on. It could have been otherwise, but the theory and evidence display a remarkable congruity (Masten, 1995, p. xi). Recent empirical surveys include Shelanski and Klein (1995), Lyons (1996), Crocker and Masten (1996), and Rindfleisch and Jan Heide (1997).

Not only has this research been broadly corroborative of the predictions of transaction cost economics, but the importance of risk aversion to commercial contracting has been placed in doubt (Allen and Lueck, 1999). To be sure, transaction cost economics, like everything else, will benefit from more and better empirical work. I have no hesitation, however, in declaring that the NIE is an empirical success story. Joskow concurs: "this empirical work is in much better shape than much of the empirical work in industrial organization generally" (Joskow, 1991, p. 81). Those who have done this modest, slow, molecular, definitive work deserve enormous credit.

The NIE is predominantly concerned with Levels 2 and 3 of the four levels of social analysis shown in Figure 1. These are the levels of the institutional environment and the institutions of governance, respectively. Between them, they cover a lot of ground.

The formal features of the institutional environment — the laws, polity, judiciary, bureaucracy — are crucial in examining the development of nation states (North and Weingast, 1989) and for making intertemporal comparisons within and cross-national comparisons between nation states. Indeed, this last has come to be a growth industry to which many economists who are only slightly associated with the NIE have made contributions. It is nonetheless noteworthy that the NIE has done much of the pioneering work in this area.

To repeat, any issue that arises as or can be posed as a contractual issue can be examined to advantage in transaction cost economizing terms. Examples for which contractual issues are evident at the outset include contracts for intermediate products, for labor, for final goods and services, for the rental or lease or purchase of land, equipment, and buildings, for professional services, for marriage, and the list goes on. Even, moreover, if contractual features are not immediately evident from the outset, many issues can be reformulated so as to disclose their contractual qualities, the choice between debt and equity, the oligopoly problem, and the multinational corporation being examples (Buckley, and Casson, 1976; Gatignon, and Anderson, 1988).

Many public policy issues, moreover, turn jointly on the combined use of Level 2 and Level 3 reasoning. In the area of privatizing telecommunications, for example, Levy and Spiller examine the institutional environments in five countries through a comparative contractual lens in which issues of credible contracting are featured (Levy and Spiller, 1994, 1996). The recent study of reforming urban water systems by Menard and Shirley (1999) likewise makes clear that ownership is not determinative but needs to be examined in conjunction with the support, or the lack thereof, of the mechanisms of governance. Again, issues of credible contracting are salient. The same is true of commercial contracting in Vietnam (McMillan and Woodruff, 1999).

Broad reach notwithstanding, the NIE is not and does not pretend to be an all-purpose construction, as the reform of economies of Eastern Europe and the former Soviet Union illustrate. Thus Coase in his Nobel Prize lecture observed that (Coase, 1992, p. 714):

> The value of including … institutional factors in the corpus of mainstream economics is made clear by recent events in Eastern Europe. These ex-communist countries are advised to move to a market economy, and their leaders wish to do so, but without the appropriate institutions no market economy of any significance is possible. If we knew more about our own economy, we would be in a better position to advise them.

Two years later, North, in his Nobel Prize lecture, expressed similar precautions.

Thus even if we are confident that "polities significantly shape economic performance because they define and enforce the economic rules," whereupon "an essential part of development policy is the creation of polities that will create and enforce efficient property rights," there is the further problem that "we know very little about how to create such polities" (North, 1994, p. 366).

Real-time events, however, cannot be put on hold. Hard choices have to be made. Economic reform in Russia is an example.

The team of Boycko, Shleifer, and Vishny responded to the perceived need to give shape to the reform with the recommendation that the Russian economy should be privatized quickly and massively. Considerations of both Realpolitik and economic theory were invoked in support of this recommendation.

There being widespread agreement that "political influence over economic life was the fundamental cause of economic inefficiency" [in Russia], Boycko, Shleifer, and Vishny (1995, p. 11) declared that:

> ... the principal objective of reform was ... to depoliticize economic life. ... Privatization fosters depoliticization because it deprives politicians of the opportunity to allocate goods. ... The goal of privatization was to sever the links between enterprise managers and politicians. ... There was no other way to achieve restructuring and efficient operation of firms.

The two strategic actors in this reform program were the official bureaucracy, which was viewed as "the enemy to be fought at all costs" and the stakeholders — managers, employees, and local governments. The Boycko *et al.* team "consistently and generously recognized stakeholders' claims, and thus ensured their eventual support of privatization" (Boycko, Shleifer, and Vishny, 1995, pp. 13–14).

This political prescription for massive and rapid privatization was reinforced by the economic theory of the firm on which the Boycko *et al.* team relied. Specifically, they appealed to the aforementioned work by Grossman and Hart (1986), which views ownership as a system of control rights and treats the appropriate assignment of property rights as determinative (Boycko, Shleifer, and Vishny, 1995, p. 13). Upon privatizing state-owned enterprises, therefore, effective restructuring by the new stakeholders would presumably follow (op. cit., p. 150). In the confidence that the future would take care of itself, the mass privatization program that was begun in the spring of 1992 had purportedly reached a "triumphant completion" in June 1994 (op. cit., p. 8), by which date two-thirds of Russian industry was privately owned.

Had the Boycko *et al.* team consulted the new institutional economics, a more cautious and selective program of privatization with greater attention to implementation would have resulted. Consider first the literature on franchise bidding for natural monopoly, where the property rights approach and the governance approach reach very different conclusions.

The property rights approach to the problem of natural monopoly is to conduct an *ex ante* bidding competition and award the right to serve the market to the group that tenders the best bid (Demsetz, 1968; Stigler, 1968; Posner, 1972). Very much in the spirit of Boycko *et al.*, the future will take care of itself once the assets have been privatized in this way.

That sanguine view does not withstand scrutiny if serious *ex post* implementation problems are in prospect. Under the governance approach, the award of a monopoly franchise needs to be assessed comparatively. This entails Williamson: The New Institutional Economics 609 looking ahead and uncovering *ex post* contractual hazards, thereafter working out the ramifications for alternative modes of governance (Williamson, 1976, pp. 79–91). Because franchise bidding works much better for some natural monopoly industries than others (Williamson, 1976, pp. 102–103), the use of franchise bidding will be reserved for those industries where comparative net benefits can be projected — but not otherwise. Privatization, it turns out, is not an all-purpose solution (Goldberg, 1976; Priest, 1993).

Although privatizing an entire economy is a much more ambitious undertaking than privatizing a natural monopoly industry, the key lessons nevertheless carry over. Specifically, privatizing needs to go beyond the *ex ante* award stage to include an examination of possible *ex post* implementation problems and, in consideration of the differential hazards, to proceed selectively.

Recall, moreover, that the NIE operates at two levels. Upon moving from the level of governance to that of the institutional environment, the rules of the game come under review. The Levy and Spiller (1994, 1996) study of privatizing telecommunications in five countries reveals that the decision to privatize and the nature of privatization turn critically on the condition and quality of judicial independence, the division of powers between the executive and legislative branches, the competence of the regulatory bureaucracy, and contractual safeguards. Whether and how to privatize telecommunications should therefore be made conditional on these features.

As Black, Kraakman, and Tarassova detail in their paper on "Russian Privatization and Corporate Governance: What Went Wrong" (1999), the "triumphant completion" of privatization in Russia was a premature verdict.

Thus, although privatization was evidently a success for small firms, it was deeply problematic and attended by massive corruption in others. But for undue reliance on *ex ante* property rights reasoning, some of these problems could have been anticipated by looking ahead and examining the hazards of *ex post* implementation. Greater appreciation for the shortfalls of the institutional environment in Russia would have led to more cautious pronouncements (Aslund, 1995). Whether added respect for the rules of the game (to include an appreciation for the limited efficacy of Russian law enforcement) would have resulted in rule improvements in Russia could be disputed. Arguably, however, the effort to reform Russia would have proceeded in a more modest, slow, molecular, deliberative way.

None of this is to suggest that the NIE could have done it all. The Boycko *et al.* team made heroic efforts. My claim is much more modest: the NIE is informative and should be included as part of the reform calculus.

4. Concluding Remarks

The new institutional economics is a boiling cauldron of ideas. Not only are there many institutional research programs in progress, but there are competing ideas within most of them. With reference to history, for example, we see North (1990) and Greif (1999) pursuing complementary but separate agendas. The institutions of embeddedness (Level 1) are an important but underdeveloped part of the story. Within transaction cost economics we distinguish between governance and measurement branches. The attributes of mixed ownership modes (alliances, joint ventures, franchising, and the like) as well as the mechanisms for supporting credible contracting between autonomous firms are incompletely worked out. Incomplete contracting of semiformal and fully formal kinds differ in consequential ways, although the gap has been closing. Evolutionary economics of selections, population ecology, and ontogenetic kinds are in progress. Path dependency is a real and important condition, but its interpretation is actively disputed. The merits of privatization are real but are not uniform and need to be assessed with reference to both the rules of the game and the play of the game. The firm is variously described in technological, contractual, and competence/ knowledge-based perspectives. How best to describe human actors is still unsettled, although evolutionary psychology holds promise. Politics is judged with reference to a hypothetical ideal by some (North, 1990) and in comparative institutional terms by others (Williamson, 1999). Efficiency arguments have mainly prevailed over power interpretations because the latter are tautological, but power issues refuse to go away. Bureaucracy remains a poorly understood condition no matter what lens is brought to bear. Private ordering approaches to contract have made progressive headway, but legal rules remain important and their relation to private ordering is incompletely worked out. Positive political theory has made major conceptual advances, but an overarching understanding of polities does not appear imminent. And the list goes on.

The upshot is that, its' many accomplishments notwithstanding, there is a vast amount of unfinished business — refinements, extensions, new applications, more good ideas, more empirical testing, more fully formal theory. I conclude that the new institutional economics is the little engine that could. Its' best days lie ahead. Who could ask for more?

References

Alchian, Armen. 1961. *Some Economics of Property*. RAND Corporation.

Allen, Douglas and Dean Leuck. 1999. "The Role of Risk in Contract Choice." *Journal of Law, Economics, & Organization*, 15(3), pp. 704–736.

Arrow, Kenneth J. 1971. *Essays in the Theory of Risk-Bearing*. Chicago: Markham.

Arrow, Kenneth J. 1987. "Reflections on the Essays." In *Arrow and the Foundations of the Theory of Economic Policy*. ed. George Feiwel, pp. 727–734. New York: New York University Press.

Arrow, Kenneth J. 1999. "Foreword." in *Firms, Markets and Hierarchies*, eds., Glenn Carroll and David Teece, pp. vii–viii. New York: Oxford University Press.

Aslund, Anders. 1995. *How Russia Became a Market Economy*. Washington, DC: Brookings Institution.

Bajari, Patrick and Steven Tadelis. 1999. "Incentives Versus Transaction Costs." unpublished paper, Stanford University.

Banfield, E. C. 1958. *The Moral Basis of a Backward Society*. New York: Free Press.

Barnard, Chester. 1938. *The Functions of the Executive*. Cambridge, MA: Harvard University Press.

Baron, James and David Kreps. 1999. *Strategic Human Resources*. New York: John Wiley & Sons.

Black, Bernard, Reinier Kraakman and Anna Tarassova. 1999. "Russian Privatization and Corporate Governance: What Went Wrong?" unpublished manuscript, Stanford Law School.

Boorstin, Daniel. 1998. *The Seekers*. New York: Random House.

Boycko, Maxim, Andrei Shleifer and Robert Vishny. 1995. *Privatizing Russia*. Cambridge, MA: MIT Press.

Buckley, Peter, and Mark Casson. 1976. *The Future of the Multinational Enterprise*. London: Holmes and Meier.

Buttrick, John. 1952. "The Inside Contracting System." *Journal of Economic History*, 12(3), pp. 205–221.

Coase, Ronald. 1937. "The Nature of the Firm." *Economica*, 4(6), pp. 386–405.

Coase, Ronald. 1959. "The Federal Communications Commission." *Journal of Law and Economics* 2(2), pp. 1–40.

Coase, Ronald. 1960. "The Problem of Social Cost." *Journal of Law and Economics*, 3, pp. 1–44.

Coase, Ronald. 1964. "The Regulated Industries: Discussion." *American Economic Review*, 54(3), pp. 194–197.

Coase, Ronald. 1988. *The Firm, The Market, and The Law*. Chicago: University of Chicago Press.

Coase, Ronald. 1992. "The Institutional Structure of Production." *American Economic Review*, 82(4), pp. 713–719.

Commons, John R. 1932–33. "The Problems of Correlating Law, Economics and Ethics." *Wiscosin Law Review*, 8(1), pp. 3–26.

Crocker, Keith and Scott Masten. 1996. "Regulation and Administered Contracts Revisited: Lessons from Transaction Cost Economics for Public Utility Regulation." *Journal of Regulatory Economics*, 9(1), pp. 5–39.

Dawkins, Richard. 1976. *The Selfish Gene*. New York: Oxford University Press.

Demsetz, Harold. 1967. "Toward a Theory of Property Rights." *American Economic Review*, 57(2), pp. 347–359.

Demsetz, Harold. 1968. "Why Regulate Utilities?" *Journal of Law and Economics*, 11, pp. 55–66.

Demsetz, Harold. 1969. "Information and Efficiency: Another Viewpoint." *Journal of Law and Economics*, 12(1), pp. 1–22.

DiMaggio, Paul. 1994. "Culture and Economy." In *The Handbook of Economic Sociology*, eds., Neil Smelser and Richard Swedberg, pp. 27–57. Princeton, NJ: Princeton University Press.

Dixit, Avinash. 1996. *The Making of Economic Policy: A Transaction Cost Politics Perspective*. Cambridge: Cambridge University Press.

Elster, Jon. 1994. "Arguing and Bargaining in Two Constituent Assemblies." unpublished manuscript.

Fogel, Robert. 1999. "Catching Up with the Economy." *American Economic Review*, 89(1), pp. 1–21.

Furubotn, Erik and Rudolf Richter. 1991. "The New Institutional Economics: An Assessment." In *The New Institutional Economics*. eds., Furubotn and Richter, College Station, TX: Texas A&M University Press.

Furubotn, Erik and Rudolf Richter. 1997. *Institutions and Economic Theory*. Ann Arbor: University of Michigan Press.

Gatignon, Hubert and Erin Anderson. 1988. "The Multinational Corporation's Degree of Control over Foreign Subsidiaries: An Empirical Test of a Transaction Cost Explanation." *Journal of Law, Economics, & Organization*, 4(2), pp. 305–336.

Georgescu-Roegen, Nicholas. 1971. *The Entropy Law and Economic Process*. Cambridge, MA: Harvard University Press.

Goldberg, Victor. 1976. "Regulation and Administered Contracts." *Bell Journal of Economics*, 7(2), pp. 426–452.

Granovetter, Mark. 1985. "Economic Action and Social Structure: The Problem of Embeddedness." *American Journal of Sociology*, 91(3), pp. 481–510.

Greif, Avner. "Impersonal Exchange and the Origin of Markets: From the Community Responsibility System to Individual Legal Responsibility in Pre-Modern Europe." forthcoming In *Communities and Markets*. eds., M. Aoki and T. Hayami.

Grossman, Gene and Elhanan Helpman. 1999. "Incomplete Contracts and Industrial Organization." NBER Working Paper 7303.

Grossman, Sanford and Oliver Hart. 1986. "The Costs and Benefits of Ownership: A Theory of Vertical and Lateral Integration." *Journal of Political Economics*, 94(4), pp. 691–719.

Hart, Oliver. 1995. *Firms, Contracts, and Financial Structure*. New York: Oxford University Press.

Hart, Oliver and John Moore. 1999(a). "On the Design of Hierarchies." unpublished paper, Harvard University

Hart, Oliver and John Moore. 1999b. "Foundations of Incomplete Contract." *Review of Economic. Studies*, 66(1), pp. 115–138.

Hart, Oliver; Andrei Shleifer, and Robert Vishny. 1997. "The Proper Scope of Government: Theory and Application to Prisons." *Quarterly Journal of Economics*, 112(4), pp. 1127–1161.

Hayek, Friedrich. 1945. "The Use of Knowledge in Society." *American Economics Review*, 35(4), pp. 519–530.

Henisz, Witold. 1998. "The Institutional Environment for International Investment." unpublished Ph.D. dissertation, UC Berkeley.

Holmstrom, Bengt. 1989. "Agency Costs and Innovation." *Journal of Economic Behavior and Organization*, 12(3), pp. 305–327.

Holmstrom, Bengt. 1999. "The Firm as a Subeconomy." *Journal of Law, Economics, & Organization*, 15(1), pp. 74–102.

Holmstrom, Bengt and Paul Milgrom. 1991. "Multi-Task Principal-Agent Analyses: Incentive Contracts, Asset Ownership, and Job Design." *Journal of Law, Economics, & Organization*, 7: (Special Issue), pp. 24–52.

Holmstrom, Bengt and Paul Milgrom. 1994. "The Firm as an Incentive System." *American Economic Review*, 84(4), pp. 972–991.

Huntington, Samuel P. 1996. *The Clash of Civilizations and the Remaking of World Order*. New York: Simon and Schuster.

Joskow, Paul. 1991. "The Role of Transaction Cost Economics in Antitrust and Public Utility Regulatory Policies." *Journal of Law, Economics, & Organization*, 7: (Special Issue), pp. 53–83.

Kreps, David M. 1999. "Markets and Hierarchies and (Mathematical) Economic Theory." In *Firms, Markets, and Hierarchies*, eds. Glenn Carroll and David Teece, pp. 121–155.

New York: Oxford University Press.

Levy, Brian and Pablo Spiller. 1994. "The Institutional Foundations of Regulatory Commitment." *Journal of Law, Economics, & Organization*, 10(2), pp. 201–246.

Levy, Brian and Pablo Spiller. 1996. *Regulations, Institutions, and Commitment: Comparative Studies of Telecommunications*. New York: Cambridge University Press.

Lyons, Bruce. 1996. "Empirical Relevance of Efficient Contract Theory: Inter-Firm Contracts." *Oxford Review of Economic Policy*, 12(4), pp. 27–52.

Macneil, Ian R. 1974. "The Many Futures of Contracts." *Southern California Law Review*, 47(2), pp. 691–816.

Maskin, Eric and Jean Tirole. 1999. "Unforeseen Contingencies and Incomplete Contracts." *Review of Economic Studies*, 66(1), pp. 83–114.

Masten, Scott. 1995. *"Introduction To Vol. II."* in *Transaction Cost Economics*, eds., Oliver Williamson and Scott Masten, Brookfield, VT: Edward Elgar.

Masten, Scott. 1996. *Case Studies in Contracting and Organization*. New York: Oxford University Press.

Matthews, R. C. O. 1986. "The Economics of Institutions and the Sources of Economic Growth." *Economic Journal*, 96(4), pp. 903–918.

McMillan, John and Christopher Woodruff. 1999. "Dispute Prevention without Courts in Vietnam." *Journal of Law, Economics, & Organization*, 15(3), pp. 637–658.

Menard, Claude and Mary Shirley. 1999. "Reforming Contractual Arrangements: Lessons from Urban Water Systems in Six Developing Countries." unpublished manuscript.

Mitchell, W. C. 1945. "The National Bureau's First Quarter-Century." 25th Annual Report, NBER 612, Aslo available in *Journal of Economic Literature*, Vol. 38 (September 2000)

Nee, Victor. 1998. "Sources of the New Institutionalism." In *The New Institutionalism in Sociology*, eds., Mary Brinton and Victor Nee, pp. 1–16. New York: Russell Sage.

Newell, Alan. 1990. *Unified Theories of Cognition*. Cambridge, MA: Harvard University Press.

North, Douglass. 1990. "A Transaction Cost Theory of Politics." *Journal of Theoretical Politics*, 2(4), pp. 355–367.

North, Douglass. 1991. "Institutions." *Journal of Economic Perspectives,* 5(1), pp. 97–112.

North, Douglass. 1994. "Economic Performance through Time." *American Economic Review,* 84(3), pp. 359–368.

North, Douglass and Barry Weingast. 1989. "Constitutions and Commitment: The Evolution of Institutions Governing Public Choice in 17th Century England." *Journal of Economic History*, 49(4), pp. 803–832.

Olson, Mancur, Jr. 1996. "Big Bills Left on the Sidewalk: Why Some Nations Are Rich, and Others Are Poor." *Journal of Economic Perspectives*, 10(2), pp. 3–24.

Pinker, Steven. 1997. *How The Mind Works*. New York: W. W. Norton.

Posner, Richard. 1972. "The Appropriate Scope of Regulation in the Cable Television Industry." *Bell Journal of Economics*, 3(1), pp. 98–129.

Priest, George. 1993. "The Origins of Utility Regulation and the 'Theories of Regulation' Debate." *Journal of Law and Economics*, 36(1), pp. 289–323.

Putnam, Robert D; Robert Leonardi and Raffaella Y. Nanetti. 1993. *Making Democracy Work: Civic Traditions in Modern Italy*. Princeton: Princeton University Press.

Rindfleisch, A. and J. B. Heide. 1997. "Transaction Cost Analysis: Past, Present, and Future Applications." *Journal of Marketing*, 61(4), pp. 30–54.

Riordan, Michael and Oliver Williamson. 1985. "Asset Specificity and Economic Organization." *International Journal of Industrial Organization*, 3(3), pp. 365–378.

Rosenberg, Nathan and L. E. Birdzell. 1986. *How the West Grew Rich: The Transformation of the Industrial World*. New York: Basic Books.

Rubinstein, Ariel. 1998. "Review of Herbert Simon: An Empirically Based Microeconomics." *Journal of Economics. Literature*, 37(4), pp. 1711–1712.

Shelanski, H. A. and P. G. Klein. 1995. "Empirical Research in Transaction Cost Economics: A
Review and Assessment." *Journal of Law, Economics, & Organization,* 11(2), pp. 335–361.

Simon, Herbert. 1957. *Models of Man.* New York: Wiley.

Simon, Herbert. 1985. "Human Nature in Politics: The Dialogue of Psychology with Political Science." *American Political Science Review,* 79(2), pp. 293–304.

Smelser, Neil and Richard Swedberg. 1994. "Introduction." In *The Handbook of Economic Sociology.* Princeton: Princeton University Press.

Stigler, George. 1968. *The Organization of Industry.* Homewood, IL: Richard D. Irwin.

Summers, Clyde. 1969. "Collective Agreements and the Law of Contracts." *Yale Law Journal,* 78(4), pp. 525–575.

Wang, Shusheng and Tian Zhu. 2000. "Contract Law and the Boundary of the Firm." unpublished manuscript, Hong Kong University of Science and Technology.

Whinston, Michael. 1997. "On the Transaction Cost Determinants of Vertical Integration." unpublished manuscript, Northwestern University.

Williamson, Oliver E. 1975. *Markets and Hierarchies: Analysis and Antitrust Implications.* New York: Free Press.

Williamson, Oliver E. 1976. "Franchise Bidding for Natural Monopolies — In General and with Respect to CATV." *Bell Journal of Economics,* 7(1), pp. 73–104.

Williamson, Oliver E. 1985. *The Economic Institutions of Capitalism.* New York: Free Press.

Williamson, Oliver E. 1991. "Comparative Economic Organization: The Analysis of Discrete Structural Alternatives." *Administrative Science Quarterly,* 36(2), pp. 269–296.

Williamson, Oliver E. 1996. *The Mechanisms of Governance.* New York: Oxford University Press.

Williamson, Oliver E. 1998. "Transaction Cost Economics: How It Works; Where It Is Headed." *De Economist,* 146(1), pp. 23–58.

Williamson, Oliver E. 1999. "Public and Private Bureaucracies: A Transaction Cost Economics Perspective." *Journal of Law, Economics, & Organization,* 15(1), pp. 306–342.

Printed in the United States
By Bookmasters